MELANIE the BADGER

MELANIE
the BADGER

FRED L. TATE

REDEMPTION
PRESS

Table of Contents

Memory

I can't remember my name. No, I do remember. My name is Melanie, and I remember my mother gave me that name a long time ago. Remember also that my mother is gone because I left her long ago to become a forest dweller, with my own burrow and territory. She used to cradle me beside her and comfort me when I cried before my eyes were even open, and now this human cradles me beside him and comforts me, and it is so hard to keep my eyes open.

He holds my graying older fur gently as the other human sitting alongside us strokes me with his own human paws. Their eyes are wet, and I do not know why their eyes would be wet, but do I know these humans from somewhere. They should stroke me because I have just saved their lives with my warning scream of rage.

Once again I am allowed to be proud predator instead of a weak prey thing. I can have pride again, and not go without the pride any female badger should have. Not crawling through the forest in pain like some lower prey creature and not trying to find anything to eat while starving slowly, instead of hunting prey on four good paws.

Kekuit waits beside me. For some reason the humans can't see him waiting patiently beside me, even though I see him clearly. He crawled across this field today to guide me home, he crawled here once before.

The monster is dead, and I am proudest of that. I have pride and try not to whimper with gratitude as the human holding me strokes me. It is just so hard to think now. I lick his human paws as he strokes me and tries to ease the journey we both know I am going on. The humans know, as I know, what is coming for me because I am a predator. I know death when it calls. Kekuit waits beside me, and I know he is beside me to help me answer death's call.

They gave me something to eat! These humans gave me their food instead of keeping it for themselves when they saw my need for it, saw how thin my sides were, saw how impossible it would be for me to ever hunt properly again.

Both humans gave me something to eat, and it was so delicious and so wonderful to actually have meat again. I have not had enough food for so long, and am so old and useless. A prey not a predator anymore, reduced to licking the paws of humans in gratitude. Kekuit waits beside me.

I know both humans, but it is just so hard to remember. Their human scents are familiar as their stroking human paws follow the traces of the scars that have never left my face and body from the murderers of my young more than a full set of seasons ago. Their stroking human paws follow the four furrows in my side that the monster gave me in this season of warmth and new growth; four deep furrows, unable to heal properly because I could not turn enough to clean them.

Their stroking human paws follow the twisted thing that is now my back. The two humans stroke me gently, and their eyes are wet. Why are their eyes making water? Why would these humans sorrow for me? Kekuit waits beside me.

Memory

My lover Akycha strokes me, grooming me gently at sunset in the heat of this season as we sit together outside our burrow watching darkness grow around us. Waiting for it to be cool enough to hunt, as he tells me I am not too old, and he will love me no matter how strange and different our lives are now from the common habits of our badger kind.

He came to me so late in life and is younger than I, but he is the one that chose me, and I am happy with him. I remember that he came to me after the young female rabbit left.

She and I are so different, I the predator and she the prey. No, the young female rabbit left me when Akycha arrived. No, Akycha is dead, killed by this huge monster that took him from me when he was my last chance in life for love and new young, and the monster that followed tried to kill me in hate and anger for what I did.

It lays dead where they stopped its charge as it prepared to kill all three of us; and this time there will be no extra chance for him to survive, to kill again in any form. The humans are stroking me, my mind is drifting so much, I am so very old, and I have been hurt so very badly. Kekuit waits beside me.

The young rabbit strokes me with her tongue in the falling white coldness around us, grooming my injuries where my face and body are ripped and torn by the human-bred creatures that slaughtered my young, the last young I might have so late in life. She cares for me even though I am her enemy.

How can I let prey care for me? I do not know her name; how can I know her name when I do not speak the same language as prey?

But she is so small and young, and my own small young lay dead behind us, being covered by the falling snow along with their killers.

I want her to be my new young so badly, as I whimper with pain and loss, and she cares for me, her enemy. No, she is gone; she left early last spring when I found my lover Akycha. He strokes me instead of her, grooming me gently. No, he is dead. It is so hard to think. Kekuit waits beside me.

My young stroke me in our snug burrow with their little tongues as the leaves change colors and fall outside. My young show me how much they love me even though it should be impossible for me to have had them so late in the seasons, so close to the winter. They should have waited inside me to arrive in the spring, not arrived this early, not now. How can I see them through the coming winter when they should be grown and gone by this season?

No, they are all dead, and falling snow is covering them, along with their murderers. I fought so many so hard with all the fierceness that is ours and I failed to save my young. I am so useless; a poor prey creature that has to be held by humans and stroked by them and it is so hard to concentrate anymore. Kekuit waits beside me.

I try not to whimper with gratitude for the gentleness with which the two humans stroke me. I remind myself sternly that I am predator and not prey. Predators do not whimper, and I will not cry for myself!

The humans stroke me, and they seem to know this also, because their eyes are wet as they both try to help me, the predator that saved them. Kekuit waits beside me.

I remember now. I do know both humans trying to comfort me because they shared food with me in the forest after they took the deer seasons ago when we first met, and they shared with me in seasons whenever we met again. We have an understanding, these two humans and I. We are both predators in the forest, and we are the same under the fur, or at least we would be if humans had decent fur.

I could not save my young and I could not save my lover, but I saved them. They remember me. They know me. They cry for me. I tremble in human paws as he holds me, strokes me, comforts me, and cries for me. Kekuit waits beside me.

Their human paws touch me as they try to sooth me, and I would have let few humans touch me before. But now I am some pathetic prey instead of a decent predator, and they helped me to kill the monster. No. They killed it. I had no choice; I could only wait to die and scream my rage at it from behind and below the humans as it came charging, roaring rage across the fresh spring grass of the field to kill the three of us.

I lick this human hand as he strokes me. My mind is drifting so badly. I am so old, and my back hurts so badly.

I hear my mother calling me from so many seasons ago.

She is so beautiful and fierce. No predator will dare touch us with her around.

No, she must be dead; that was so long ago.

She strokes me, grooming and cleaning me. She is calling me, and I have to go to her.

Kekuit is still beside me, waiting patiently for me to join him in our final hunt together. He grooms me gently, comforting me on this last journey while reminding me that his mother must be stronger than this. I must go with him soon.

The young rabbit strokes me in the cold, winter whiteness around us as she cleans my wounds. The humans stroke me in this new spring grass I crawled through to come here as they comfort me. My lover strokes me in the heat of summer as we love and then sit together to wait for the darkness to come. My young stroke me as the leaves change colors and fall around us.

They all stroke me as one; and Kekuit, who once could not stand, now stands up beside me while my mind drifts back to when there were no young, no lovers, no humans, and Kekuit had not yet been born.

Alive

I am back in the dark, warm place again, and there is food. I love food so much! All I have to do is work my way over to the large, warm thing in this dark, warm place, and I can have all the food I want from the large, warm thing.

I drink greedily along with others beside me that I can hear but can't see, for my eyes are not yet open. Then I sleep, until it is time to awaken again and feed from the large, warm thing that loves us. The large, warm thing strokes me, and that makes me feel good as it grooms and cares for us.

Sometimes the large warm thing that cares for us must go away, and then we whimper and cry with need for it to return, and it is back to care for us again.

I know that is us, and not just I, because I can feel the others beside me as we all compete for the food from the large, warm thing. Then we huddle together again to sleep, and the large, warm thing that loves us cares for us strokes and grooms us, cradling us close beside it again until we awaken again to feed from it.

Darkness and light pass across my closed eyes, and then I see things through the dark and light. I can see shapes begin to appear. Shapes, and the large warm thing is like me but much larger.

She gives me the food from her, and now I can see to go to it instead of just following my instincts to reach it.

"Melanie," the large, warm thing that cares for us says gently to me. "It is the name for all of us, and you are so beautiful you are all of us. Your name will be Melanie."

I love her, and I know she loves me in return. My name will be Melanie.

The male beside me she calls Tigranuhi. "Your fur is darker than normal, almost all black, instead of brown with black markings. It will soon be all black as you grow to be an adult. You will be a great hunter in the darkness, and your name will be Tigranuhi, which means 'the moon and darkness.'"

The female beside me she calls Shareesa. "You are beautiful and brown, as you should be, and wild. And you deserve a beautiful, wild name."

"I am Asaseyaa," she tells us tenderly, "the mother of you, and the mother of many others."

We understand now. The large, warm thing that loves us is our mother, and she is Asaseyaa.

She tells us, "Remember I am Asaseyaa. You come from me, and someday you will return to me again."

We do not fully understand why she says this, but we love her as I look at Tigranuhi and Shareesa.

Both of the others are like me, and like me, they are all so very much smaller than the large, warm thing we now call *mother*. Our mother, Asaseyaa, cares for the three of us in this snug burrow, well lined with things to keep us warm and safe. And we know she did it just for us as we tumble over her while playing together in the burrow.

Bouncing and rolling with fierce, young joy, playing the games that later in life will be used to hunt and strike at our prey, and also to fight for our lives if we have to.

All we know at our young age is that it is fierce fun to pounce and strike while we play with each other and our mother is so approving when we do it.

"You will be fierce predators!" she tells us. "Not weak prey to be eaten!"

And we are fierce, proudly challenging each other as we roll over her body in fun and chase each other back and forth.

She goes and returns, bringing us back things not like us, which are not moving but have a strange scent on them that excites us fiercely. She teaches us to eat them. We preferred the warm food from her body, until we taste these new things and play with them. She sighs and patiently tries to teach us how to eat our new food instead of just playing fierce, instinctive games with it.

We learn to eat the new things, and they make us fierce with joy at their taste while we discover our heritage as predators, not prey, and now we understand that this is food!

She goes and returns again with more of this new food; and we eagerly await the new food she brings back to us. We stop drinking the warm liquid from her in preference to this new prey food as the dark and light time pass; until it is finally time to go outside our snug, warm burrow.

For the very first time, our mother takes us to the opening. Before Asaseyaa would not let us go near it, and now we are to go out into this far too bright world we see in front of us as we reach the entrance of our burrow.

Too many smells! Too many new things, and all too big!

We are too cautious for good predators, and we hesitate, while she sighs as a mother does at our reluctance, gently pushing us out in spite of our resistance.

We are careful not to let her get too far away as we try to understand all of the huge, bright new around us, and it is far larger than we ever thought it would be! We are not good predators yet because we act more like bewildered prey than good predators.

As she leads we follow, tumbling all over each other to be closest to her while walking and staring at everything around us. Our startled, young eyes wide with wonder at this huge, immense new surrounding our mother is guiding us through.

Barely paying attention to her as she tries to instruct us of what we are seeing, and what we should know about it, she tries to herd us into some kind of order, as we stumble over each other and over other things under our paws while staring in wonder at all of this.

She sighs again, trying to make us listen and not just fall over ourselves and her as we follow.

The forest ground is almost never really level or smooth and definitely not for ones that walk as close to it as small short-legged badgers do. We stumble over things in the forest while following our mother, and try to listen to her as she guides us to new things.

So many smells and colors we have never even imagined in our burrow with her, and the bright blue of the huge thing over our heads, and the white things moving across it far above us, the big brightly glowing, far too bright to look, thing in the huge blue above us.

The green of the brush she easily passes through slows us with its thickness: the green of the trees so high above us, and the green of the grass we walk through, and the darker green of the moss on the ground and trees' sides, and the browns of those tree trunks, the colors of the flowers, and the colors of the rocks.

We lose our fear in the excitement at all the new, and we are most fierce as we play now!

And our mother, Asaseyaa, is proud of us as she teaches us. "See what things are around you and what they will mean to you in terms of survival in your lives when you finally leave for your own lives away from me."

We are confused. Of course, we would never, ever leave her. She will always be with us, and we will always follow her.

She teaches us how to dig, which is our main route for both food and survival. We watch Asaseyaa disappear as she tunnels far faster than many other creatures can.

Then we hear a small scream from underground, and she returns with something small and bloody in her mouth.

She shows us our next lesson by eating it in front of us, and now we know where the prey she has been bringing us in the burrow can be found underneath the ground we walk upon.

We watch her dig again after we have walked some more. She is quick, and there is the small scream again from below us as we watch our mother return above ground with another small, bloody thing in her mouth, dropping it in front of us.

We sniff and taste, and our excitement grows at the sight and smell of the prey she has found and brought for us. We tear it apart without much grace, and by the time we are finished playing with it there is not much left to eat, but we try anyway. It is an excitement to eat!

We start to mimic her and begin to dig, but we are unschooled and do not know where to go for more of this new foodstuff.

Asaseyaa teaches us again. "Listen for the small sounds from beneath the ground."

We try but we still can't hear those noises yet, but she teaches us patiently, until we learn how to hear the sounds from below the ground that says, "Prey is here!" She teaches us how to tell the difference between the sounds of different prey animals and how to hear them below us even if they try to hide quietly.

She teaches us until we finally understand how to dig without wasting time or energy when hunting the prey out from their below-ground burrows. She teaches us how to look for the entrances where the ground is mounded up with fresh dirt because prey is somewhere below those mounds of fresh dirt.

To go directly down into the ground above the prey, and not just follow the tunnel the prey has made for us because the prey may have gone out another entrance when we dig into the existing one. If we come straight down to the faint sounds of fear we will get food every time.

She teaches us to watch out for predators that may harm us, such as the bear and the wolf. There are very few others that would be foolish enough to attack us when we are grown because our claws and teeth are very good indeed, and our fierceness is virtually unmatched.

But for now, our mother, Asaseyaa, teaches that we must watch for the things she calls *hawks* during the day and *owls* during the dark because our present small size will make them want us as prey now, but not when we are older and larger.

"And above all," Asaseyaa tells us, "watch out for the humans' dogs, for humans sometimes turn their dogs loose upon the forest and let those dogs run wild, and those human dogs gone wild have no fear of anything, not even humans."

We ask our mother why, and she tells us.

"Human dogs running wild kill more humans in each set of seasons than bears do. Human dogs gone wild also form packs so fierce they can't be stopped by the simple fear of humans. They will also stalk and kill humans. They kill not just for food as we do but for the joy of killing, and they kill the weakest among their own kind when they form the packs they run in."

We ask what these humans look like and what their scent would be like. Asaseyaa instructs us in human's appearance and scent, and we find the description of these tall, two-legged creatures amusing, until our mother tells us that humans have the power to kill from a distance, and you may not even see them when they kill you.

She tells us more of these creatures called humans who are predators like us, but who can kill from a distance, and who might not want us just for food, they might want us instead just for our fur or part of our bodies!

We can't understand this. To kill not for food but for the fur that covers our bodies, why?

We have never seen any of these tall, two-legged creatures she describes, but she is fierce in reminding us of this thing, and insistent on us clearly understanding what they look like and what their scent should be like.

She also tells us that there are other creatures we may never see, but that may still harm us.

When we ask, "Why learn this if we may never see them?" she only tells us that she is Asaseyaa, and not to question her, as if she herself does not want to talk about them.

But she then also tells us these are "Others not as they should be; creatures of evil that walk when and where they should not."

We do not understand, but later in my life I will understand it far too well.

She teaches us not to annoy the things called *skunks*, for while they are not our equal in battle, they seldom have to fight, and if we annoy them we may spend many days in the stream trying clean ourselves again, and regret the encounter afterward.

She tells us never annoy or try to eat the creature called a *porcupine* because it can hurt us badly and leave us in pain with a mouthful of its needles, making us unable to eat, and we may starve.

She also teaches us the way to safely kill those long, slim things without legs that have rattling tails.

Asaseyaa tells us we are night creatures when hunting or roaming, although many of us hunt and roam in the daytime by choice. In darkness the prey is often sleeping or not fully aware, and it makes it easier to get them in their burrows or when they are sleeping in the open.

Also, when it is dark and raining, the delicious things that come from the ground will be on top of it, and then we can easily grab the things called *worms*.

Our mother then tells us that she has brought us out now to teach us how to daylight hunt, as well as other things we must know of the daylight.

Asaseyaa explains to us that while we are normally creatures of the open areas and not of this forest around us, she has chosen to live here with others of our kind because food is so abundant here, including wonderful, tasting things that badgers of the open areas never get to see or eat. There are also many areas for burrows in this forest that are safely under tree roots or in the rocky sides of the hills.

"Our burrows can be as elaborate as we can choose." she explains to us. "The only thing that matters is that you make them safely in good ground, which will not collapse or become soaked with rain when the rain comes from the sky each season. They also should be comfortable and well lined with grass and with the leaves that fall from the trees. Grass and leafy things that only plant-eating prey eat."

We laugh with her at actually using things those weak planteaters eat, the very things we use for our own comfort in our burrows.

We laugh and learn to hunt those planteaters. We learn to dig them out of their burrows, we learn to wait in ambush for them in the darkness as they wander by, and we learn to let the sound of the stream hide our sounds as we wait beside it for them to come and drink from it in the darkness; for darkness is our friend and hides us well as we hunt.

Of course we do not always just come out at darkness to hunt. Sometimes the warmth of the sun is just so nice to sit and bask in, and to warm our bodies before we go out to hunt the night. And sometimes we also just like to wander in the daytime to see all of the things that are here in our forest for us to enjoy.

Day or night, very few other predators will even think of annoying us as we wander with our mother, for she only has to show those terrible teeth and claws of hers, and the fox, the hawk, and the others leave her and us alone.

The bear we fear, but it is usually a creature only of the day, and we are usually creatures of the night, and we seldom meet.

Even though we fear it, the bear seldom touches us when there is much easier prey to find here in our forest. Only when winter is approaching does the bear need vast supplies of food to survive its long sleep, and then the bear thinks of us as prey. We do sometimes feast on the bear's prey after the bear has dined.

When it has made a big kill, feasted, and left for sleep, and then there is plenty of food left for the rest of the forest to find. However, Asaseyaa cautions us to never ever feast on a bear's prey and stay there because the bear is very jealous of its food and will strike out in a rage at whomever it finds near that food.

But we seldom see a bear, and when we do, it seldom tries to actually dig out one of us from our snug burrow. If it tries to dig out one of our burrows, its nose might regret finding our claws and teeth embedded in that nose, and the bear knows this well and stays away.

We discover that our mother has not just one but several burrows as she takes us from one to the other in our travels, now both in the day and in the dark.

"All should be nicely rounded out, with a sleeping area to be comfortable inside and well lined with grass and leaves to rest on and help keep you warm in the winter," Asaseyaa tells us.

We do not know what this winter that she describes is because it is the beginning of the warm season for us.

As we grow we change, and we each become our own badgers. My brother, Tigranuhi, now loves to roam by himself in the forest, finding his own trails, and finding his own prey. Tigranuhi hunts well at night; his fur is now all black, and with his darker fur, prey simply can't see him until his teeth and claws are already into it.

Sometimes our mother, Asaseyaa, my sister Shareesa, and I both follow Tigranuhi through the forest at night as he hunts.

Asaseyaa says, "He will always have something by the time daylight is here for all of us to share."

Shareesa is more reserved in her hunting as am I, and we both prefer to let Asaseyaa show us how to hunt, and then share her catch until daylight is here, before it is time to roam back to the burrow.

We roam with her. We grow, until we three of her young begin to hunt more and more on our own. She lets us hunt proudly, and she is especially proud of us when we catch something that is very hard to catch. I make her the proudest, though.

I was only waiting by the rabbit's burrow and hadn't even started to dig yet when the rabbit came bounding out!

I pounce on it before it even knows I am there, and my teeth and claws stop its cries as I kill it. To actually catch one of these fast-moving creatures in the open is hard to do, but I have managed to get this one right outside its burrow, without even having to dig for it!

There is pride as our mother, Asaseyaa, arrives at the scream of the prey, with Tigranuhi and Shareesa. My brother, Tigranuhi, is jealous that I have actually managed to catch one of these prey creatures in the open; this is something not even he has been able to do yet. My sister, Shareesa, is envious because this is one of the tastiest of all the prey creatures.

Asaseyaa is proud; telling my brother and sister that they should also learn to hunt like this. But they are far too busy trying to help me share this feast to really listen to our mother talk, and she finally gives up trying to get through to them.

Enjoying some of the prey herself while she tells me how proud she is of me. I get the best pieces, which is only right since it is my kill.

Asaseyaa is not so happy when we meet our first predator that can kill us easily: the bear.

She stiffens and freezes beside us. We are traveling in the daylight, as she chases us into concealing brush while giving a soft, warning growl for us to remain still.

We freeze as she commands; we understand that Asaseyaa's word is law in matters of danger. We still can't see any danger ourselves, but then our badger eyes are not our best sense.

The sound is first, a steady, heavy walking, and then the sound of the deep, heavy breathing of some very large thing walking this way.

Now we know, and are very careful to remain still and concealed as he comes. For the first time we see the creature that could kill us. I had no idea that this creature our mother mentioned would actually be this large. I thought we were the very best predators.

He shambles by, unaware of us. The wind is with us and he can't smell us, even this close.

We remain still until he is gone, and until now we had thought Asaseyaa was just telling us stories about the bear to make us more careful in the forest, but now we will be more mindful of this bear-thing that can kill us.

The season grows still warmer as we grow larger. Most of our time outside is in the dark now, when the forest sleeps as our prey also sleeps.

We find the tasty grubs under fallen trees and in dark places, and we find them to be delicious also. We find burrows and dig them out quickly before prey can escape, although, prey that has learned the lesson of a second entrance sometimes surprises us, and runs away too quickly for us to catch it.

We can run very fast for short distances, but creatures that can run fast for longer distances will escape us, so we are creatures of digging quickly, of ambushing, and we are not above finding prey already killed by others and eating some of it.

We find the nests of the birds that live on the ground and raid their eggs, which are also delicious, and if the parents are not cautious enough to fly away in time, we have them for food also.

We find the hopping food that comes out of the stream each night, such as the frogs. They are so slow and foolish; it is almost not a challenge to catch them. They are also tasty and will fill us up to prevent hunger, even if it is not really hunting to catch these frog creatures.

We roam, and find that ground squirrels are the easiest to catch when we tunnel swiftly down into their burrows. They almost never have a second entrance to leave by as we come tunneling down, and they are too foolish to try simply run out their entrance as we come in above them. They become our main diet, along with other things, that we can catch at night.

Our bodies are rounding out as we realize that our mother was right: life in the forest can be easy.

We are now almost the way we will look for the rest of our lives; even our colors are becoming fixed; narrow, black noses that go back to a widening head, making our faces and heads look pointed in front, with a stripe of white on top stretching from the black of our nose to the front of our backs and over the top of our heads, where our faces have white cheeks, with black above and below them, the black below going upward in front of our ears, presenting a powerful, pudgy flat-looking body on short legs behind our pointed head and very short neck.

Our fur course stiff hair covering a full layer of thick skin, which protects us from the harm of claws or teeth, as does the fat layer beneath it.

I am proudest of my looks. Although my brother and sister feel the same about their own looks, I am the one that looks the most like our mother, Asaseyaa.

My brother, Tigranuhi, has fur that looks all black, my sister, Shareesa, has fur of lighter reddish brown with black stripes like myself. In contrast, my own body fur is a lovely brown, with stripes of darker black fur running down each side from top to bottom mixed in with the brown.

Our paws are also black, as is our short tail. Our paws also hold one of our most powerful weapons we use in hunting, self-defense, or digging, and our very long claws, almost as long as the paws holding them are very strong and very sharp.

Our eyes, while not that good in the daytime, are more than good enough for what we are: night hunters. Our senses of smell and hearing are both fully developed now and almost as good as our mother's. We can now find our own prey below the ground without our mother's help.

Asaseyaa has taught us well. We also find smaller prey that does not run at all or does not run well. Grasshoppers and crickets, beetles and caterpillars are not as good as fresh meat from prey but it will help us to survive if we need to.

As the season moves onward, we survive more independent from our mother now, and although we do still follow her back to whichever of Asaseyaa's burrows she chooses to use when day is coming again.

When we do travel with her now, her growing distances separate us because it is almost time to leave our mother and go on our own. We are grown and feel the call for our own families.

The season is growing colder now, and trees which are not green for all of the seasons have started to turn to other colors and lose their leaves.

We will sometimes stay longer outside the burrow, and sitting in the sun after a colder night just to enjoy the vanishing warmth of sunlight before going to sleep.

Asaseyaa is also spending less and less time with us, encouraging us to be more on our own as we travel. She even tends to push us away now, as if to tell us to go. But we love her still and stay as long as possible, even though our instincts say it is now time to find our own burrows and forest to live in.

She still loves us as we love her, but there is a new separateness about our relationship now when we hunt together. We often go off on our own, until we find each other again and return to the burrow and sleep.

Asaseyaa knows, as we know, what will happen soon with us, and we sense our mother's growing sadness. But it is a part of our lives to leave her finally because the lives of all creatures must move onward, as is the case with all things in nature.

Asaseyaa reminds us of what we must know above all. "Starvation kills many of us in the first two full sets of seasons we go through; always find a place to make territory where there is a good and plentiful food supply."

Asaseyaa reminds us, "When you establish your territory, you must defend it fiercely against all others because your very survival depends on finding a good, territorial place, where you must make sure you are strong enough to keep it yours."

"You are predators, not prey!" she reminds us fiercely. "Do not ever allow yourselves to become prey by lack of alertness. Few can kill you, but those that can are also a part of nature and are better predators. Watch out for them!"

Asaseyaa reminds us, "When you sisters have your own young, you must train them equally well, and for their only survival depends on how well you have taught them when you become their mother."

Asaseyaa reminds us again, "Beware of the humans and the dogs they turn loose upon the forest through their thoughtlessness or deliberate intent. The humans can kill from a distance, and the dogs fear nothing when they roam in wild packs. Humans' dogs gone wild kill far more than they need to eat; they kill just for pleasure, they never have enough pleasure in killing, and they can kill humans also."

The call to go and find our own way through the forest grows stronger as the leaves begin to fall from the trees that do not stay green throughout all of the seasons. Soon the call is finally too strong for us to resist.

We can feel it inside ourselves, urging us to make a burrow, our own burrow, and stay in it for what is coming.

We go out at dusk.

My black brother, Tigranuhi, looks back, walks into the forest, and disappears into the trees.

We go out at dusk.

My sister does not feel well and stays behind.

My mother and I return to the burrow as light grows in the sky, and my sister lays cold and stiff inside it.

My mother weeps beside me, as I try to understand this new thing, one of us dying.

We leave for another burrow. As we walk there, my mother covers her sorrow with instruction.

"We are predators," my mother reminds me. "Death is always with us."

We go out at dusk.

I feel the call. I look back at my mother and she smiles at me. We both know, and as I walk into the forest she cries behind me. I never see her alive again.

Alone

I roam through the night forest until dawn lights the sky before making a safe burrow.

Finished, I look at my first burrow, and it may not be as complex and well-made as Asaseyaa taught me to build, but it will do until it can be finished.

Then I sleep through the day, and I cry with the new aloneness, and there has never been a time of aloneness before. Now, it is new and fearful to me, and I wonder if Asaseyaa still cries behind me.

Night finds me roaming, looking for food without the protection of my mother for the first time in my life.

The night noises seem different without Asaseyaa's strong body and good claws alongside. Most of this night is spent jumping at shadows instead of feeding. I finally give up and return to enlarge my burrow, and always looking back over a shoulder to see the threat I know is behind and closing in on me as I return.

The second night is better. I am actually out before dark to enjoy sun's warmth before hunting. I remind myself sternly that this time I am a predator, not prey, and my mother, Asaseyaa, would be very unhappy to see me shivering at night like some weak prey animal.

Then it is time to wait beside the stream while the sound of rushing water covers the sound of my breathing, and the mouse that goes to drink gives me a meal. I wait again and am rewarded by another one, and then I find some tasty grubs under a rotting log by the stream, and fill myself. I return at dawn, and satisfied, because I am a good predator after all and I have pride in this new alone now.

The forest moves onward, and I move through it as the season changes. My burrow is enlarged in time to become a proper burrow for one of us, which is a well-lined sleeping chamber with fresh grass and leaves to help me rest comfortably and be warm.

I branch off and make other tunnels, with one tunnel leading out to another entrance for safety in case a larger predator is outside my main tunnel or tries to dig me out through the main entrance. Other tunnels serve as places to eliminate waste without my having to ever leave the burrow.

This burrow is truly a home to take pride in when it's fully finished, and as I go hunt again the gathering darkness, I know that this burrow will be ready for my return.

But when dawn arrives over the trees, instead of returning to my first, real burrow, something moves me to a new place in my forest. It is time to dig another burrow in another location.

Digging new burrows is instinctive for us, and also ensures that if one burrow becomes unusable, there will always be another one to go to.

Over the next full set of seasons, there will be several good, livable burrows dug and enlarged the way they should be, but for now, I am happy with just this new one and my first one.

Sleeping alone, I dream of prey food and wake at dusk to hunt again.

The dawn is colder when I return to my first burrow, and I discover that a prey animal has tried to take up residence in my absence. I kill it and it tastes good, and then it is time to sleep again.

I will have to remember the trick of coming back to all of my burrows on a regular basis to see if any prey has tried to use them.

The next night is even colder, and the knowledge comes from instinct as much as it comes from mother's teachings that I will have to eat as much as possible now to round out my body for winter.

We do not have true, deep all-winter sleep like the bear; we sleep more lightly, and are often out in the winter to hunt or roam.

By now I know what my mother meant by *winter* when she trained me, and I will have lots of nice snug burrows ready before winter comes, and the best and warmest will be my home.

In the meantime, the sun is there to enjoy each day, in all of my growing, plump beauty as I bask in the sun's warmth and stay out longer each time. It's nice to feel the sun's warmth for just a little longer before the growing cold covers this forest in white, just as my mother said it would. She called it *snow*, but I have never seen it before and can only guess.

Prey is harder to find now as they also prepare for winter, and I start eating different things, and like berries and roots for my diet, until my body is plump for the coming cold.

The living has been good here, and while sheltering for my first winter, I fully understand why our mother lives in this forest. My primary burrow is the one I will use as my winter burrow because it is well lined with leaves and grass to help me stay warm.

I sleep the days, until it is time to roam again at dusk for food, and although I do not really need any, it is still an instinctive action among our kind.

The nights grow colder as daylight lessens, until one day, winter comes home to my burrow. The white things high in the blue overhead have been moving faster each morning when I return to my burrow. I have already noticed that the air is much colder when I emerge for my night hunts.

I know that I will spend this winter alone, but we are solitary creatures and live alone unless with our young or a mate, and there is no mate for me yet. Some of us have mates by the first winter. I do not and awaken alone to darkness coming through my burrow entrance and into my sleeping chamber before it should be dark outside, wandering for the entrance to see this new thing. Darkness has been much earlier and much longer each time it comes, and this added darkness is curious to me.

I notice the increased cold before reaching the entrance, and then see the whiteness falling outside onto the other whiteness already on the ground. I stop in wonder at the burrow entrance to see this new thing coming down from the sky. This cold white that becomes rain when I taste it, this thing my mother called *snow*, and then I really feel the added cold and decide to go back to sleep instead. I'm not hungry anyway.

We are not true deep sleepers in the winter, but we do sleep more than in the other seasons, and I make use of that now. Curling into a ball in the grass lining of my snug, burrow sleeping chamber, I let my body slow down into the deeper sleep we do during this season.

After sleeping for two full days before deciding to look outside again, I discover it is still the same, but the snow is now much deeper now and much harder to walk through when I do decide to get some warming sunlight.

Still it feels good to have sun on my body while I travel, using the weight of my body and the power of my legs to push through the winter whiteness.

Coming back will be easy. I will just follow the trail that I made with my own body back to my burrow. Meanwhile there is all of the new to explore and investigate. Everything is totally different. I have to stare around in wonder while traveling, looking for directions. Old landmarks are rediscovered by guesswork in all of this newness, and I finally find the stream to drink from before heading back, but then I discover the fun of this new snow.

I only meant to catch that incautious creature of a mouse still out in the snow; it was foolish enough to hop right in front of me across the snow. Plowing through the white in full chase, I try to get to the mouse as it runs easily across the top of the snow.

Until suddenly realizing that I am not so much interested in a meal as in bouncing in and out of all the whiteness around me. Digging my nose into the snow and throwing it up in curving arcs of white before my face, only to watch it fall again; running back and forth, while chasing imaginary prey that happens to be always just beyond the deepest white areas. Sometimes almost burying myself completely in all of the new snow around me!

Finding fun in this entire cold, new white thing; until I finally grow tired of throwing the snow everywhere, and leaving happily exhausted, for my burrow. Sleeping snugly for another two full days until the call in my body that tells me how long

I have slept brings me awake again to enjoy the sun for a while before I go back inside again to sleep deeply again.

Days become not so much for hunting but to feel the sun on my body, and on the nights I want to avoid the cold, I just sleep in my snug, warm burrow until I feel the urge to roam again.

I roam now, not so much because I have to, but just to be out roaming, not even bothering to look at the full extent of the area I have claimed. It is much simpler to stay closer to the area where my primary winter burrow is and make sure it is secure from any new arrivals that might want it for theirs, but then, another new thing happens by accident when I go down to the stream for a quick drink that makes for more winter play.

It is very cold now and a little uncomfortable to drink the water, but I need some, and so I ramble down through my thickly, white-covered forest to satisfy my thirst. Instead of finding a flowing stream with decent noise like it should, the stream looks shiny and still.

I am puzzled by this for a little bit before I decide to investigate. After all, it is my stream, and if something has been happening to it, I should know.

I discover the thick, shiny top is solid and cold, and while slowly sniffing and testing it with a paw, I see why it now looks this way. I start to slowly test the surface with both my front paws when suddenly my paws slide outwards as I rest weight on them!

Growling with surprise, I try to get back, but my front paws will not obey me as they slide further out with each movement in my scramble to get back. I manage to slide all the way onto the cold, shiny surface of my stream instead. Paws scrambling frantically for a grip, and failing, my paws now refuse to obey me at all!

Managing not to fall, my naturally low body and short legs help me. I growl fiercely at the new and strange stream, and discover that if I move very slowly and very carefully I can make my way to the other side of my stream. It is out of the question to turn around. I try, and fall, paws scrambling frantically for a grip again on this new, slick surface!

But I can actually get out on the other side, as soon as my front paws are on good ground that is not slick and shiny, which amazes me when I stop to think about how to deal with this thing. I will have to cross it somehow to get back to my burrow, but I do not trust this new thing enough to try going over it again.

Somehow, I know that if I fall through the new, smooth shiny surface, it will not be good. Turning to move cautiously down to the stream again, this time I am careful not put my weight on the shiny surface as I test it.

It works! I am not slipping further outward, and I realize that there actually is water here below the entire shiny surface.

This new thing is keeping me from my burrow. I decide to try crossing it again.

Now that I know the trick, I slowly let my front paws back onto this new, shiny surface, and I find those paws can be controlled if I move very slowly back onto it.

It is cold, but fascinating, and there is another feeling as I deliberately let myself slide out on the new, shiny stuff this time.

The same feeling that was there when I was playing in the white snow that covers the forest is the same feeling when my brother and sister and I would scramble all over our burrow and chase each other and mock fight. This is that same feeling of fun!

I run as best I can across the shiny top and slide as I try frantically to stop, but I slide all the way into the white stuff on the other stream bank, pick myself up, and run as fast as my scrambling, slipping paws will allow to slide again all the way over to the other side, and then I turn and do it again the other way.

My original reason for coming here has been totally forgotten in fun as I learn to control my sliding. I growl with fierce joy at the sensation of turning around and around, all out of control on this new thing.

I spend far more time than I had intended to, riding the excitement of this new plaything, and day is almost gone before I realize it is time to roam homeward again.

I finally did get my drink by finding a softer spot near a bank and breaking through the shiny stuff there with my powerful front claws, but that is not important compared to the fun of today.

I sleep for a few days and awaken to do it again before simply giving up on this coming out into the colder air for a while. I want to let my body slow down as we do when we find winter boring, and I decide to just sleep winter away.

I will awaken again a few times, but most of the time now is spent sleeping. I have a nice sleeping place of dry leaves and grass, and the burrow is comfortable and warm. Why bother going out at all?

Only awakening from time to time to check on my territory, I roam through a much-reduced range now, preferring to stay near this primary chosen winter burrow for the rest of my first winter; until something awakens me, and I shamble upward to my entrance to see the new thing outside.

The sun is out, and it feels far too nice to stay in this stuffy burrow, no matter how much a home it has become, as I shift, stretch, yawn, and go out to greet the sun's warmth.

The white stuff is already almost gone, and melting quickly in sun warmth as it would melt in my mouth when I would taste it, and the sunlight outside this stuffy burrow is nice as I rest in it, basking happily in an open area of warm sun.

While we are creatures of darkness normally; this is just too good to pass up with sleeping, and there is a new need for food to fill my winter-depleted body as I go to find some prey.

The stream is out, no frogs, and I finally have to settle for some roots, and the few mice that can be caught in the open.

Then it is time to go for a drink at the stream and back to the burrow for some more sleep until tonight when I will hunt for real. I sleep, and dream of delicious food things, until it is time to go out again and resume my normal life of day sleep and night hunt.

There is a bit of luck when it is dark. I find a big kill. I do not know what killed the deer but am happy to find it lying there. It has a bloody hole in one side, and it must have already been found by daytime predators because some parts of it are gone, which is puzzling because those parts are not gone as if they had been torn off by teeth, they are cleanly gone.

Still there is more than enough left, and I feast while wondering why I don't scent any predators that might have killed it around this area.

A new scent is here, but no scent of any forest predator I know of large enough to have done this, and my nose is very good.

I also puzzle at the hole that seems to have killed this creature; the hole is so small to have killed something this large, but that doesn't matter as long as the meat is still good.

I do remember hearing something like the loud crack sound in the sky that happens when the bright light flashes and then rain comes down out of the sky. But that loud crack sound was only once just as I woke up to come outside, and there is no rain around now, so it couldn't have been the flashing, sky light thing.

Giving up puzzling this thing as I feast, I am still curious as to why I can't smell the smells of predators around the deer kill, just this new smell of a new creature I do not know and have not smelled before.

I give up puzzling the crack noise to concentrate on eating the fresh kill, and it is good meat and that is all that matters to me, then I return to my snug burrow before dawn to sleep, full and happy.

Awaking, there is a new sense of wrong, although not of danger, just a sense of something I need to do? I am almost a full set of seasons old now, and feel I am missing some part of me, now that spring is here, as if something is not complete in my life.

There is an instinct that bothers me and makes me feel restless and uncomfortable. I do not know what it is; I just have it. I know the killed deer will be there for me, but I instinctively freeze in place before reaching it. There are sounds and the scent of another newly awakened large one near the kill, and he is noisily feasting on my kill!

It was not actually my kill, but I found it and it should be mine. Remaining hidden in the surrounding brushy cover watching the bear eat, I snarl soft resentment at him for having the nerve to invade my territory to feast at what by rights should be my food.

Not his, mine!

I shake with fury at him daring to eat what should be mine. He doesn't belong here. Mine. My food! I found it and it's my kill to eat!

But he is far larger than any other bear I have ever seen before, and he can kill me easily, and so I have no choice, and can only watch as the bear eats what should be mine. Chattering my teeth, I shake with rage until he is gone. Strangely I have sensation that something is alongside him as he eats, and that it knows I am watching. But I can't see anything alongside him?

I go for what has been left for me after he leaves, still full of fury, wishing my body were the size of his so I could have hurt him; he and the others that have been here before him while I slept didn't leave much, but there is enough.

At least the fact he was here had kept some of the smaller predators away, and so I can have some now, without having to devote my time in chasing others away.

I notice that he has already left his territorial claw marks high on the trees around here to let all other bears know that this is now his territory and not theirs. But something is wrong with his claw marks: they are much higher on the sides of those trees than any of the other black bears of this forest have ever left their claw marks on trees before, and his coloring was all wrong.

Not black like the other smaller bears of this forest; he was brown in color, and much larger than any bear I have ever seen before, much larger than any of our smaller black bears.

There was also some kind of large hump over his front shoulders, and he walked differently from the smaller black bears of this forest.

Knowing what my mother told me about a bear's fierce jealousy concerning kills they consider theirs, I remember to carefully keep watch while eating. It is not his kill, but he might consider it so and return, and if he does come back, it will be time to forget all about this "mine" thing and run quickly! Eating until I'm full, I then head back into my favorite burrow before dawn, to sleep through the daytime until it is dark again.

I can't sleep because the feeling that there is something wrong in my life is worse the more I try. I am restless, unable to sleep, and feel like I am missing something, and there is a desire to roam and find it.

Finally, I just give up trying to think of what it is that is needed and manage to go to sleep. I will sort this whole, and restless, missing-something-in-my-life thing all out when I awaken.

I awaken hungry again, still restless and missing something in my life. Night will be here soon, and it is time to see if any of the bear's kill is left. I shamble up to my entrance but stop before reaching it, and for some reason decide, rather, to do an old predator/prey trick and dig out a secondary entrance to this burrow, instead of waiting to do it later as I intended.

The instinctive decision to dig that second entrance for safety saves my life.

Turning and returning to the main chamber, I go to the other side of it and start digging. We badgers dig very fast and it takes no time at all to get a good long tunnel up to the surface again, and now my second burrow entrance is finished; then comes all the hard work of getting the burrow back in order, and clearing all the loose dirt out. With the burrow cleaned up to the way I like it, I am finally satisfied with my hard work and now ready to get some food.

Darkness is outside now, the food is either roaming or sleeping, and I find my first one still sleeping. The snake that had come out to roam in the sun on this nice spring day had foolishly stayed out of its hole when darkness fell.

I am on it before its body can react; the air is too cold now for this creature, and the snake is too slow to get its head around in time to reach me with those fangs. I kill it and feast.

We can kill these things with the rattling tails in the daylight when they are fully aroused, but killing during daylight is more difficult and dangerous, even though our thick layer of skin and fat will protect us from them, unless they get very lucky.

This one had no luck at all. But he is delicious and fills my tummy nicely as I roam some more. Checking all of the territory and making sure my burrows have not been taken over by others, I look for that something else that seems to be the need making me so restless. But I do not know what it is, for it is just a want that I do not know how to fill.

Still there are things to keep me busy, and some of my other burrows need work, and if I busy myself it seems to make the need go away somewhat. But the need is still there when I return to my primary burrow and move back into it before dawn and sleep soundly.

I will try to think this thing out tomorrow when it grows dark again and it is time to roam again.

It is just before I would normally awaken at dark when something else makes me awake, I do not know what . . . a feeling, a feeling of "Wrong! Wrong! Wrong!"

I wonder if this is just that need-thing happening again, but it is not, it's an uneasy wrong feeling for some reason. My predator instincts tell me something is wrong even if it is not obvious yet to any of my other senses. Wandering up the tunnel to my entrance, I can see it is still light before even reaching the opening, but the sense of "wrong" grows worse the closer to that opening I come. I stop.

I hear nothing; but there is the scent of something, a new something, not a forest scent I am used to?

Until suddenly I realize the "wrong" is that I hear nothing, and that gives it away. Shouldn't I hear birds and sounds of the forest? There were always birdcalls just before dark, now there is nothing as I edge cautiously upward, and I do hear something just as I begin to stick my head out. I hear the sudden sound of rushing air and duck my head quickly back inside!

It saves my life. The huge, brown paw misses me as it slams into the ground over the entrance, and I scramble backward down my entrance tunnel as quickly as possible!

The new, larger brown bear was waiting patiently outside the entrance for something to come out, and I am still scrambling all the way backward down into my sleeping chamber when I hear him starting to dig furiously! I sense something else as I scramble frantically backward down my entrance tunnel. I sense rage from above me, and directed at me. Not the rage of a hunter; this is deeper rage, and I have the strange sensation it is not from the bear.

I don't have time to consider it! He can dig, I realize; turning in the sleeping chamber, and running for the second entrance on the other side! The other smaller black bears can dig also, but they cannot dig as well as this larger bear can!

My mother did not mention that there was a huge type of brown bear that could dig as fast as he can and now he is now coming through the ground far faster than I would like for him to, digging down into the entrance he has found, coming for me!

I feel pure rage that this creature would dare to try to dig me out of this, my favorite burrow; he is ruining it completely, and I will never be able to return to it, now that he knows where it is!

But there is fear also: this one can kill me, and he is not afraid of digging a badger out of its burrow, like the far smaller black bears of the forest are. So I do not stop to object to him invading either my entrance tunnel or my burrow as he digs furiously down into both.

I am much too busy running up my second tunnel to the second entrance of this burrow and out of that second entrance, and as I hear him digging furiously behind me until he finally reaches the sleeping chamber.

His roar of frustration would be funny, if I were not so certain he could run me down in the open. Contenting myself with just getting distance between us, I can still hear him back there digging furiously, still trying to find me in the burrow that I will never use again.

Running from where he roars frustration at the discovery that the prey he wanted has tricked him and is gone, I am only interested in simply putting distance between us. Trying not to shake with the fear of what almost happened as I run. It is not good for a fierce predator like me to be seen shaking like some small, weakling prey animal!

While running from him, I notice his roar is far louder than the other bears that normally stay in this forest, but I am safely away from him, and it is getting dark now anyway. While I am good in the dark, he will be clumsier, and it will be easy to hide from him, just as long as he is far enough behind me before I stop running.

I have seen bears before like the one our mother showed us, but they were the smaller, black types of bears, and while they are our enemies and consider us as prey, they do respect our claws and teeth, and usually leave us alone, especially if we are secure inside our burrows.

This bear is far different from those simple black bears; he is brown, and is more than three times the size of the simple black bears that used to rule this area.

This huge, new brown bear also marks his territory by clawing trees much higher on trees than any black bear does, and in the brown of the fur on his head there is a strange marking I have not seen before on the head fur of any black bears of our forest: a thin white scar from front to rear in the fur on top of his head.

He is also much smarter than the simple black bears of this forest, smarter than any bear should be, and he is not afraid to dig a female badger out of her burrow. Worst of all, as he tried to dig my burrow out, I had a sense that this bear was not just hunting for prey. There was a deeper rage with this bear, a rage not out to just hunt prey; this rage was out purely to kill.

There was something else I sensed, a sense that something had been with him when I saw him, but I couldn't see anything else with him when I sensed the unseen something alongside him, and when I sensed the rage directed at me as the bear tried to dig me out of my burrow. Suddenly realizing that I did not sense the rage from the bear at all, the rage directed at me was from the unseen thing that had been alongside him!

He is new, and he is dangerous, and far more dangerous than any other bear that has been in this forest before. I will make a new, favorite burrow, among the many others that will be dug this season, but I have also learned a valuable lesson. From now on all my burrows will have second entrances and they will all be under things brown bears can't dig through easily, like tree roots or rocky areas.

I roam until dawn, and roam far away from that burrow. The burrow I choose to stay in this morning is as far away as I can get from where I know the new brown bear roams, and let him have that area back there. My own territory is opening up in this direction, anyway.

Second Home

The newness of this area is slowly replaced by my own markings as I extend this territory in the new direction to let any intruders know who marks the territory here, and who will be ready to fight for it.

This is my territory, and I will defend it fiercely; unless it is the bear again, I am not fool enough to try to tell him that this is all mine and he can't roam here.

The area chosen as my new territory gradually enlarges with new burrows in the most protected places I can put them. Before I had no idea that the bear could dig so fast into a good burrow; this time all my burrows are dug under tree roots or rocky areas in this forest.

I do find a nice place for my new primary burrow; on top of a little hillock in the center of an open meadow, with a stream flowing down the center of it from north to south. Curiously there are no other hillocks in this meadow, just this one.

I would expect to find several hillocks in any area holding small hillocks, but except for this one the meadow is flat, and this hillock is almost in the exact center of the meadow as if it were somehow placed here intentionally.

I give up on this puzzle. The top of the little hillock will always keep my burrow dry even in the heaviest rains, no matter how high the stream in the center of the meadow floods. It is my new burrow, and that is all that matters as I explore and mark territory to make this new territory my own.

There are a few tall, older trees in the meadow with one near the hillock I have chosen, but not enough to spoil my view. In this open meadow from up here on my little hillock, I can see all of the meadow and the tall, old, thick forest around the meadow, secure in the knowledge that I own all of this.

My burrow is deep inside the little hillock, with the main opening near the top on one side of the hillock, allowing me to emerge and still see in all directions without rain falling inside my burrow. I make a second entrance on the other side of the hillock, in case I need to run from my burrow unseen again. For both warmth and protection, the main entrance tunnel and my other entrance do not come straight into the sleeping chamber now, as the last burrow had.

This entrance tunnel wanders as it comes inside, which makes it harder for any other bear or other predator to dig straight inside with the hope of finding someone easily available in a sleeping chamber. If that bear returns now, he will have to dig the hillock apart to find my sleeping chamber.

The skies darken, open, and water falls on my little hillock in my meadow, and the grass flourishing in the rain allows me to make a nice warm lining in all of my burrows, with the thickest grass layers inside for comfort and warmth.

When the rain does come down I can simply be inside here, snug and warm in my comfortable sleeping chamber. I also remember to make little side tunnels in here, to make it possible to have a place to make waste, without having to be outside at all if the weather is too bad out there.

This entire area is mine now; unless the bear wanders down here to see me, and then it will simply be time to move again.

But for all his intelligence, he does not appear to be bright enough to have figured out that I have moved, and I like it that way.

The few other predators that might be able to hurt me are all of the daytime, and when I hunt it is of the primarily night-time, so we seldom see each other.

I also have many burrows dug along both daily and nightly routes of travel to go into if threatened.

Best of all, the food is abundant with ground squirrel homes in the meadow, and a nearby stream flowing south through my meadow will be available for catching those delicious frogs and for drinking water.

Sometimes it is only necessary to wander a short distance from this little hillock burrow before finding needed food. Roots, good for food, are also are here in abundance in the tall, surrounding, older forest. Of course, it would not be right to concentrate on eating roots; that would hardly do for a good predator such as myself, and I do have pride.

It is easy to roam through the ferns growing along the stream, and to shelter inside them, waiting for prey to come through them to me. And easy to hunt each night for new types of food preys, or simply to find old types. Sometimes I do not even bother to wait until darkness to start my hunt because it will be necessary to pick up a lot of body fat for the coming winter season.

But that is still far away from this season, and the primary reason I hunt now is because food is available here, and I so love to hunt and to eat!

It is also necessary to make sure all the burrows that will have to be dug in the new areas of this larger area I am now claiming are prefect and well lined with grass for comfort

I stay busy digging and preparing burrows, and checking of all of them while I roam to make sure no one else has tried to claim a burrow in my absence.

While doing this near the far edge of my territory in the middle of the day; there is suddenly the scent of a new trail in this territory, markings she has deliberately left to antagonize this territory's owner.

She is in my territory! My first scent of her is while I am out in daytime, hunting and checking all of my burrows in this area; there are more than enough dug by now, but all are still worth defending from any rival, and I shiver with rage, and go hunt her instead.

It is not hard to track her either; this one is deliberately leaving her scent to be found where any other rival for this area can find it easily.

She wants my territory, and I fluff my fur to make myself appear larger in her eyes when we do meet, and grinding my teeth in anger, I follow the scent to her.

This is my territory where I have my very best burrow on my little hillock overlooking my forest; she is not going to take it away from me!

I can tell from the places she has walked through that she may be larger than I am but that is not the point. I do not care how larger she may be, this territory is mine and she will not hunt or roam here unless I will it!

She is easy to spot: arrogant and proud, and she must know who this territory belongs to already because she is deliberately making her own scent territory markings right over my scent territory markings!

Now I am beyond rage, growling and making an anger noise loud enough for her to hear easily. I want her to fight me if she dares!

She is waiting for me to come to her in the small, cleared area, and she is proud and arrogant about trying to take over what is mine.

She does not give me her name, and I do not ask for it as I rush at her, showing teeth and claws to let her know who is ready to fight for this! I do not care if she is larger, and she is. I do not care if she is ready for me, but she is.

I stop just before reaching her to see if she is actually trying to take my area away from me or is just bluffing. My mother, Asaseyaa, had explained to me that sometimes when two rivals meet on the borders of adjoining territory, they simply exchange insults and then each potential rival will turn and go back the other way into its own territory without fighting, but only if the aggressor is not really serious about taking territory away from its owner.

Sometimes even that does not happen, and two rivals simply see each other as they approach, and each recognizes they are on the boundaries of claimed territory. Then both will turn away; pretending not to have seen each other, without even exchanging growling insults as they go back to their own claimed territory.

This is not one of those times. I can see from the way she sets her body aggressively, and the way she shows teeth, that she seriously wants what is mine. She is not going to simply turn and leave; she wants to fight and claim this as we circle each other, still apart, still trying to evaluate each other's fighting ability before we actually attack.

Fur as erect as possible to make our sizes look larger than we really are, we try to bluff the other into leaving without a fight, if possible. To fight is to risk crippling injury that might leave one or both of us unable to hunt, and we might starve to death. Or we might be unable to defend ourselves if injured, and become prey ourselves to the first predator that comes along afterwards and finds us helpless.

Each of us evaluating the other in tactics, size, and movements to find any opening or any advantage as we circle; both our mouths growling with insults and threats as each of us tries to make the other be the first to charge, to see who is the most aggressive, and who might have weakness and be ready to run first. My advantage is that I already mark this territory; as she fights in it, she is considered the weaker one, despite her greater size.

We both decide at the same time and rush each other, circling, circling, trying to get to the weaker, less defendable backside of the other as we circle each other furiously, trying not to let the other behind, and snarling, biting, swiping at each other with our claws as we each try to make the other leave, without actually fighting.

Looking for the weakest side of each other, and then giving up on any hope of not having to fight, both of us rush into each other at the same time, trying to use weight for a quick tumble of the other and to advantage at the weaker stomach. Joining into a biting clawing mass, we two fighting creatures become one big ball of biting, scratching, snarling, and angry fur!

The thickness of our skin and fat layer may protect us from serious harm, unless one of us gets lucky, but she now knows I will fight for what is mine, and I do!

I fight, screaming with my rage at her intrusion as she fights to take what is mine away from me! But my mother, Asaseyaa, trained me well, and the fierce games we would play as young had also trained me well. This one is backing off from this territory before I will as we roll and rage and claw and bite, and until she breaks free and runs first!

I snarl with triumph and rage while chasing her from my territory, and my forest, my food, and my home, and I still rage even after stopping the chase!

Only after realizing that I now hurt badly in some places on my body will I even consider forgetting her intrusion into what are by all rights mine and mine alone. Then it is time to check my body, as I look sadly at my now missing sections of fur, and go to the stream to soothe my body.

I hurt, and am missing some of the beautiful fur I was so proud of, but although my injuries are a little painful, I am still able to hunt and not so crippled as to become prey myself, which was my biggest fear of having this fight with her. For now, I just want the cool waters of the stream to sooth my injuries. Going to it and drinking after I reach it, I sink into the stream to sit in the flowing cool water.

While we are not fond of having water all over ourselves, we can and do swim. This time I am grateful for the cool water of the stream. I learned some time ago, when one of my paws was hurt by the bite of a prey animal I was trying to dig out of its burrow, that if the hurt parts rest in cold, running water, it helps the pain go away. I sit and let the coolness of the stream soothe my hurt body.

Only after resting in the water long enough for the wounds to go from pain to dull throbbing ache do I return to the long job of remarking all of my territory, especially where she had the nerve to put her markings over mine! Everything she had scented now must be properly re-marked with my own scent for territorial possession.

Only when everything is properly re-scented with my own markings do I finally get around to the hunting thing I started to do today. By that time it's nearly dark anyway, so I simply stay out and hunt the night, and then sleep when daylight returns.

Although we badgers are tough creatures, and hard to hurt, my body will hurt for the next few days, and for those next few days it will be hard to dig burrows or hunt.

Still, there are enough burrows dug already, and there is enough prey not in burrows this time of the seasons to allow me to put off the digging to spend more time in my best burrow on the little hillock, watching the forest and clearing that is mine. Not forgetting to note all those places, I watch ground squirrels go into their own burrows in my clearing.

I will go see some of them later for dinner, but for right now, I try to understand this feeling thing happening to me, and still do not know what it is. Every time I think of young now, there is a little fluttery feeling inside me. Is this a way for a good predator to feel?

Reminding myself sternly not to give in to little fluttery feelings and to concentrate on being a good predator instead; my mother, Asaseyaa, would be ashamed of me if she knew that I was taking time off from the hunt to sit around the entrance of a burrow and sigh in the sunlight.

The seasons are also growing warmer now, and it may be necessary to find a new source of water if the stream becomes dry, which is something far more important than these silly feelings I don't fully understand yet.

Firestorm

As the seasons move more fully into the hot season, it becomes more noticeable that the rain falling from the sky is much lesser this set of seasons than the last hot season when I was still with my mother, sister, and brother.

I still think of them from time to time and wonder what happened to my brother, Tigranuhi, and my mother, Asaseyaa, but there is so much to do it is just impossible to consider going back to check, and at least not yet, maybe later. The worry now is that the rain falling from the sky is much lesser this set of seasons.

The rain still has not come from the sky as the season moves still deeper into the hottest of seasons; the stream that used to be so wide is now just a trickle of water when going to drink, and the creatures here in the meadow must satisfy themselves with less and less water.

The forest around me is no longer the beautiful green it used to be; now it is brown, except for the trees that always remain green, and even they are drying and browning in the deeper heat of this season.

The forest grows still browner around my meadow as the season moves onward into greater heat, until it is even hot at night now when it's time to hunt as I notice that some prey creatures are now leaving to find new homes closer to water.

If all of the planteaters are moving away or hiding, there will be need to go find new territory, and I love my beautiful, primary burrow in the hillock overlooking my meadow. The grass in that meadow is as brown as the trees around it now, and the only good thing is that there are now more of those long snake things with the rattling tails to eat, since they are staying out later in the warmer evening air. True, they are dangerous to hunt, but they taste great.

I sense the "wrong" again and am instantly awake! It is the midday, but there are too many loud, new noises outside my burrow, and I am angry at having to get up this early for any reason as I wander grumpily up the entrance tunnel to see what is making all the new noise.

The wind is up again today. I can hear it blowing hot and dry from the north to the south across my burrow entrance, but it sounds much stronger than before and something is wrong. A new wrong smell I have never smelled before is on the rising wind.

Looking outside cautiously, in case it is a dangerous thing, I finally see my very first humans, and far too many of them are around my hillock, using their human mouths far too much, keeping me awake during my sleep time.

It is easy to tell what kind of new creature these are by their scent. My mother had described it to me, and I remember now that my mother, Asaseyaa, had also said, "They can kill from a distance!"

As I catch the full scent of these newcomers, I suddenly remember this was the same strange, new scent I noticed around the deer with the small hole in its side on my first spring night in my first territory. It was humans who had been there and made that kill.

I had not connected the scent to the look of these creatures until now; but now as I watch them making too much noise near my burrow and look closer at them, humans hardly look like decent predators at all.

They have no fur, and their teeth are also too flat and small to be decent predators, from what can be seen of the two humans making those loud, annoying, human-mouth noises to each other.

And both of the humans near my burrow entrance have no claws at all. If these are the dangerous, two-legged predators my mother described, I don't know how they do it.

They are also wearing some kind of brown skin-covering things, with no difference between them in looks; how can they tell each other apart to mate?

However, they do seem to be very noisy, excited predators, no matter how poorly equipped they are with no teeth and claws, but now it is easy to see that even these noisy humans are not making the noises that had awakened me.

In my meadow are new, far too loud, far too large, roaring yellow clanking things, with one human each riding on top of each one as they move north through my clearing.

I notice through my irritation that the huge roaring, yellow, clanking things have large flat things across the front of them and no decent paws at all on any of them. Instead they move on other flat things that go around and around on each side for the full length of the side making the loud clanking noises.

They are going to scare away all of my food with these things! I give up on the idea of sleep to just watch all of this human stupidity keeping me awake.

I also notice now that all the humans passing north through my clearing on top of the yellow clanking things also seem to have the same kind of all-brown body covering, but not the beautiful brown with darker stripes of my fur, these are all just plain brown with small markings on them.

I barely have time to notice this when something huge flies overhead, making an incredible noise as it heads north!

I have never ever thought a bird could be that large or make that much noise as it passes overhead, as I duck quickly back into the burrow for safety; looking out again just in time for another one to go overhead, making me duck back inside again!

This is really infuriating. I snarl our rage sound to both humans still out there making all the yelling noise.

"This is my territory, get out of it, Humans! Shut up and go away!"

They both turn to look at me with amazed looks on their human faces as if they were not aware that all of this would annoy me! Of course they do not speak badger any more than I would speak human, but they do understand my raging snarl.

Then both humans actually have the nerve to try to get me to leave my burrow and head south away from here with motions of their arms and paws. I ignore them. If they annoy me, I will bite them!

Instead, I turn to look where the huge monster-flying things went, in case they are still here and come back for me, and only then do I finally see the rapidly rising cloud to the north of my meadow.

Rising, rolling red soars upward from hillside to hillside under that smoke, riding the wind southward; and even from here I can see that the rising red is easily far above the tops of even the tallest trees to the north, and the trees of this forest are very tall!

I know instantly, as a shiver of fear passes through me in spite of its distance from here. I do not have to have seen this before to know. We all know instinctively, and I can see creatures beginning to drift past my hillock now heading south away from it.

Heading south as the loud clanking things head north toward the cloud with more humans heading north with them, I watch, thinking how truly foolish these humans must be to head north to that thing when all of the other creatures have the brains to head south, away from it.

Not only are humans the most poorly equipped predators I have ever seen, they are also the most stupid, poorly equipped predators. I can now hear the distant roaring, even this far away from the fire, and hear the distant sounds of loud cracks as I watch it grow larger to the north.

Every time there is a loud, distant crack some red things fly up and out of the area where the rising red is, and something starts red in a new location where they fall. Rising red joins rising red and the red grows larger to the north.

Then I realize that the wind from the north is now rising rapidly in our direction; the fire is riding the wind blowing toward us, and the red is coming my way fast!

Even if this is my first fire, I know that there is something terribly wrong with this fire; it is far too large to be normal, and the center of it suddenly seems to have risen higher, opening up into the sky above it.

Suddenly I also know a new terrible wrong; the center of the fire has started to turn into a giant circle of flame as the fire roars south! The entire center of the fire in the valley has turned into a giant circle of fire now rising far up into the sky, with smoke soaring higher above it, and I know that this is not natural! The wind coming south is also now bringing me not just the scent of fire, there is death smell with it; creatures are dying up there, and we all know because the creatures moving south around my hillock are beginning to move faster south through my clearing.

They smell the same scents; they know what is happening up there where the red is, and they do not wish to join the dying ones behind them. I don't worry; my burrow is safe, I will just go into it and let this thing pass. I will certainly not drift south in fear like the planteaters are doing.

More of them are passing my favorite burrow, running now as they head south away from the fire, and the humans in front of my burrow are still trying to get me to go with the creatures fleeing south by waving their silly, helpless non-clawed paws at me. I snarl a warning to let these creatures know that touching me might not be a great idea as one of them seem to want to do.

They give up and go back to yelling into a flat thing they hold in their paws, with a thin silver thing sticking up from it.

Silly humans; to talk to things in your paws and expect them to talk back to you, this species are definitely not predators!

Then the things they hold in their paws do talk back to them, as I look amazed at this wonder, and then duck back into the burrow as the roar passes overhead again.

I watch this time as one of the huge flying things goes overhead. Curious as to what these new flying things are doing; not bothering to go all the way back into the burrow.

Badgers eyes are not the best of our senses, but I could swear that as the flying thing got over the rising red to the north, its belly opened and a large cloud of something came out and fell away from it.

I wonder if it was hurt, but then another passes overhead and heads north to do the same thing and they both fly away again without appearing to be hurt, so I guess that it is just something these flying creatures do.

I watch for a while from my little hillock as the flying things continue to go north over me, open their bellies, and dump something on the rolling cloud with the red beneath it.

The fire ignores them as it continues to grow and come this way faster. They have no effect on it at all, and I could easily have told them that; from hilltop to hilltop now, across this entire wide valley, it rides the wind coming south. It is too big now, and they are too small to stop it.

I am thinking of going back into my burrow to simply wait until this all passes. Until suddenly, I do not know why, it seems important to do something. It is not anything my mother taught me for survival, just an instinct as I go through the burrow to my second entrance and fill it in from inside, sealing it off. It saves my life.

That job completed, I shamble back through my burrow to the main entrance to watch the humans do foolish things again, and hear all the noise before even reaching the entrance; the loud, clanking, yellow things are coming back from the north by the sounds, and there is an incredible amount of human yelling from outside my entrance!

The noise of the loud clanking things stops suddenly, and there are more and more loud crack noises growing louder, with a steadily increasing roaring noise outside. I rush quickly up to the entrance to see what is happening with these foolish humans who are so noisy in my forest.

Before reaching the entrance I notice the wind is there, and suddenly is no longer blowing rapidly south with the fire. It stops. The wind stops for no reason, and then begins again as it changes and shifts, but in the wrong direction!

The wind grows stronger, and suddenly is now howling to the north across the entrance of the burrow, toward the fire in that direction! But the northern direction the fire is in is not what catches my eye first.

The humans are running! All of them are running south, including the ones who were on the yellow clanking things before. They are off them now and running to a human-carrying traveling thing that has round things below it. They all climb into it, and then it runs itself on the round paws things that spin around as it runs.

I had no idea that humans had these things, but it is making far greater speed than the loud, yellow clanking things did as it runs south, while carrying the humans inside it.

I ignore the roaring cracking sounds to my other side while watching these humans leaving in their human-carrying thing. What stupidity; these can't be decent predators at all to run like that while leaving their loud, yellow clanking things in my clearing! They are totally ruining my meadow for hunting. If those huge yellow things stay there, it will scare away all of the prey.

Then among all the other rising, cracking noises from the north where all the roaring is, there is a much louder crack as something very large flies, flaming in front of me all the way across the clearing from north to south! I just have time to realize that it was the entire top of a tree flying past on fire, and for the first time, I look to the other side, shriek like a pathetic prey creature myself, and run back into my burrow!

It is here, and it is huge; a solid wall of flaming, roaring red as it eats the trees, and they explode, throwing pieces of the trees across the clearing! The huge flames are many times the height of the treetops now in a giant turning circle of fire, and the terrible wind is now roaring back into the fire! The wind is pulling things from the ground and turning trees into towering flames before the fire even touches them, as the flames roll back into the fire with the wind!

I feel the terrible heat fully for the first time, and run frantically back inside my burrow to do the second thing that saves my life. Now I catch the smell, despite the wind blowing itself back into the fire outside, and I do not like that smell!

Kicking dirt frantically behind me to seal up the entrance tunnel leading out of the sleeping chamber, I am inside, hiding like some pathetic prey creature in my sleeping chamber, shivering as the noises outside come through the thickness of the hillock above me.

The ground is vibrating with the roaring above and around my hillock, and even through the thickness of dirt above this burrow; there are sounds of things hitting the ground up there! The loud crack sounds can be heard even down here, and suddenly there is the sound of something huge falling on top of my burrow complex as the ground shakes!

But the burrow is built strongly, and only some dirt falls on me from the top of my burrow as I shiver in fear in darkness and wait in fear until the roar above me is gone, and still I wait, shaking in fear.

I have enough air inside here with the size of this burrow complex, and have no intention of trying to go anywhere near the outside of it until everything up there goes away, far away!

Waiting, shivering, until it is long past the time to normally go out at dusk and hunt; waiting, shivering, until it is time to be outside in the early sun enjoying myself in its warmth before coming back inside to sleep for the day, and waiting, shivering, until I am absolutely sure. And only then, cautiously, I begin to dig my way outside.

The smell is the first thing noticeable, making me wrinkle my nose in disgust. Somehow the air is bad in the tunnel leading up the main entrance. Hurrying upward through air that is hard to breath and gasping by the time I am at the end of it, looking out over what used to be my beautiful meadow with the beautiful forest around it. It is gone.

It is still there, but it is all wrong; everything I loved about it is gone, everything is blackened and burned. What used to be a tree near my hillock is now what is left of a burned still-smoldering tree trunk, as the remains lay on top of my hillock. The tall, older trees I loved to hunt beneath, in the forest around the clearing, are all gone, except for the few ones still standing as blackened, smoldering tree trunks that go to nothing above them. Trees lay fallen and smoldering over what used to be my lovely forest around the clearing, and the grass that was my clearing is now gone with them.

Even the huge, clanking yellow things left in that clearing by the humans who ran from them are not yellow anymore; they are all black and burned.

I do not like anything I now see or smell. Where will the food be, and how am I going to hunt in all of this new ugly that used to be green?

In the south there is some green visible in the far distance above all the blackness that used to be forest and meadow, so I decide to go that way.

The ground is still warm, and the black stuff over what is left of my meadow is hard on my paws, but when I try to clean it off, it hurts my mouth as I try to lick the black from my paws. Giving up I decide that it is better just to accept the black stuff on my paws instead.

One look at the stream and I decide not to even bother trying for water there. It is full of the black stuff covering what little water was there before, and if the black stuff tastes bad just trying to lick some of it from my paws, then the black which fills the entire stream will probably be worse. Better just to roam south and find that green; where there is green, there will be fresh forest and fresh water.

Roaming, I use the green in the distance as a landmark, since everything else is different.

I pass fallen trees that still smolder, and standing ones with no limbs left on them; still upright, black and burned.

Roaming until I find the humans again, standing in a large cluster at the edge of where the fire stopped at a newly cleared area, stupidly exposed to all dangers out in the open like foolish prey creatures, not like the predators they are supposed to be.

The stuff that the flying things were dropping is everywhere, all over the trees and the plants in front of me, stuff covering even some of the large yellow clanking things that are here, some even covers humans in the newly cleared area around them. It's too messy; it's ruining my forest, and I hate it!

The humans are not even looking as I come toward them through blackness around me; bad predators indeed not to notice me by now, the one creature emerging from all of the blackness behind me. Any real predator would have had all of them by now! They continue to make their foolish mouth noises to each other, until one of them finally does notice me.

I recognize from both mouth noises and scent he is one of the two outside my burrow, as he yells something to the others, and suddenly, all the humans are staring at me as I shamble toward them through all of the black. I do not mind them all staring at me, but if they annoy me I will bite them!

They continue simply to stare at me in apparent foolish human amazement as I walk onward through them, past the huge, yellow clanking things, toward the forest I want to be in again.

For some reason the humans all seem overly excited about my emerging from of all the blackness behind me, unhurt and unburned, but I have no time for humans or their excitement. I just want a new place to have territory and some food, and not necessarily in that order as I pass, unconcerned, beyond them into the forest on the other side.

Once I get past the stuff the flying things dropped, there is real forest, with real green trees, around me again. There will be food here, there will be water here, and there will be a new home in this new territory that will be mine.

At least it will be mine as soon as I have finished marking it with my scent and digging all the necessary burrows. Right now I just want some water and some food, and a good burrow to sleep in before tomorrow would also be nice.

I find the food quickly. Far too many of the prey things have neglected to dig their way to safety, and that long, rattling tail snake tastes nice, even if he was fully alert and dangerous for me to catch for food. There are also some of the nice plants whose roots taste good, although I would never admit to any other badger that I actually ate planteaters' food.

Still the plants taste nice, and they fill me until I can eat later, when I roam from a decent burrow for decent prey food like I should. There is some water in a spring not fouled like the stream was fouled, as I drink from the spring.

By the time it is dark I have started to dig my new home; digging, when I should be preparing to roam for the night, and walking around in the daytime when I should be sleeping. I wonder what else will be strange in my life now.

The urge is there again, but I need to get this finished and start claiming territory. Giving up on trying to think of what the urge means, I try to turn this digging into a suitable burrow, with a decent sleeping area, some side tunnels, and of course that important second entrance in case that new far too large, wrong-colored bear, or other dangerous predators like him had made it out of the fire as I did and happen to be down here with me now.

Actually, I hope he did not make it out, but he is obviously a tough, experienced predator and probably did. I sense that he will not die this easily. Somehow there is an instinctive feeling I might see him again, and I have to be prepared for him when I do.

Few black bears, who used to be the only bears in this forest, will try to dig us out of our burrows because they respect the teeth and claws of badgers waiting for them inside those burrows. But this new, huge brown one with the thin white scar on top of his head does not fear our teeth and claws at all, and does not fear digging us out of a burrow, and has already shown that he can dig out burrows very quickly.

There is something different about him from any other bear, something more than size or color, something wrong, and something my mother told me once before. Something about the way he roams, something about the unseen one that I sensed beside him; something she told me about "others not as they should be." But in the need to have a safe burrow, I have to put unimportant thoughts aside for now as I concentrate on digging instead.

The new burrow is finished by the time I would normally be out roaming, and since it is easier to just simply settle into it instead of going out to hunt, I do. I need to try to get my life and schedule in at least some kind of order with some much-needed sleep. For the rest of the dark time and much of the next daytime, I sleep and dream of delicious food things.

Ardor

Awakening before it is even near darkness yet, I wonder if the new bear has found this burrow also.

But it is not the bear; it is something else, and I scramble out to follow the feeling that is so strong now. I can't quite understand why, but my urge to roam is strong.

I have to roam and find something. It doesn't help that this is all new territory and I might have to fight a rival for it again; and this time as challenger not defender, I will be the weaker in the fight, as the one who challenged me was the weaker in that fight.

Still for all the caution in this new place, I have to admit that it is beautiful, even better than the old forest and meadow I will return to someday when it is green again.

I already miss my lovely primary burrow in the little hillock overlooking my meadow, with all those delicious ground squirrels to keep me company there.

Here the forest is old and tall, beautiful and green, and thick with trees and plants. Not knowing this new place, I will have to be more cautious in its thicker cover; one of the few enemies that can harm me could be concealed in this deeper cover, waiting for me to pass.

I remember the bear that tried to dig me out from the burrow, and hope that he did not make it out of the fire ravaged area behind me, and then scent water as I find a wide field and wander into the thick grass covering it, passing under some strange new thing as I do, a series of short upright things of wood, but not trees. The short things growing from the ground stand in a long row, with four long thin things on each one; each long, thin thing, one above the other, stretching from short not-tree to short not-tree along the length of where they grow from the ground.

I wander under this new thing and stop to taste the lowest long, thin thing in case it might taste good. But the long thin thing tastes hard and not good, so I leave it alone to taste the wood of the short not-trees also. They are of real wood, but they have no branches like a small tree would have, and I wonder if the long, thin things actually are the branches of these not-trees?

I puzzle this, and then wander into the overgrown field. Finding a deer trail where they have pressed the grass down traveling in here makes the going easier. I simply follow the deer trail through this field, until reaching the other side where the ground rises and passes into what, at first, looks like a green forest of the tops of tall trees.

But as I near it, the forest in front of me somehow doesn't seem thick enough, and it puzzles me at first why I can see so far while nearing the top of the small rise to enter the trees.

The sun is starting to set as I enter the forest on the other side of the field, and it isn't that thick after all, at least not in front of me, but it is thick below me as the forested ground slopes downward from this higher land that I didn't realize I was traveling on.

Below me, at the bottom of this sloping, forested hillside is more water than I have ever seen before. Then I see the full view in front of me, and stand amazed at something so beautiful that I stop, gasping like some amazed prey creature instead of the decent predator I am!

The sun is setting over the hills on the far other side of this impossibly large place of water, and for the first time in my life I see gold as the huge red setting sun turns the far larger than I could ever imagine, place of water golden before me!

The water stretches as far I can see to either side of my view from up here on the hilltop, and across all that water the hills are thickly green with forest.

This side of the thickly forested hillside of old trees I am standing on stretches down to the large water on both sides of me, and I already know where my new primary burrow is going to be. On this hillside stretching down to that water where I can catch the last warming of the sun each day as that other favorite burrow I had in the meadow somehow seems just not that important anymore.

I roam to find the perfect spot to dig and find a tall, wide-limbed tree to dig beneath near the top of my hill, and one of the trees whose leaves turn to colors and drop every winter, these always have nice, wide sheltering roots to place my burrow underneath.

Let any bear try to dig this one up to get at me. Digging my new burrow below my chosen tree, with a nice flat area in front of it that will be perfect for sitting to watch that sun setting, and I work on the burrow until well after dark.

For some reason it just seems important that this burrow be more elaborate than any other burrow I have ever dug, but I am also hungry again, and it is hunting time; the rest of the work of making my new burrow perfect can come later.

It is easy to hear where the next meal is, as I roam down the hillside for some of those delicious croaking frogs I hear below me near the water. Food is going to be plentiful here and I sense that I may need extra soon, but do not know why.

Feasting until full, and then before it is even light, going back to work again, digging, cleaning, and pulling lots of the abundant grass from the field into my center sleeping chamber. Again, I am not sure why, but it just seems necessary to make it larger this time.

This burrow has to be extra safe, so this time I do not dig the second entrance all the way to the outside from inside. Instead, there is simply a partially dug tunnel leading upward to that second entrance from the sleeping chamber. A tunnel I can finish digging out in a hurry if a threat appears at the primary entrance, but not something a predator can see from outside or use to enter this burrow.

I have that urge again, very strong now, and it makes me whimper as I sleep through the daylight because I still do not know what it is.

Still, the frogs taste delicious, and I feel happy enough to start another new burrow closer to the water. Not as good as this one, but the new borrow burrow is closer to the food around the large water, and I will not have to roam as far to find more delicious frogs at night. If I am lucky, those delicious frogs may even hop right into this burrow in the dark and save me the trouble of bothering to roam for them.

I then want to sleep as the sky begins to lighten, but for some reason can't, for the urge to roam instead is simply too strong now. I caught just the faintest trace of scent from over the top of the hill behind me when the wind shifted, and for some reason it seems to excite me until it is just impossible to stay in the burrow and sleep.

Going back and forth through the forest on this side of the hill with no luck, I am sure what I need is not even on this side of the hill as I finally decide to go back uphill through the field to see if it might be something on the other side.

I sniff the air carefully. This is so frustrating when I do not know what it is, but I do know what it is at the same time. Clearing the top of the hill and roaming back through the field while still looking, I try to catch that scent again.

There, the very faintest of smells. I am instantly aware of something and still not sure just what it is, until I catch a stronger scent where markings have been left for someone like me to find in the thick forest on the other side of the field.

For the first time, all of my natural instincts come forward, and I know now the scent is one of ours, another badger, but not a rival that will have to be fought in the new territory I have found and claimed.

I run, before slowing down into the proud, assured walk of an adult. I have pride and it would not be prideful to rush and meet this one; I will let him come to me instead. The scent is faint, but still there as I go further into territory not yet claimed as mine yet.

I don't care; his scent is there, where he has left it, so any females will know he is here, and to let rivals also know he is here among them.

I try to make my fur look its very best as I fluff it up and growl with pride to let him know that I am a proud, adult predator and worthy of looking at, even if I am still a little small.

The scent leads off to the other side, and I follow, trying to not look too eager, as I hear him through the brush nearby.

Breaking through the surrounding brush into the cleared area he is in, I can see him fully, and he is gorgeous! Full-grown and delightfully plump, with perfect reddish-brown fur just like mine, but his fur is even more beautifully red brown, and so soft with such beautiful markings, good teeth and claws, proud as any badger should be, alert, and so lovely fierce . . . I want him!

He sees me almost as soon as I see him, and since he is interested also I fluff my fur with pride again to let him see that I truly am an adult, and worthy of notice. Then I growl fiercely to also let him know I am just as proud and independent as he is, and that he will not enter this territory without my permission. Of course, neglecting to mention that this is not actually my territory yet as he snarls, and I snarl back just to let each other know that we understand each other.

We begin the meeting ceremony together, fluffing our fur to make ourselves look larger in each other's eyes while circling and growling;, letting each other also know that we are both proud and independent, even if we are to be mates.

We exchange names, and he tells me how beautiful my black markings are mixed into the brown of my fur, as I smile back at him with pride. His name is Red Fur and I understand why; his fur is such a soft and gorgeous dark red.

Only after we find each other suitable do we mate, although I will not know fully until this next spring if it happened, I do know that Red Fur is handsome and he loves me as we roam happily together, and stay together in my burrow overlooking the large water place.

We sit snugly together just inside the entrance of what is now our burrow together; enjoying the breeze as the forest whispers in the wind around us, enjoying the white things passing overhead in the sky making the large water darker as they pass overhead, enjoying the dark gray of the water stretching outward below us when rain comes from the sky, while we sit snug and warm together watching it.

Enjoying our sunsets together, he watches them with me, before we go to hunt in darkness; and I am proud to hunt alongside him as we seek prey together.

But Red Fur stays just a short while; for we are solitary creatures except with our young, as my mother had instructed me, and we prefer to live alone, except in certain rare cases if we are older or just prefer the company of another.

Then Red Fur simply leaves, and I miss him, but not as much as I should, I suppose.

The days are becoming colder, and winter is coming, and it is time to feed and fatten before it arrives. For some reason it seems really important now to eat more than normal, and even for an approaching winter.

I have to concentrate on work also; there are other burrows to dig, and the areas forming the boundaries of this territory to scent up, so rivals and others will know that I am here, and this is mine.

There is the beauty of the forest on the other side of the field above this burrow to admire in all of its greens and browns, and to admire the colors of the leaves of trees that shed their leaves in this time of the cooler season.

Leaves make a colorful, soft ground for me to walk on as I explore and hunt, or as I rest in the daytime on the flat area in front of this burrow, content to feel the sun warming me.

When the sun sets huge and red behind the green hills on the other side of the large water, the beauty of the sun makes my large water all golden, turning the white things that move across the blue above me red as it sets under them.

I enjoy watching it at every day's end, sitting in front of my primary burrow, catching the last warming rays of the sun. Winter will be here soon, but for now I enjoy my large water and my forest, as the reds and yellows of the leaves I sit on turn to browns and then fade and fall apart beneath my paws.

Winter arrives in white falling snow one morning, and I have accumulated so much extra fat this season, I look as round as a fat frog instead of a sleek predator. Still I feel the need to eat and eat, wondering where in my body I am going to put all of this food.

Until I sleep before coming out again to enjoy the white stuff falling, then hunt before going back into my snug burrow to sleep again.

Letting winter pass as I sit outside sometimes in the last of the day to enjoy the sun before my burrow; enjoying the sight of it setting in golden beauty over the now white hills on the other side of my large water.

Discovering that unlike the stream I was at last winter, this large water seldom seems to grow solid and clear like the stream once did, except around its edges. Here I never have to break through the solid clear of this water to get a drink as I did at the stream, although I do have to be more careful on the clear solid edges of this one, since the only time I am incautious enough to try to go out on the solid clear for a drink I fall through the surface.

I thought it would be hard like the steam was; however, it was not as I finally manage to scramble out of it by clawing my way over the solid clear, until enough of the solid has broken to allow me to find solid ground again.

On cold but safe solid ground at least, but with freezing water all over my body, I run for the safety of the burrow to get warm again, and sit, miserable, before finally drying off as sunlight warms me. Having learned another lesson and survived it, I realize that we often do not survive the lessons of the wild. I am lucky this time.

Most of my time is now spent sleeping and waiting for warm to come again. When it is warm again, there is also a strange sense of anticipation, one I never had before as if something were about to happen.

The days pass and it is time to play in the snow, but not as much as the last winter; now it seems more tiring to play, and most of my time is spent sleeping inside my snug burrow. Winter passes, until the day the white stuff begins to melt again.

Emerging from my burrow only to find I have slept for most of the last few days with no urge at all to hunt and now am hungry, the first thing to do is hunt for food; even plant roots would do now, anything to eat, something to dig up and eat greedily.

I was not this hungry after the last winter, but now for some reasons I just want to eat and eat as the season passes into warmer spring days, and something very strange seems to be happening to my body.

I roam restlessly even when not hunting, just to be out walking sometimes, and realize that I am definitely getting plumper. Worst of all, there is something wrong inside me; I can feel my body moving inside as I grow plumper still during the passing of the days and nights. I hope I do not have sickness of some kind, for sickness kills us so easily.

There is also less urge to roam now, with more need to stay close to the burrow, and for some reason, an urge to also make the burrow extra warm and special. Dragging almost enough grass into the sleeping chamber to fill it, I continuously try to improve the burrow and make it better, even though it is already as good as it can possibly be.

There is also a need to just sit in the last of the daylight each day; enjoy the sun setting, and try not to worry about what is happening inside my body.

Something is moving in there. I feel it all the time now, as if something were trying to get out of me. It moves as I sit and wait until it stops. Lately it seems to be stopping less and moving more, and there seems to be more than one movement inside me, and I am really afraid now of what is happening to me.

Afraid of this strange new sickness I might have, I wonder what my mother would do in a case like this and wonder if I will be like my sister, dying alone in a burrow without anyone to come back and mourn for me, as my mother and I did for my sister. I will die, and no one will know it or even miss me!

Attachments

Until the day I drag myself deep inside the sleeping chamber; something is wrong. I am dying. I am dying, just as my sister, Shareesa, died inside the burrow we shared with her; but I am alone, and no one will cry for me. I will die, unloved and alone.

I weep with frustration as I prepare to die, and then something happens, and I do not know what it is. I am so afraid, until the sleek, wet young one emerges from me as I lie on my side, and look in wonder at what I have done. The next one follows it into their new world of this burrow they are being born into. Now I know what my mother went through to bring me into this world.

Fear of what was happening is gone; these are my very own young to groom and teach and love. The third one emerges, and I wait hopefully for another. However, that is all as I turn to clean and groom and love my very own special little ones!

Cleaning their wet, beautiful, little bodies, making them so perfect and beautiful for this world they will be living in, I know that they will love the sight of the sun setting in all its red beauty over the green hills on the other side of the large water as much as I do. I know they will love all of my forest in all of its greens and browns and grays and all of the other colors of its life, and I know that they will love me just as much as I love them now.

My mother had three, and now I have three like her; two females and one male, just as she did. As I finish cleaning their little bodies, I love all three so very much, then move them so very gently to where they now have to be. Remembering this from what I knew of the large, warm thing that fed me. And as I once drank greedily to feed, these three begin to drink greedily from my own body also while I look on in wonder, and, like my mother before me, feed my very own beautiful young.

There must be names for them, but I simply do not know what those names should be, and that I could actually have young never occurred to me, and now what will I call them?

One of the females is striped and colored just like me, and I am so proud of her for looking so much like me I think of giving her my own name, but she is a proud predator and should have her very own name.

She will be called "Melinoe." Smugly satisfied after I name her, for she will have her own name, but it is still very much like mine.

I can tell already that the other female will be a proud little hunter, and she is pawing at me so demanding as she feeds. I will call her "Menhit," which means "the huntress."

The little male who needs so much attention from me I will call "Kekuit," the name for "ruler of the dawn and twilight."

I have so very much to teach them, so much to do, so many things they will have to know about: predators, prey, and survival, before they can leave me and be safe on their own. They will be trained so well to be ready for this world by the time they leave me, like I had left my mother before them.

But for now I watch my beautiful young sleep peacefully against me, safe and warm and perfect. And I already know that when they do leave I will cry behind them as my mother had cried behind me, but for now, as they sleep against me, I am content that I am their large, warm thing now, as my own mother had been mine before.

I awaken to feed them again, and have no urge other than to just groom them and groom them, and make them so perfectly lovely, until I have to sleep again.

Food can wait until later; I just want to be here with them, only leaving once before rushing right back to be sure nothing has crept into the sleeping chamber to harm them while I was gone. They are all right, and I groom them again while they sleep.

When I do have to leave to get my own food, they start to cry in their need for me to be there before I can even get out of the entrance tunnel, and I have to rush right back to them and comfort them, letting them know that the food from the large, warm thing that loves them so much is right here for them.

Only when they are fully fed and sleeping so beautifully and snug will I try to go out again for my own food, and even then, I find prey quickly, make a quick kill, and rush right back with it still in my mouth.

Afraid to stop and take the time to eat it there, I am terrified some creature has been inside the burrow while I was gone and has killed all my beautiful young ones!

They are all right as I check them anxiously for any damage. Only when it is clear that they have slept peacefully in my absence will I eat quickly, so I can snuggle them right beside me and keep them so warm and safe.

Over the next few days, I will not go out at night at all, but then I begin to understand that they will not miss me for a little while if they are sleeping.

I am hungry, and no predator other than the bear will dare to enter the burrow of a female badger to try to get them. My mother had told me this, but it is so hard to believe that they will be safe because they are my very own young ones to care for and protect.

I go out for food and find that the wonderful, croaking frogs have come back, and they are still delicious. Feasting well until it is dawn, I am surprised at how famished I was. Eating frogs is hardly hunting because it is far too easy, but they are close, and I will not stray far from the burrow, even if I do prefer ground squirrels and other warmer prey.

My life soon settles into the routine of hunting and trying to make sure I am always back to our burrow before the young ones can awaken.

Little Kekuit, my beautiful little male needs so much attention from me, while little Menhit is so much more independent, even at this early age. Her sister, Melinoe, is between both of the others in her need for me to be there. And if I hear their need from their little cries while I am returning from a hunt, I curse myself for being selfish to run off and feed myself while they are hungry, as I wonder if my own mother had felt the same way with us. I am certain now that she did.

Their little eyes open for the first time, and I smile with joy at all their wonder as they look at what is around them. It is only a simple burrow, but they are so fascinated with everything in it, including me, their large, warm thing that has been feeding them, grooming them, and loving them.

They make the cutest little cries of fascination at everything they see, and as I groom them, their little tongues kiss me back, letting me know how very much they love me, telling me that they will stay with me and follow me forever.

They tumble and roll across both burrow and me in mock fighting, playing with each other as they tear up all my carefully arranged grass inside the chamber. I love them so much as they play, even if it does mean extra work for me to get the sleeping chamber back into some kind of order for the next sleeping time.

Even at her young age, Menhit is fierce and usually wins these fierce games; she will survive and live long.

They grow. I bring them their first prey and they are not ready for it yet. However, as they play games with the prey, I am patient with them as my own mother had been patient with me. Then my young watch me fascinated as I eat it. The idea of food coming from something other than from me is still too new for them, but they are learning.

As they grow, I bring them prey, and they still play with it, tearing it apart in their fierce instinctive games as I watch them proudly.

They grow, I bring them prey, and they taste it, and for the first time they try it as food, not as a plaything to simply to be tossed around the burrow.

They grow, I bring them prey, and they eat it eagerly.

They grow, I bring them prey, and now they prefer it, stopping their nursing from me in exchange for this new food. I feel sad, and as my mother had known with me, I now know it is time to go outside with them for the first time.

I wait deliberately for the right time of the day, wanting to show them something very special, and it is time for them to see the sun setting over the hills on the other side of the large water above on this hillside where we live. Their first colors other than this burrow will be something that they will remember forever.

They have already been wondering where I go when I am not here with them, but they have not had permission to go near the entrance yet, and my word is law in matters of safety. Now I try to keep them in some kind of order through their fierce excitement at being able to see the new outside for the first time. Taking them up our entrance tunnel as they stumble all over themselves to see this new thing.

The forest, sloping down to the large water on either side, is full and green in this season of new growth, and the sun is on top of the opposite hills by the time I manage to get them to the entrance. The sun sets in all of its red beauty over the green hills on the other side of the large water, turning the surface of that large water golden in its light as the white things passing high overhead turn red in the setting light of the sun.

I proudly listen to the gasps of my young while they stare frozen with awe at the sight of the beauty in front of their perfect burrow, until it is time to get them into some sort of roaming order again.

Unlike my own mother who had taken us out in the daytime to hunt first, I am going to take my little predators on a night hunt, and it will be an easy hunt to be sure; after all, we are going after frogs, and the moon in the night sky is full and bright. There should have an easy first hunt, and they can learn of the hard ones later.

Leading them down to the edge of the water in the growing darkness, I marvel at their desire to see and feel everything around them all at once as they try not to fall all over each other. They are so eager to learn, and I am so proud of them.

Even prouder am I when they start to ambush the frogs by using the method I have taught them, as they creep up very slowly up from behind, for the frog can't see slow movement as a threat.

They are good at it, only missing a few at first because of too much eagerness, and moving too quickly at the excitement of the hunt. But I remember when I was that excited the first few times I had hunted and had missed prey also. The thing that makes me proudest of them is when they start to work together for the prey, something even I didn't do with my brother and sister.

It started by accident. Melinoe is behind a frog, and Menhit is in front of it. Both sisters are stalking the same prey at once. When Menhit in front of the frog moves a little too fast upon the frog they are both after, it turns to flee and hops right into Melinoe's mouth.

They have learned something, and soon, all three of them are taking turns; one getting in front of the frogs, causing the frog to turn around and rush right into an eager mouth.

After watching this new thing, I even join in. The frogs are delicious, and this fierce game of catching them is fun in this way. Soon, we return, full, to the burrow for sleep.

They will be allowed to sleep for most of the day, but I want them to be up before dark to teach them how to dig for prey, it is important that they understand that many of us die of starvation within the first two full sets of seasons.

As they hunt today I want them to know how important it is to hunt for all kinds of prey. They may prefer one prey over another or one type of prey may be easier to catch than another, but it is important for them to remember that some prey, like the frogs, is seasonal prey, and is not found in all of the seasons.

They tumble all over themselves and me in their eagerness to see the new things I promised them today, as I lead them up and over the top of the hill and into the field. It has not skipped my attention on our previous trips through that tasty ground squirrels are also here for us.

Finding a mound that says one is below here is easy, but trying to get my young ones to pay attention is much more difficult. They love to wander and explore instead of realizing that teaching time is here. Finally, after explaining half of the field to them, I manage to get them to watch, and teach my young how fast an adult badger can tunnel as I dig down into a prey burrow.

The prey is quickly killed, and I back out with it in my teeth just as my own mother had backed out that first day of teaching me to hunt with prey in her mouth. Just as hard as it was for her to teach me what prey food was, it is hard for me to teach my young that they really should eat the prey and not play with it.

They are so fascinated by this new idea of digging to get food that they fail to realize how important it is to hunt this way, as they tear their new food apart and scuffle for the best pieces, losing most of what I have gathered for them in the process, I sigh and try again at another burrow. This time my young remember to watch and learn, and they try to eat with at least some manners.

The day continues, until I am sure that they are all well fed and have learned something. Then it is time for them to try on their own while we are still in this field filled with prey.

They are eager little badgers as they tear at the soil. By the time my overeager, inexperienced young get into the prey's main chamber, most of the prey they try to dig out have long ran out through escape tunnels.

But they are learning, and I help a little by sometimes staying at the prey's entrance and catching it for them as it runs out so my three little ones will not have to dig up this entire field just to catch one ground squirrel.

By the time they are backed out of the overly large hole they have dug, I have left it for them to find at the entrance. If they ask, I tell them that they probably scared it to death in their frenzy to get at it. But they learn, and I take them for a walk through the forest, after they have had time to rest from the unnecessary amount of work they have done just to catch prey.

They are well fed now. We find some water in the stream that runs through the forest and I continue to teach them, showing them some of the plants we can eat if we have to survive, as well as some of the plants they should never eat because these could make them sick.

Some of this is learned the hard way by all creatures, and I want to make sure that my young do not have to learn it the hard way themselves.

When I am finished with today's instruction I take them back into the burrow for more sleep; we will come out again in the daytime for the instruction that only daylight will allow.

We roam again by day, and I teach them how the stream will mask the breathing sounds we make while we wait beside it for prey to come drink. I also teach them how the stream can be a place where predators may wait for us to drink, with their own breathing masked so they may harm us.

I teach that the stream I had followed to come here flows in a waterfall into the larger body of water we live above.

"Do not fall into the stream near that, or it will take you over the waterfall," I advise them. "You must always be alert by the stream, whether for prey or for protection."

They must understand this, although they now ask me many questions about what can kill one like us. They can't understand how anyone who hunts like we do should fear another creature. But they are still small, even though they do not understand the many ways badgers can die in the forest.

I teach them the ways they can use the darkness of their fur to hide in shadows in daylight or night. I teach them this as we relax away from the stream in some sheltering brush, where I can watch for any enemies without being seen.

I tell them of the bear and see the disbelief in their eyes as I describe its dangerous size. But they will have a chance to see one safely if I can find one, just as my own mother had once showed a bear to me.

They will find its scent first, where I can show its territory to them without it seeing us, and only when it is safe will they get close enough to actually see a bear.

I teach them that the hawk by day can swoop down and seize them to carry them away, or simply kill and eat them where they are, and my young look at the sky above us with new respect, which is what I wanted them to do, before they then ask me why that is so important since they have already been told we hunt mostly by night.

I tell them of the owl by night that can do the same, and then I make sure to tell them that as they grow older and larger, neither hawk nor owl will bother them, for both hawk and owl fear the claws and teeth of the adult badger. I tell them that by the time they leave me they will not have to fear either the hawk or the owl; they will be large enough to defend themselves against both.

They want to know why they will leave me "since we will stay together forever."

It provokes a memory of the same thoughts in my own younger life, and then they want to know why I am sad.

I wonder where my mother, Asaseyaa, is as I tell them that it is nothing, and they should also remember to watch out for the wolf. I have never seen one of these creatures, although my mother had described them to me once.

My lover, their father, Red Fur, once told me that wolves are gone from this forest now because the humans killed all of them.

I then teach them about this human creature, which brings me to teach them of the greatest threat they will ever face other than the bear: humans and the dogs they turn loose upon the wild.

I teach them that humans can kill from a distance, even as my own mother had once taught me, and then tell them of the deer I found with the strange hole in its side.

As my own mother taught me, I now teach them that humans may want them only for their fur, and they want to know what kind of predator kills just for their fur and not for food.

I can't tell them the reason for this when they ask because it puzzles me also. How can someone kill a creature just for the creature's fur and let the food go to waste? The humans I saw beside my burrow in the little hillock when the fire came were not wearing fur, and they did not seem to need it. Why would humans want the fur of another creature?

I leave this puzzle to describe a more serious danger in the forest because I want them to understand this danger, although I have never seen it myself. My mother had been so serious in describing this threat to me. My own young must also know and understand the threat of dogs running wild in the forest.

I tell my young that humans will sometimes dump their dogs in the forest when they do not want them, which allows those dogs to roam free and become wild. Then because they do run wild, they form packs that are most fierce and vicious, for only the most fierce and vicious survive.

These pack dogs do not fear humans, because they had lived with humans before. These dogs will even kill their own kind and eat them, and if they catch humans unaware, the dogs can even kill humans in the forest.

My young ask me how this can be, and I tell them it is because humans do not always think when they do things.

I will teach them more tomorrow, and more in the remaining days they are with me.

I already know that I will cry for them when we go out at dusk and each one leaves, just as I had left my own mother, Asaseyaa, and she cried for me. I fully understand now why she cried behind me as I left her, but it is time to return them to the burrow for another chance to see the sun setting outside before they are taken inside to rest for the night. Then my little ones sleep snugly against me, tired after trying to dig up an entire field for the few ground squirrels they caught today.

The rain falls from the sky in the daylight when we awaken again, and they see something that amazes me each new time it happens. A bright thing of colors arcs up from the water through the falling rain in the area of sunlight and curves all the way over the large water as another bright color thing joins it. My young gasp at the sight of these two brightly colored things rising above the waters!

Over the next few weeks they learn how to tunnel quick and straight where the prey's sleeping chambers are and kill quickly so they can move on to the next one. They must know how to feast well while it is available because only whoever has adequate body fat will survive the winter.

My little ones must survive, and I worry about them in different amounts; my two females are fierce little predators who will have no problem hunting on their own, but my little male Kekuit is still too casual about finding food, as if he believes food will always be there waiting for him.

I think that the abundance of it around here has spoiled him, and worry about what he will do when it is time to go off on his own. He seems to believe we will always be together and still does not pay enough attention in the search for food; however, he is fierce about the other things he needs to learn to survive, so he will not be some other predator's prey.

He easily enough learns from me about the ways we fight, and learns also from his sisters in their rough play together.

The play is not really play; rather, it is there to teach them how to fight for their territory, and how to kill if they need to. For now I supervise; to make sure it does not get too rough as they roll across me in their fierce little games with each other, and to make sure that it does not take up too much of my resting time.

The seasons are changing into the hot one when I will teach them what they need to know about finding water. Since we are mainly of the darkness we do not need as much water as the creatures that have to wander in the hot part of the daylight, but my young ones still need to know where and how to find water should it become scarce during the season of the fire like I had survived.

Creatures there were lucky because the stream never really dried up, even in the hottest part of the season, but in other places creatures are sometimes not so lucky and die of thirst. My young ones will not die!

They are curious as to why I would even bother to tell them this since the large water below our burrow will obviously never ever dry up. I am fierce in teaching them that they may not always be beside large water like the one near us now, and they may need to know the rules of survival without it. They are still curious, but my word is law in matters of survival, and so they accept it and learn.

They grow until my little ones are not so little anymore, and there is sadness in knowing that far too soon they will be leaving to find their own lives, but for now, I try to teach them every last little thing they may need to know. I also show my young the monster for the first time, but only when I am sure it is safe for us.

I know that he is to the north as we roam toward his territory, making use of previously dug burrows along the way for protection, making sure not enter his territory too quickly. I do not want my young to be his prey, and even if he has not yet started to fully fatten up for that long winter sleep, this bear is still dangerous to our kind.

He is a creature of fixed habits and of a fixed territory, unless someone or something drives him from that territory he should not be too hard to find. Personally, I hope the fire actually did kill him as we continue to travel north into his territory.

I use more caution as we grow closer. But my young must know of this, our most dangerous enemy, and I have to actually show a bear to them so they will not discover him by surprise later on and waste time trying to figure out what he is, when they should be avoiding him or fleeing him.

As my mother, Asaseyaa had wanted to show a simple black bear to me once, so I now show a bear to my own young, a bear that is far more dangerous and larger.

He is here, and I have deliberately chosen the hottest part of the day when he is most likely to be sleeping. Using more caution when it becomes obvious from his scent and from the markings he has left high on the sides of the trees with his claws that he is still in this area to let other bears know this is his territory and no one else is welcome here.

I move more cautiously with my young, I do not want to die here today, trying to defend them from this creature.

He sleeps, and this one is totally arrogant about it because he sleeps in the open. Movement toward him now is very cautious; we have to be downwind from this bear as we approach, and I have already taught my young what downwind means.

The downwind side is where the breeze is blowing toward, and if you are there you will not give your scent away but can catch the scent of what you are interested in as the wind blows down toward you.

The creature on the upwind side often loses in the fight for survival, but we are on the correct side as we approach him, and my young can hear his breathing as I move them quietly through the surrounding brush to see this monster that can kill us so easily.

We move until we are finally in position to see through the brush where he is snoring as if nothing could ever harm him, the arrogant fool! I always teach my own young that you should never ever let your guard down in the wild or someone else may have you for lunch!

This one does not care; he sleeps far too exposed for safety, and I silently wish he would find some other predator that could kill him, so he would no longer be a threat to my young.

But my mother had taught me that the only ones that can kill a bear are humans, and even they might have trouble killing this one. Then I finally see him again myself and immediately see something wrong with him.

He should not be larger because he already was an adult male, but he looks larger than before. I put it off to him just feeding well this season, and try to ignore his new largeness, but it still puzzles me.

They are suitably impressed by his size and danger, and we move back away from him, slipping quietly through the brush until it is safe, and I lead my young quickly away from his territory. It is important they not be near should the wind change to the other side, or should he wake for some other reason.

They have the same questions I had asked my own mother when we are safely away. I teach then again about always having a second entrance to your burrow, and my young now understand why it may be needed as they hear of how this bear almost managed to dig through that burrow of mine before I could leave quickly through my second entrance.

This suitably impresses them also, and the next instruction is finding one of the snakes with the rattling tales and showing how to make them meals safely. It is easy to kill if you are careful. The thickness of our fat layer and fur protects us. This teaches them also, and the rattling tail snake tastes delicious as always.

Fed and happy, we trek back to our real territory, my young are becoming large enough to leave and I want to have as many days as possible with them before that happens.

My two little huntresses find plenty to kill and eat on the way back, although they are not too fond of the lesson about how we can also eat insects. Grasshoppers are just too hard to catch for the small meal they provide, but they have to understand that if the seasons become hard and you are hungry, you must eat everything to survive.

The real treat comes for them when we find a fresh berry patch on the way, and they are introduced to sweets for the first time. Not sure at first if they really want to eat "planteater's food," and then they are unable to get enough once they have the taste of this new thing, as my little ones demolish and devour the berry patch and are plumper by the time we leave.

The only one that worries me now is my little male. Kekuit is still far too finicky about what he eats and too lazy to really hunt for food by himself. I spend far too much time teaching him the importance of finding food, and he spends far too much time playing instead of listening to me.

We relax in the sunlight outside the burrow overlooking the large water, and my little ones are no longer my little ones, now they are grown, and the sadness is here.

I know what is coming, but I have taught them everything possible of how to survive, and they have grown large enough to be on their own. They will leave soon as I had left my mother, and it will be lonely without them tumbling over me in their mock fights while trying to sleep inside the burrow.

The season has turned to the one of leaving, for the leaves are now turning to their colors and beginning to drop to the forest floor, as my no-longer young spend less time with me and more time roaming on their own. It is coming, and the sadness comes deeper with it.

We go out at dusk.

My little Kekuit looks at me and walks into the forest, and I try not to cry in front of his sisters when he leaves without looking back.

We go out at dusk.

My little female, Melinoe, does not feel well and remains behind. Before I even reach the edge of the field with Menhit I panic at the sudden memory of my sister Shareesa; running back to the burrow to care for the sick one.

Melinoe is better before dawn.

We go out at dusk.

Melinoe goes with us this time, looks back at me once, and then enters the forest. I never see her again.

We go out at dusk.

My last one, Menhit, looks back at me from the other edge of the field, and then she, too, enters the forest and is gone as I cry from the new "alone."

They have left, and this winter will feel even more alone than the last one.

This winter will be harder than the last one; the blue above me runs with darkness more often in daytime, and the white things that move across it turn darker as the air grows colder. The winter will be harsh for any who are not ready for it, and it will be here soon.

Alone now, I prefer to hunt daytime instead of darkness, trying to get as plump as possible. Roaming and searching, looking for the one I met this last season, Red Fur, and knowing where his territory is, I go in search for him.

I want more young ones, and he was such a lovely strong, fierce adult the last time I saw him; it would be simply perfect to meet him again, even if it is later in the seasons from the last time we met and mated.

I hope he has not forgotten where this territory is by now.

I roam until I find Red Fur, or at least what is left of him; his red fur lies dead and torn apart in the red of the falling leaves lying around and on him. The predators have found him and there is not much of my lover left but enough of his scent to tell me it was him. I cry for him; he was handsome and proud, and for a far too short time I loved him.

I roam, still searching and cross into the new territory of another male, as I move anxiously until I find him.

He finds me suitable after we have gone through the growling, erect fur thing that we do to show each other that we are proud and beautiful and adult enough to mate.

Then we mate, and I ask him to follow me back to my burrow to stay, but he wants to stay where he is instead, and so do I as long as he is here with me. But I miss the sunsets and miss the area that was mine, and I miss the place of my very first young ones. I want to go home to the burrow where the sun sets over the hills on the other side of the large water.

After a few days I simply leave. We are lonely creatures in our lives, and he will not miss me. If I do not return next season, there will be another for him.

Days grow colder still, until the snow begins to fall as I enter my burrow and sleep, and only come out to look at the sunsets when I want to.

I feel the alone so badly now, the sense that there may never ever be young again and I may be by myself forever. But I did mate, and there is hope for the next season to once again have young to love, teach, and care for, and then to cry for when we eventually go out at dusk and they leave me also.

I sleep more as winter deepens and the forest around becomes whitely cold and barren, and then the season of death is fully upon all of us.

The nights are for hunting when I do awaken from time to time, but the prey I would feed on grows scarcer in the growing cold of the nights, and I find myself hunting more in the daytime to keep my protective layer of thick fat to keep me warmer.

The days grow colder still, until the white is thicker, and no longer fun to push through when hunting or roaming. There is now less time out even in the daytime, and so little prey is out roaming in this harsh winter, it is not worth the trouble to go outside at all.

I feel the call while still sleeping in daytime, and can't understand it? I hear nothing with my ears, but the call is there inside my head, and instinct says I must go to it.

I roam from the burrow, feeling the cold first, even with my thick winter layer of fat. The forest is silent and frozen, even in daytime now; the birds are mostly gone, and the ones that remain shiver silently today. The bleak and barren winter forest around me and across the large water is solid with white that even covers the always-green trees.

I shiver not just from the cold around me and try to think of why the call came and what it was. Suddenly the call I can't hear with my ears is there again, more urgent now in its need for me to come, and closer this time. But I am hungry and stop to find food.

The call becomes even more insistent, begging for me to come to it, but then it's suddenly gone as I eat.

There is suddenly a strange, sad feeling of someone standing alongside me, wanting desperately for me to see them, and then that too is gone as I look up from my meal.

No one is beside me. "First it calls, and then it is gone?"

I return to eating and then remember something about the feeling of the sad one I sensed alongside me. Suddenly, I realize I know the voice I had heard calling and recognize the sad one I sensed beside me!

I shiver; there is suddenly a terrible sense of something, as I abandon the food and begin to run through the snow! Running toward the top of the hill behind my burrow, running uphill through the white, frozen forest, running faster and scattering white on both sides of me, not bothering to go around the edges of the deeper areas, simply running through them.

Up and over the edge of my hill, I run into the white-covered field behind it and see the brown lump with the black markings lying on top the snow halfway across the field as I run desperately to him, wailing my grief before I am even close enough to be sure it is Kekuit.

But I already know before I even reach the too thin body, and see his tracks behind him, leading from the other edge of the forest and across this cold white field, wandering as he had grown weaker.

Tracks leading toward home, where he was desperately trying to reach the only one he truly knew could hunt; the one who might have been able to find him food again. My poor starved little Kekuit, who did not learn enough about how to hunt to survive this harsh winter!

I wail my grief! If only I had understood the wordless call when I first heard it! If only I had not stopped for food myself before running up here! If only I had just been more insistent on his learning how to hunt better! If only I had simply kept him with me longer!

He is still warm; his eyes are open, staring at me. I have a sudden hope as I take him quickly into my mouth as I had done so many times before, when Kekuit was younger and I needed to move him somewhere.

Half carrying, half dragging him back through the white bleakness around me I move us both toward home again, crying as I bring him into the burrow and wrap myself around him so Kekuit will be warm again.

Crying; as he grows colder, while I try to groom his thin starved little body back to life. And finally give up; my first little male is dead, my little Kekuit who did not learn enough to survive.

I wait until almost sunset before carrying him from the burrow and placing him on the flat area in front of our burrow, turned so he can see the sun setting red and huge across the white of the hills opposite us.

I wish that those hills were green instead so we could watch the sun set over them together again as we once did; but then I wish Kekuit were warm and alive, and I will never have that ever again.

I simply sit with him as we watch the sun setting over the white hills together. Only when the sun has gone completely below the hills, and the whiteness around us darkens, will I leave to hunt for myself.

When I return, his body is gone, and the scent of the fox is around the front of the burrow. The other winter predator has taken him.

I will never again allow any of my young to take an easy attitude toward hunting. If they fail to pay attention to the lessons, I will be most fierce with them. The rest of the winter passes unhappily as I spend most of it sleeping, waiting for the spring to come again, and for life to begin again inside me.

Abaddon

They are so beautiful, my two little females; both of them so perfect, with such beautiful markings just like mine on their lovely brown fur. It is impossible not to love them so very much!

This time there was no panic of wondering what was happening to my body. I simply ate and ate and grew delightfully fat while they moved freely around inside me, enjoying their share of the food I ate for them.

Then spring returned, and the white melted again to make my forest grow again; everything winter, bare and barren turning green again, grass growing full in the field above my burrow again, with lots of delicious mice to eat in it.

Of course, I pay those mice visits from time to time as they snack on that grass, for they are a little snack of my own. Feeding until the day comes when I have to enter my burrow and lay down to watch as two beautiful little perfect females come out of me for their own lives. Both of my girls will carry the names of huntresses; they will be my two little huntresses, and both will be so good at it before I allow them to leave me.

These two will learn to hunt, and they will not ever leave me until they understand the need for it, as well as the need to never ever totally relax in the forest even when you must rest.

I am the large, warm thing they can't see yet, the large, warm thing that cares for them and gives them the food they need from my body. For now, they both need to be cleaned and groomed properly to begin their new lives.

I do that while admiring my two little beauties; they do not have their full adult colors yet, of course, but as a mother I can tell what those colors will be.

One of them has more darkness in her fur than the other, with more blackness in the markings of her forehead and face. She is so lovely and fierce even with her small size, without her eyes even open yet. I will call this darker one "Cetnenn," which is a fierce, fighting female name.

The other one is as beautiful in her lighter markings and wails so lovely for her food. I will call her "Caoineag," which means the one who wails for the dead. She will kill often and well and will never wail for lack of food or starve like my little Kekuit did.

They grow, they see, they stare at me in wonder, and try to comprehend how I can look so much like them, and still be so much larger.

I smile down at them while grooming them, remembering how I had once stared upward at a large, warm thing grooming me, trying to understand it also for the first time.

They grow as I feed them from my body, and then bring food back for them. They do not understand, just as I did not understand at first with my mother.

They play their fierce, instinctive games with it instead of eating, but they do get some as they grow and begin to taste it.

They grow and decide that they like it as much as they like the food from my body.

They grow and begin to prefer it.

They grow and forget about me to eat greedily of the prey instead, and sadness is in me again.

They grow, and I love them so much, knowing they will grow and leave me someday. We all leave in our own time and I will have yet more young after they leave, but it is still sadness to consider them leaving.

They grow until it is time for them to see the outside world, theirs to take for territory, and the first sight they see will be the same sight that had amazed me so much when I found this place.

We go from the burrow at sunset to watch the sun setting in all its glory over the large water. They hesitate at the edge of all this large, new, scary openness that is theirs, and I must gently urge them from the burrow, as I had been urged from our own burrow by my mother seasons ago.

Cetnenn and Caoineag stare in wonder at all the huge blue openness above them. They stare at the white things floating across the high openness above their heads, which will soon turn red as the sun passes below the green hills on the other side of the large body of water in front of them.

They stare in wonder at that water and stare in wonder at all the tall, huge, brown things with the green on their limbs, towering around and above them. They stare at all the things around, and then stare at the thing I had wanted them to watch when we first came out here.

They stare and gasp, as I had gasped when I first saw it setting in all of its glory, and they stare as I had stared before at the sight with my other young ones for the first time this last season, and then I remember that they are staring at it as I had stared at it beside the body of my poor starved little Kekuit this last winter.

After they get over their awe at the sight of the sun setting huge and red over the hills, they want to know why I am suddenly crying, and I can't tell them. Instead, I take them for their first night hunt, fiercely determined that they learn well what must be taught tonight.

They are small of course, and little legs tend to stumble across things in the forest often as we travel. I guide them while stopping from time to time to make sure I still do have two small young ones traveling with me, since they both tend to wander at this age as all young do. The owls roam now in this time of the darkness. The owls will not have these two because I am their protection.

The owl finds us as I roam with them. Huge and white, he drifts overhead through the dark trees as I snarl softly below.

I have not missed his presence while watching these two, ensuring they do not fall over too many things as we roam the darkness for the first time.

He spots us easily with eyes as designed for hunting in darkness as mine are, his eyes better actually. Without alarming my little Cetnenn and Caoineag, I move softly to the side he is on above us and make my claws ready to kill him.

He drifts overhead silently, waiting for the chance while I wait below for him to try, and if he does my little ones will feast on owl this night!

I move my little ones closer to the sides of trees, trying to move them nearer to the burrow away from him. The owl follows above, flying back and forth, waiting for me to make the mistake that will give him one of these two.

He is not that much of a fool above me as he drifts silently back and forth, while I move from side to side below him, always matching his movements above.

He knows that a female badger with young will kill him to protect those young, no matter what his size. He watches my continuous movements to match his as he drifts back and forth through the trees above us, and knows from my movements of keeping my young always on the side away from him, that I see him and I am ready for his move.

He decides that death is not an acceptable risk in trying to take one of my little huntresses and glides silently away to find prey that will not get him killed.

I relax only when I am certain he is gone. My two little ones did not even notice, which means Cetnenn and Caoineag will need training on this. They should have seen him. They will be taught this lesson, but for now there are other lessons for my two little huntresses to learn this night. I teach the easy lessons first, the ones of digging for prey.

Both love to dig once they begin doing it. These two learn to dig for the prey below much quicker than my other three did, and I am proud of them.

We travel for the large water, but there are no frogs yet, so teaching frog hunting will come later in the season. For now, I show them the other burrow closer to the water, and they want to know why.

"Why are there two burrows since we are going to stay with you forever and one is all we will ever need?"

I explain while trying to ignore the twinge at their words. "The more burrows you have, the more places to be safe from predators that may harm you, and the more places a predator will to have to search for you. Also, if you keep returning to the same burrow over and over, predators will learn of it sooner or later and simply wait for you outside that burrow."

I remember the huge brown bear well during this lesson to my two huntresses.

They want to know, "How any predators will ever be able to harm us since you are there to protect us and will always be there to protect us?"

They must understand that there are other predators far larger than I am, but I cut the lesson short to return to our burrow. They are young and tire easily, even if they do not feel tired yet, and so we return to sleep, and I walk in front of my two perfect little huntresses so they will not see me crying as we return. I groom them extra specially after we return and cuddle both Cetnenn and Caoineag very close to me as they sleep the rest of the night.

When I take them into the field in daylight looking for the ground squirrel burrows, it only is necessary to show them once what to do. They learn, and I have two perfect huntresses here. They get it right the first time and dig quickly into the burrows and come up with prey. Until Cetnenn and Caoineag are soon better at it than I am.

As they grow, they both work at learning the lessons they must know to survive, learning of prey that they will need to catch to live, of predators that will kill them if they are not cautious enough, and learning of the plants they can eat, and the ones that they should never touch.

These two will never starve. I only must show them once and they know. They amaze me with their own self-taught skills and while they are still small they both team up to catch the hardest of prey, the rabbit in the open.

I was only trying to teach them how to dig into this swift prey's burrow after seeing where it had entered to hide from us.

I am still digging down into its burrow for them when the rabbit flees from the second entrance I haven't noticed.

But my two little huntresses did notice as they run it down in the open, working together, running not directly at it but toward where it would be running, forcing it to turn in a large circle as they chase. They work together to exhaust the faster moving prey, and I watch them do something I have not taught them.

While Cetnenn rests in an easy run to keep up but not chase, Caoineag chases hard then rests into an easy run just to keep up, and then Cetnenn takes over the hard running.

While it is trying to evade Cetnenn, Caoineag, who had been running over to where it would be as her sister chased it, manages to cut it off and kill it.

It is hard to catch one of these things out in the open when it has a good start on you, but they did, and as I watch, the understanding comes. These two may form the rarest of groups among badgers of our kind, badger-pairs that stay together and work together to survive.

We share this prey together and I remember to praise them both while we eat. They are still so small, but they know this already, and most importantly, they learned it all by themselves.

I have been watching them while training. This is not the first time these two have shown how they can think up new things together, and then do those things without guidance from me. Cetnenn and Caoineag will not starve; these two perfect huntresses will hunt together and live together.

We trek back to the burrow and sleep for the rest of the daytime, full and happy.

They are big enough to travel long distances. We roam together, and I take them to all the many other burrows that I have dug in this territory. Watching me as I inspect and do minor work on each burrow, they are fascinated by the small differences in the burrows. I explain that the ground and the need for safety when deciding where and how deeply you dig each burrow.

They want to know, "Why bother coming back to all of these burrows, since each burrow is already dug?"

This makes me explain to Cetnenn and Caoineag how necessary it is to ensure that each burrow we come to be cleaned and ready for use if needed at some future time. It is safety from predators, as well as for a comfortable place to pass the day until it's time to hunt the next night.

I tell them of the bear, how large he was, how quickly he could dig into a burrow, and how a second entrance had saved my life.

Cetnenn and Caoineag both stay very close to me as we travel to the next burrow for inspection and cleaning, and on the way there I teach Cetnenn and Caoineag another lesson, the lesson of how some prey creatures may come and try to take up residence in one of your extra burrows in your absence, which makes for a tasty meal if you find them inside upon your return to that burrow.

This they understand very quickly, and at their age both Cetnenn and Caoineag love food more than anything else. When we reach the next burrow to inspect and clean it, they both try to get inside the entrance first to make sure any tasty prey creature inside there belongs to them.

Then they receive the lesson I dread, the one that may make me fight to the death for them if he discovers us, the lesson of the largest predator that might harm them, but not really the largest of its kind.

I have no intention of taking them into the territory of that monster brown bear that tried to kill me before; thankfully, this is just a smaller black bear of this forest. It is at night while he sleeps that I show them the one to fear.

We slide through brush shadows in the moonlight, using the stripes of our sides and the darkness of our fur to hide and disguise our shapes within the shadows of plants and trees. They have both learned well, and Cetnenn and Caoineag move noiselessly beside me as we go into the territory of this black bear.

He snores loudly, the fool. Another predator, including that monster of a brown bear, would not have to search for this one. My young could simply track him to where he sleeps by his snoring.

We track him now to where he sleeps by both sound and scent, and he sleeps so soundly I can get both of my two little huntresses closer than I really care to, so they can have a good look at him and memorize his scent.

We leave as he snores onward, totally unaware that creatures normally prey for him were close enough to bite him this night.

Cetnenn and Caoineag grow larger as the season moves from the fresh one of new green to the warmer one of heat, both of my huntresses still too small to let go, but they learn perfectly as I teach them how to catch and kill the long snakes with the rattling tails.

My fierce little huntresses want to do it themselves without any instruction, but my word is still law on matters of survival, and they will not try this without my instruction. I catch and kill while they watch, and then we all share the food, knowing that it will not be necessary to show them a second time, for these two will kill the next one together.

They kill the next one for themselves as I watch, proud but nervous, hoping they remembered all that they were taught about this creature, and how to kill it safely.

They kill the snake without any effort, once again, working together. It can't possibly watch both at once, and the snake has no chance as one of them distracts it while the other one rushes in for the kill. It is delicious, and I am proud of them.

We roam the darkness, and the huge white owl returns, but these two are well trained huntresses now, and not some little prey for some owl to easily carry away. Unlike the last time he saw them, Cetnenn and Caoineag both notice him above as he drifts silently back and forth above, looking for opportunity.

He sees three badgers below him in the dark forest: one adult, two young but almost adult, sees their claws and teeth ready for him and sees how delicious they might find him to be if he decided to come down to us.

He is looking for prey, not trying to be prey, because he knows that my huntresses are now grown enough to consider him as prey and not as threat. He decides to go away instead and try to find smaller, less dangerous prey in the darkness.

We sit in the entrance of our burrow overlooking the large water, watching moonlight shining down as the shiny things that swim in the large water jump for insects near the water.

Cetnenn and Caoineag want to know why we do not catch those shiny, swimming things also, and I must explain that, while we can swim, we do not do too well underwater where those swimming things live.

Only if we are lucky will one be brought to the side of the large water for us, or be dropped from the talons of an eagle that has caught one of them for itself.

I have tasted these shiny swimming things very rarely, but there are other things that live around the large water for us to feed on. I rise from where we sit watching the water, to take Cetnenn and Caoineag to find those frogs waiting for us down there.

Cetnenn and Caoineag are so close now, and think so much alike when they hunt, it is almost like watching one animal with two bodies' hunt the same prey.

They both show me this rare joining of two far better when they are attacked together as they defend each other together before I can rush up to save them.

The forest has predators for all creatures. No one is ever truly safe in the forest no matter what their size or fierceness, not even the badger, and we are known for our fierceness.

We are out in the daylight when the hawk thinks he has an easy kill in a still young badger, but either his shadow or the rushing of his wings, or both, gives him away. Giving my little Cetnenn and I warning at the same time as I see him begin the dive above us while out in the field behind our burrow, cursing myself for the stupidity of letting my young get so far away from me!

I charge at the sight of him diving on my little one, my beautiful little Cetnenn who is far too exposed in the open of this field, and I am too far away!

She is far too exposed, but I have taught Cetnenn well as she runs to one side, instead of rushing blindly straight ahead to evade him. Trying to run straight ahead, he could simply correct his dive to catch her in his talons; Cetnenn evading to one side forces the hawk to correct instead to land beside Cetnenn and take her with beak or talons.

He does neither. Caoineag is on the other side of him instantly, snarling rage as he tries to get past the claws and teeth of my little Cetnenn to kill her and take her away.

He stays on the ground, torn between which of the two he wants to take as they both lunge at him. He dodges both, trying to evade the teeth and claws of these smaller creatures that should have been easy prey. He stays on the ground still trying to decide, and confused at how fiercely these two prey creatures are fighting back at him from either side as if they were both one animal!

He stays on that ground, still trying to decide for just a little too long as I land on his back in rage, crushing him to the ground, ripping through his feathers. He suddenly realizes he forgot to account for my position, and he dies, screaming under my claws and teeth, now prey instead of predator.

My first thought is of my two little huntresses who stayed together to save each other, and I am so proud of them. No predator will ever take them because they will be such incredible huntresses, and they will never starve!

Only after checking them both anxiously, making sure they are not hurt, do we all three turn back to this one who tried to kill my little Cetnenn.

And as we eat, we three agree: "Once you get past the feathers, this is delicious!"

We hunt the darkness and day together, finding food is easy with these two; they both know how to dig swiftly down to the prey's burrows and both are so good at running down faster prey that I would never dream of running down. But these two now know the secret of making prey run in circles while they chase, letting prey tire itself as they take turns running it until the prey has no chance to run further. Then we all three feast well again.

I do not want them to leave me, but the season is near, and the call will come for them as it came for me, and they will soon go out at dusk as my other three had done. Then I will cry as they leave together for their own burrow or burrows and start their own lives.

I do wonder what any future mate will think if they do stay together; both are very strong willed by now, and both are very strong in body. Any mate they take should be cautious not to annoy them while around them.

The weather is warmer now, the days sometimes too uncomfortable to hunt in, especially when you consider our thick skin and fat layer. We hunt more at night, and this time no longer simply mother and daughters. Now we are three huntresses together.

We are all three also plumper now as we prepare for the turning of the seasons and the need to choose burrows for the coming winter.

They of course will leave by then for their own burrow or burrows, and I strongly suspect by now that it will be a single burrow, for these two are bonded for life as hunting sisters.

I try not to let them see how sad I am at the thought of their leaving as I continue to teach them all they need to know for survival. I know the leaving will be soon because both Cetnenn and Caoineag are hunting more on their own in the darkness and need me to guide them less.

I have so little time left with them now and I cherish every bit of it as I try to share each new sunset at our burrow entrance, with them near me.

Rain comes down steadily from the sky in the darkness of this cooler than normal hot season night. We three sit, warm and dry, at the entrance to the burrow overlooking our large water and watch the sky flash with light in the darkness, hearing the loud crack and rumbling in the sky following each flash of light. They shiver in delight at the sight beside me as flashes of light show water and hillsides in the darkness of falling rain from the sky. Then it all disappears into dark falling rain again, until the next flash lights it all up again.

We watch for a while, but there is more to train them in, and this is the perfect time for the next lesson. It is time for another treat, and when the flashes have stopped, I take them out of the burrow and up the hillside behind it while rain falls from the sky above.

We go to the field where worms come out in darkness from the rain-soaked ground. They will be on top of the ground in this falling rain, ready for three hungry badgers to find them. By the time we are full we are all three soaked, and it is still colder than normal for this hot season as we trek homewards in the darkness of the night for some sleep.

My two huntresses have grown fast, but they are still small to me, and I know already that they will always be small to me, no matter how large they grow.

We sleep the day, and then watch the sun setting in all its red glory over the green hills across the large water that is ours.

I feel mixed emotions as while watching it; sad that they will leave soon now, but happy at the same time to be able to share all of this with them just a little longer until they do leave me. Darkness grows as it does each new night, until it is finally time to hunt again.

But they want to stay behind and sleep, so I go out alone to bring us prey, instructing them to wait here for my return. Just before dawn, I have great luck in finding an older rabbit foolishly sleeping in the open.

Returning happily with the prey in my mouth at dawn, I know that my two little huntresses will be hungry by now, and proud of their mother for catching this swift creature. And if I happened to have caught the rabbit while it was still sleeping, without having to chase it down, I just won't mention that to them as we share it together.

Both Cetnenn and Caoineag will be full, little huntresses by the time we three finish this fine plump prey, then they will probably want to sleep again, until it is time to go out together for the next hunt tonight. There are still a few lessons to teach the two of them before they are finally ready to leave this burrow to go make their own burrows.

Entering my sleeping chamber happy and proud; both lay waiting for my return as I had instructed them, huddled together, still and stiff on their sides.

I stare at uncomprehending at them, before realizing what has happened; drop the forgotten prey from my mouth, and scream my grief. The sound of my scream bouncing off the sleeping chamber walls, mocking me by screaming my grief back to me!

Rushing to them, I try to make them move; desperately trying to make them not be stiff, desperately trying to groom them back to life, and screaming, screaming, and crying, and then I leave.

I wander aimlessly over the field above the burrow, ignoring the mice in it, without caring, walking into the forest on the other side of the field, through the forest, through the slowly passing daylight, and not feeding or even bothering to notice the rabbit prey that runs in front of me without warning.

It stops at a safe distance and stares at me, trying to understand how I could simply ignore it. For me, it is not even there, and nothing is there for me. I wander, not bothering to notice landmarks, they are not important, nothing is important. I wander, walking by instinct only, until it is darkness again, and then for the first time in my life, I do not bother to dig a burrow.

I simply sit, exposed in the open without sleeping. Nothing kills me by daylight, so I roam again until darkness, and roam until it is daylight again and continue walking because it is pointless to stop. Finally passing through the edge of the forest into a new area, I do not even bother to notice as I wander through its openness, not knowing where I am going or really caring anymore.

I roam until exhausted, and I fall over, exposed in the open in daylight, and I wait. Nothing eats me, but I do not care anyway.

Something is familiar about this area, but I do not care as I pick myself up and roam in the daylight through this far too open area I am in, with the tall-blackened things sticking up here and there with no tree limbs above them, and pass the other blacked things laying on the ground, long dead.

I do not notice the signs of old burn on these treeless tree trunks that still stand upright, do not notice all the other things that once used to be trees, which now lay black and fallen over this area of fresh grass, where smaller, younger trees have barely started to grow.

I roam until I pass into the meadow, and by instinct only, reach my little hillock overlooking the center of the meadow. I go inside the old, favorite burrow with the burned, fallen tree still lying across the top of the hillock above the entrance. I go inside and cry until I can't cry anymore, then I fall asleep, exhausted.

Sleeping I do not know how long, and thirsty and hungry, so hungry and not caring as long as I can just remain sleeping here in my old favorite burrow, inside the hillock overlooking my meadow.

Finally awakening from thirst in the heat of this season as survival takes over, even if I do not care anymore, I go to the stream that runs down the center of the meadow to drink, and notice the entrance mounds where ground squirrels have once again taken up residence around my meadow around my little hillock.

I drink until I'm filled. Life moves onward, and I go to one of the ground squirrel burrows and dig, kill, eat, and then return to my own burrow on the little hillock before darkness to clean it out.

I have been gone too long. It is untidy with too much loose dirt inside it, and far too much old grass in here that needs to be changed. I must clean it. I have no young to care for, no lover to care for, just this burrow.

I clean it and make it perfect again. I drag the old, long, dead grass out of it and clean all loose dirt out too, bringing in new grasses, until the sleeping chamber is filled and thickly lined with fresh grass again, and snug as it should be. Then I collapse inside my clean, tidy, snug, lonely burrow, and cry and sleep through both the night and the next day.

Hunger calls. I awaken, roam, dig, and kill. Returning to the burrow to work on it again, although it is already perfect, but I need this work more than the burrow needs to be worked on, so I do it anyway, until exhaustion sets in again. I fall asleep in the entrance tunnel.

Hunger calls again. I rise to kill and eat, and it tastes better this time, and I kill again and eat. Suddenly realizing how famished I am, I spend the rest of the night hunting and eating, until dawn when I simply return to my burrow and sit in its entrance, the same entrance I sat in before the fire came, and look at all that is mine once again.

The forest will grow taller again around my meadow, and the meadow is beautiful in the rising sun of dawn. I see him roaming this way through the small trees re-growing in this young forest around my meadow.

He is handsome, and he is an adult. I go to meet him. We make the by now familiar ceremony of meeting to mate, all of the fur fluffs, teeth showing, circling. His name is Thamuatz.

He stays with me in the burrow on the hillock, and I will have new young by him this next springtime when the plants begin to turn green after winter passes, and I will survive.

Sar-akka's Porridges

Thamuatz only stays for a while, but then makes his excuses for moving on and leaves.

I am alone again, but now there is a strange happiness to this alone. I feel life again, and while it will not become apparent until the white melts again after this next winter, I know that life is inside me.

I can't explain how I am so sure it is there, but I know it, just as surely as I know that the ground squirrels in my outside meadow taste good.

I hunt and survive and watch the season pass as the leaves of the young trees around my meadow lose their leaves and begin to change into reds and yellows and fall from the trees, and the other always-green, young trees never lose their green no matter what the season. All the new trees around my meadow are so small, but they will grow, as I have grown in this short life.

The rain comes from the sky, as I watch it from the shelter of this burrow entrance, and the days grow colder also.

The white things in the blue above move faster and the days grow colder as the season begins to shift into the season of death. I stay alive and watch it from my burrow entrance.

I have seen three winters come and go now, and this will be the fourth, and the coming spring will be my fifth. I am not elderly yet, but have already lived longer than many of my kind, and for the first time, I understand death. The death I have given in my life, and the death that was given to the ones I loved.

When these new young ones come, I will protect and defend and love them as much as I possibly can, but if they die, I will not cry. I promised myself that I would never cry again, not for myself and not for anyone else. I will not cry. I am, of course, lying to myself.

I hunt and gather body weight for the coming winter.

It will be fun to once again play on the top of the clear, cold, solid stream when that happens. I have not done that in so long. It will be fun to play in the white that falls. I have not done that in so long. I am going to enjoy this winter, and when the spring comes, I will enjoy the coming young ones also and also teach them how to have fun before they leave me.

I wonder how many there will be while the days pass as I wait for the winter to come. My first was three, my second was two, and this time will probably be only one. But it doesn't matter; three, two, or one, they will all be loved the same by me no matter how many there are. And I am already fussing with the burrow again, despite it is already perfect for my new young.

The winter comes, blowing white while I watch from my burrow entrance, having fed well already this day. The blue above is soon gone, while I wait and feel joy at seeing the first white flakes beginning to fall in the rising wind.

The snow grows thicker and the brief flurries become solid falling white in the cold of this day. I wait for a little while to watch, and then simply go inside to sleep for a few days. It will all be here when I emerge, then it will be time to have fun again.

I sleep two full days before it is time to come out again. My body usually tells me how long the winter sleep has been each time, but this time my body seems not to care how long I sleep, so I just sleep for the time that is needed, and then awaken to come out and see the meadow in its covering of snow. It feels strange to be a creature of the daytime now, but that is what my body tells me, and I obey it.

It is almost hard to step into the snow, but then it crunches beneath my front paws, and I go crazy!

Running through it, I push the snow aside with my body and feel the thickness of it giving way to my body weight as it flows along my sides and crunches under my paws. Having run into an area deeper where the white was deeper than it looked, I splutter as I come above the surface again

Turning and running into it again, running for the cold, frozen stream, running onto it without stopping, I skid across the cold, hard top of it all the way to the other side, where I promptly bury myself in snow on the other bank, but I am moving too fast and out of control on the surface to stop!

Scrambling up out of the snow and running back onto the surface of what used to be running water; my paws scramble frantically beneath me as I try to run. I shriek with delight at the sensation of sliding out of control into the other bank.

Then just seeing how fast I can scramble downstream on the hard top of it, I turn and do it again, until all four of my paws slip at the same time, and I slide all the way into the other side of the bank.

Any prey watching probably thinks I am crazy, but I don't care! Running and sliding to the side of the stream's bank, I run into the meadow again to play in the white that covers all of my meadow.

Running, shrieking joy through snow, I bury myself in a deep spot and return above the surface to splutter it from my mouth and nose. Running again, then turn, still running, throwing white up on all sides of me, as I run to dive into the deep snow again, until I am exhausted.

Only then do I return to the burrow to sit in the entrance overlooking my meadow, until the sun finally sets over the hills, watching darkness gather and cover everything, watching the huge, lighted thing in the sky that is the moon rise full and beautiful above the trees.

The moon lights the snow around me until it is almost as bright as day outside, and then going inside to sleep in a warm ball inside the sleeping chamber, I wait for the spring. I will not know if I actually do have young inside me until spring, but from my joy of today, I suspect I do.

We mate in the summer and fall, and then among our kind, the thing that happens inside our bodies is delayed until spring when new life has the most chance of survival, and when the prey is appearing again to give us food. I know for certain that there will be young for me again this next spring.

A creature of both daylight and darkness now, I simply awaken when I need to roam and hunt and feed.

The snow returns from the darkness of the sky, covering the meadow deeper, making it harder to hunt and even to play. I love the running diving into the white fun, but this is getting to be too much.

As the snow continues to fall, the meadow disappears even further underneath the white, until it becomes harder to find prey in all of this now. Fortunately, I did all of the hunting that was needed before it became this deep and cold, and now have my full winter fat layer.

I will not starve, but the other creatures will have more trouble, and for the first time in my life, I begin to feel sorry for prey when I find the ones that could not feed because of the snow's deepness over forest and meadow.

I find them more and more; the poor starved frozen bodies of birds, and the ground creatures who could not reach food below the thick covering of snow.

I eat them because they are available prey to me, but now there is a guilty feeling of not being a real predator each time I do, and I sense a strange, new feeling for these prey creatures.

It becomes even harder for me to wander. There are more and more days of just sleeping, and I don't even try to plow through the thickness of snow around this burrow on my hillock. The fun of running through it and diving into it is gone as I find more of the dead prey on top of the snow.

I begin to find the bodies of the other frozen ones, the ones that did not die from lack of food, the ones who could not stand the cold, which even I can feel now through the thick layer of fur, skin, and fat of my own body.

The daytime cries of the remaining winter birds grow less as the cold becomes more intense. Snow falls again from the sky, and winter birds fall dead with it.

The forest is truly barren now, as frozen snow-covered branches break in the slightest wind on these small trees around my meadow, and sometimes even the snow-covered smaller trees break, covered in the cold of snow.

The remaining creatures, except for a very few to be found out in daytime, are all in burrows and dens. The nights are empty. No one comes out to try to make it through the white darkness.

I fill in the second back entrance to my burrow and make the front one smaller also. Pulling the grass of my sleeping chamber into a thick pile, I huddle in; glad I pulled so much of it in as the cold grows outside.

The fox howls desperately for food in cold, frozen daytime, and the owl hunts for anything at all to eat in darkness.

I roam and find the frozen fox that could not find food in the forest on the other side of my meadow, his body far too thin, his jaws clenched tightly showing his teeth, lying there in the white cold where he died starving. Forcing me to remember my own poor little Kekuit, giving me shivers, not from the cold as I return to my burrow where I cry and wait.

I wait until the days grow longer and the sun begins to warm again, and then the day comes as the air warms around us enough to make the snow begin to melt.

The snow begins to melt too quickly into flowing water, rushing to find its way to someplace lower, running from all of the high places where the sun finds it first, rushing to fill all of the low places.

I watch as the day warms completely and melting snow becomes a river in the small stream that runs through the center of my meadow, taking plants and ground with it, until the ground becomes something I would rather not walk on.

All the mud and melting snow exposes the bodies of the ones that could not survive this winter. I roam for food, working my way through the mud to feed and find water that is not rushing and muddy. I do not want to go too near that stream to drink; it is not a small stream now, as it rushes south, carrying things down it.

I watch as the days warm, until the snow is gone, and the stream gradually becomes its normal, small self again.

Without the stream banks it used to have, at least it is a normal sized again. The stream's destroyed banks will grow with other plants, and the forest is already blooming again. The small trees that lost their leaves in the winter begin to show green, and life returns to forest and meadow.

The trees have creatures building in them already, and the squirrels are coming out from their own winter sleep, the birds return from where they went during this terrible winter of death. And then I see that the huge, brown bear has awakened also. He is here, and he is roaming for food after his long sleep.

I wish that he would not have awakened at all. I had no idea that a bear was this close to me now, and certainly not this one.

I know that it is the same one because he has that strange white scar over the brown top of his head as if something very thin had hit him from the front and passed across the top of his head, taking his fur with it without killing him. However, I do not know what thing could do something like that.

I wonder if his head is damaged underneath the scar, but that is not important to me, the only important thing is that he has now moved down here into this area of my little hillock. Again, I sense that something or someone I can't see is with him, and again something is wrong with his size. This time I am certain of it. His body is changing somehow, and I shiver at the sight of this wrong.

He was already an adult and should not have grown any larger, and he could not possibly have grown larger during his winter sleep. But he has become larger.

He is also different in another way. His larger shape is now changed and somehow wrong; his nose is flatter and his head is also larger, his teeth are longer in that larger flatter head and his legs seem longer.

Still, no matter how dangerous he is to me, he will have trouble digging this burrow out because the entrance tunnel wanders, and I have that second entrance to flee through, and the big, dead tree laying on top of this hillocks crest will present him with problems if he tries digging from above. He can try to dig forever through that.

The only thing that worries me is my young when they arrive, and I know they are coming because I felt the first movement inside of my body today as I watched the bear roam.

My first litter was three, my second litter was two, and this will probably be just one little badger, but it will be such a loved one, and the bear had better be ready to fight if he tries for it. Any attempt to dig into this burrow while my little one is in here will result in him receiving a face full of claws and teeth!

For some reason, he never tries as I watch him cautiously in his movements over the next few days. It is as if for some reason he can't come close to this little hillock that is my home. I roam and feed and avoid him, and he seems willing to avoid me. Perhaps there are other far easier prey creatures for him to find after all.

I avoid him and wait for the one I am expecting to arrive, and there may be more than just one as I feel the movements inside me. Possibly two or even three this time, and they will be trained to hunt for food as best I can train them, for there will be no more starved young ones trying to make it home to my burrow.

The day comes when I feel the need to return to the burrow and wait for my body to do what it needs to do.

The first emerges from me, and I feel the joy at seeing its wet little body squirming for life, and the second one emerges, wet and wriggling, and now know that there will be three.

The third is emerging as I try to clean the first two. I am so content because there will be three again. They are so perfect, and then the fourth one emerges, and then the fifth . . . and I stare astounded at the extra two I did not expect!

Five! I can't even keep two alive in a safe place, and the bear is here in my territory now. What will I do with five?

How is it going to be possible to keep track of this many young all at once? How can I train this many young to survive? How will I be able to find enough food for them? I will be hunting all day and all night to just to feed all of these and myself!

It will be a constant problem trying to keep all of them out from under my feet in the burrow, and old grass will have to be out of here every day they are in here, and new grass dragged in just to keep the burrow clean.

When we go outside I will have to herd all of them together all the time, just to keep them out of trouble. I do not know how I am going to train five at once to do anything, how am I going to handle this!

But for now, all five must be shown that their poor, confused mother cares for them, even if she doesn't understand how she is going to deal with all of them. I decide to just to tend to them now and deal with the problems later. They need to be cleaned so they will not be cold, and they need to get right over to my tummy for some food. Thankfully I didn't have seven!

I groom my little loves, making sure that they are all fed and then sleep, tucked snugly so they will feel secure and loved. I try to consider what I am going to do. I thought I was going to have one at first, but later when I felt the additional movements inside my body, I thought maybe two or three at the most, but five, how am I going to handle five?

I have so much to do when they are all cleaned and groomed and sleeping peacefully, but I check on them from time to time to make sure that they are all right while I try to think of names for my three males and two females.

They will all carry proud, hunting names, but not now, right now, I have to sleep and then to hunt for food for all of us. I will need a lot of food reserves in my body to take care of these five. They have already proven themselves to be hungry little predators while nursing from me.

When awake again, I try to decide on names before feeding them, but they are also awake now, such great little feeders, and so hungry that I have to concentrate on keeping them in some kind of order while they feed so they do not tumble all over the place and over each other, trying to reach me.

Then, after making sure that they are all sleeping soundly again, I must go out to hunt for myself at dusk before being able to make a name-decisions for these five.

The frogs by the stream are the quickest, and since there is a good amount of rain on the ground tonight, the worms are also out, and quite delicious.

I eat quickly, though, unable to leave my new young alone, certain that they will all be dead by the time I return. Running back to the burrow, I find them all still asleep; but not for long, my entrance makes one awaken crying for food, and then they all awaken, and they all want to feed again right now!

I will grow used to this. One always alerts the others to my return and then they all need me at once.

Now I get to experience the joys of motherhood to the maximum. I am continually dragging in fresh grass to replace the old, soiled grass in here, continually looking down at five hungry mouths that need me right now, and never able to hunt for myself, or even leave the burrow because they have an absolutely uncanny ability to tell exactly when I am going to leave to do something else, anything else, and they wake up needing me.

As I look down at all five of them crying for my attention at once, I realize that I am also going to have to name all of these; thinking briefly, that perhaps I will just name them all "Trouble" and let it go at that!

Then I groom them, decide I love them so very much anyway, and forget about the problems of deciding their names.

One is darker than the others, almost as dark as my brother, Tigranuhi, was, making the white of her cheek and head markings vivid against the blackness of the dark stripes below and behind those cheek markings and either side of that head stripe of white. I will call her "Akna," which means "the moon and the night," and hope she will be as great a hunter of the darkness as my brother was.

Another has even brighter, white cheek markings and a bright white stripe back over her head, and the markings almost as white as the snow that comes in winter when the sun is on it. I consider and decide I will call her "Alarana," which means "northern huntress."

The others I try to decide on names for my three little males. All three need decent hunter names. Whether our young are male or female, we name all of our young after hunters.

One of my little males looks so much like my first male Kekuit, and I will name him "Aataentsic," which means "immortal hunter, destroyer of life." He will be a fierce hunter, and he will never ever starve.

Another of my new little males has so little white on his cheeks, and the white stripe across the back of his head is so thin he looks like he is as dark as the sky when it begins to drop rain on the forest around us. His fur is as dark red as the fur of my first lover, my Red Fur, and this little one will be called "Asiaq," which means "the weather and hunting."

The last of my new males is easy, and he is fierce even at this very young age, and before his eyes are even open, he is fierce at my side when he nurses. I will call him "Atsentma," which means "wild animal."

Now I am happy, and my wild, little animal, Atsentma, is ready to feed again as he cries pathetically along with the rest of this large new family of mine, and I simply turn on my side to let them have what they need from me.

My life is my young now, and I try to spend as little time as possible for myself in hunting outside this burrow, and spend as much time as possible with my young instead as they grow and their eyes open.

They stare in wonder at the size of this huge creature that looks so much like them inside this burrow. They grow, and soon it will be time to teach them to feed from real food and not from me. The snake makes that job easier.

After hunting the night and feeding myself, I return to the burrow in daylight with the idea of taking all my young ones solid prey food soon; returning just in time to see one of the large snakes with the rattling tail begin to slide inside for the easy prey of young in a burrow.

I don't care how large it is. My scream of rage makes prey throughout my meadow run for cover as I run for the snake.

It will not have a second chance for them or any other prey as I scream fury and land on its back, yanking it out of my burrow with teeth and claws, throwing it away from the burrow entrance with a toss of my head, rushing to where it lays stunned on the ground, and tearing into the snake with my teeth and claws before it can even think of what creature just grabbed it away from the burrow where it thought it could find an easy kill inside!

The snake will not ever think again of prey as I take it apart outside the burrow of my young, and then it is time to drag its headless body back into the burrow because my young are about to have their first good prey meal. The snake wanted to eat them, but they will eat it instead.

Just as I was when younger, they are confused at first as to what I want them to do with this thing their mother has dragged into the burrow, but their instincts are good, and while they waste too much of the snake, playing fierce games with it, they do get some of it to eat.

They grow in here with me, and I teach them all there is to teach until they are ready to see the outside world. They learn that my word is law in matters of survival, and they learn to keep their fierce games at least a little under control when they play, so they don't actually eat each other. They grow, and then they are ready to go out.

On the first trip outside the burrow, they should see all there is to see, and it will be in the daytime, and we will go as far as the next burrow to sleep there.

Getting them into some kind of order is not very easy with five to control at once. Finally I manage to get all of them up the tunnel to the entrance and out into the outside world.

Then the sight of all this bright new that is so much larger than the inside of the burrow stops them in the entrance. I push patiently behind them until they decide it is not all that scary to leave their home and actually see this world instead of staying frozen with awe in the entrance forever.

Under my watchful eyes, they roam from the burrow entrance, looking above for any hawks, looking around for bear or foxes, and looking at the ground of this meadow to find the first lesson for them, how to kill prey.

The last is the easiest, and for badgers there is always prey if you look for it. There are ground squirrels in the meadow.

I take my young to the nearest entrance mound, still wondering why the ground squirrel is never smart enough not to leave a mound of dirt right in front of their entrance saying, "Here I am!" to every predator that sees it.

Their foolishness is my good luck today, and after my five young are gathered together in some kind of order to watch, I show them the speed with which we can dig.

They watch, amazed, as they try to keep dirt from my rapidly digging paws off themselves. They are not too sure of what I am doing, even if it has been explained to them that this is where the prey is.

I bring them the prey, and like me so many seasons ago, they are not too sure what to do with it even if they have already seen it brought to them in the burrow. For them it is one thing to have it brought to them inside the burrow and quite another thing to actually see how it is caught.

But they get the idea quickly. Even though one ground squirrel divided up five ways doesn't equal much meat for anyone, they fall upon it and devour it, and I am proud of them. Returning to the hunt, they follow eagerly to another ground squirrel burrow. As soon as I return from another quick digging trip underground, they are sure that more food will be delivered to them.

Their wish is granted, and they fall over each other trying to compete for it, then follow again as I try to get them to start digging on their own for these tasty things. It takes a while and two more squirrels' burrows, but then, at the next squirrel burrow, they start to dig on their own.

The only problem is that they all start on the same mound, getting in each other's way as they do, and I watch in amusement as the ground squirrel takes advantage of so many paws trying to come straight down for him. But the ground squirrel simply runs up his entrance tunnel to escape while they are still digging down for him.

I let him go, and he has earned his life today, and they can hunt him again tomorrow. Besides I now have to convince five eagerly digging badgers that he is no longer down there.

My far too eager young are missing more ground squirrels than they catch today, and I up on this particular instruction. We will go for easier prey, instead of trying for the same squirrel burrow at the same time. There will be more instruction on how to dig for separate squirrel burrows later.

They learn plants for now, the ones that are good for you with tasty roots, and the ones you should never touch because they will poison you if you do. There will also be night instruction tonight when it is dark because the frogs are so easy to catch then. But for now, there is far more daytime instruction to be given, and they follow me again as we roam into the forest around the meadow.

I remember to walk slowly for them as we go because their little bodies are close to the ground, and what I would easily walk over they manage to fall in eagerness over.

Sighing, I turn around to make sure they get back up. Instead of looking down to watch where they are walking as we go, they look upward at the same time.

They must learn to be more aware of what is around them because death is quick for the unaware in the wild.

The new amazes them as they look at all the new colors of the trees around us and the tallness of the trees compared to their own size. I do not have the heart to tell them that these are all small, younger trees, and they have yet to see a truly tall tree.

They are also beginning to show me their true selves while on this walk, which is another reason for taking it. Such a walk will tell me who needs the most instruction on each different thing they must know to survive.

My little female, Akna, is shy and tends to stay close to me. I must teach her more independence so that she will be sure of herself when it is time for her to go out on her own. Unless she can bluff them away from her with teeth and claws some predators may harm her, and she must be sure of herself before she leaves me.

The other small female, Alarana, tends to stay close to my little male, Asiaq. If their fierce games inside the burrow grew too fierce, she tended to rely on him for protection and stayed behind him before I could break them up and restore some kind of order among the five. I wonder if these two will bond and wander off together when they go, something that is unusual for us, but can happen.

Of all three males, Asiaq is the most fearless and wins most of the fighting games inside the burrow, and if Alarana and Asiaq do bond, he will fight to the death to protect her if he has to.

Before their eyes were open I thought Atsentma would be the fiercest, but now I can see that Asiaq is the fiercest one when they are all outside the burrow. Asiaq is strong and hunts well. He will be able to find food and will not starve.

He is also dark like my brother, Tigranuhi, was. Asiaq will be a great night hunter as my brother was, Asiaq is fierce and proud and prey will not see him coming in the dark.

Aataentsic is shyer than Asiaq but still fierce and has some of the look of my former lover Red Fur about him. Aataentsic's fur is also red-tinged brown and his markings on that fur are a fine black. He will be a good hunter, and he will make a proud mate for a female badger someday.

My last little hunter, Atsentma, is fierce enough but tends to stay a little too close to me now that we are outside. I must teach him to use his natural fierceness as a weapon to keep predators away and to defend his territory.

Neither Akna nor Atsentma will be safe if they can't find their own territory, defend that territory from others, and defend themselves from predators that might harm them.

I need easy prey for my next instruction. I take them to the nearest fallen tree near the stream, knowing already that the cool dampness underneath will almost always have some nice tasty grubs to eat.

We find what we are looking for and they feast. Once they understand that though this prey might look different it is still as tasty as anything else that may run from them.

I want all of them, but especially my little Akna and Atsentma, to know that prey is everywhere in all its different forms, and this will keep them from starving if they can't find any easier prey to eat.

Leading them to some plants with tasty roots so they will understand that you don't always need living prey to fill your stomach. Teaching until they are filled, I sense a great deal of sleepiness among my young, and we head back.

Over the next few days we roam to different burrows, and there is rare luck in that we find a prey creature that has tried to take up residence in one of those burrows during my absence. It tastes delicious, and now they understand one of the reasons for coming back to check the many burrows that they will dig in their lifetimes from time to time.

Soon I introduce them to other areas of the forest, and our walks become longer as their legs grow longer.

I show them how to hide in brush and wait for mice and others to come inside for shelter in the heat of the day, show them how to wait alongside the stream and let the sound of the rushing water mask our breathing so the prey can be taken when it wanders down to drink.

I show them how to find ground-nesting birds, how not to be fooled if the parents fly from the nest, and feign injury to attract predators away from their nest.

One day while teaching them, the sky grows darker and the rain comes down strongly, then I show them how to find tasty worms on top of the ground in the open areas of our meadow as the rain stops.

The rain from the sky comes again, and they watch with me, the sky flashing light, with loud cracking afterward. But these young ones stay in the burrow with me as the rain continues to come down because I will not have a repeat of what happened to my two little huntresses.

The rain comes down stronger and I wonder why. It has never come down this hard before, but my young are safe and snug, and I simply teach them inside the burrow as rain falls from the sky outside.

I teach them how to make a strong secure burrow in good, strong ground, pointing out that this burrow was dug near the top of a hillock, with its entrance tunnel sloping slightly downward to the outside, which allows water to flow past the tunnel entrance and not flood it.

I teach them a burrow should be made with extra tunnels so they will not have to go outside for any reason because some of the tunnels will be where to eliminate waste.

Remembering my own experiences, I also teach them the value of having a second entrance to escape from, should something very large try to dig them out through the primary entrance tunnel.

The rain is still coming down from the sky, the meadow runs with water as it flows to the stream, and I make them watch the stream carefully when we do go to drink.

The stream is starting to look the way it did when all the snow melted before, the water climbing higher on its banks as the rain continues to come down. I watch my little ones carefully when we go to drink from it.

Although Aataentsic loves the flooded stream, my word is law in matters of safety, and none of them are not to go near the stream without me in front!

The rain continues to fall outside until there is so much water running off the sides of the hillock where we live that there is seldom any need to go near the stream at all. This makes me happy because the stream is dangerous now, and even if the stream floods over its banks, we are safe in our little hillock.

One thing is nice about all the rain falling steadily from the sky. The hunting is good, more prey are out trying to find new burrows away from the stream both at night and in the daytime. The sound of rushing waters hides our own noise well as we hunt them.

We find some of snakes with rattling tails trying to move to higher ground. After showing my young how to kill one of these creatures safely, I watch as my little ones kill the other two, and we feast well. Then, of course, it is my job as the mother to clean out the remains and tidy up the burrow.

The rain still comes down, and until the stream is no longer safe as it runs rushing over its banks, taking them downstream with its rushing water as we watch from the comfort of our burrow entrance. Cleaning my young is harder now, since each time we go out to hunt we manage to get muddy again.

While we are around the stream I thought controlling my Aataentsic would be a problem, but my little Atsentma becomes a worse problem in managing to get mud allover himself first, and I am thoroughly tired from licking mud off all of us. Then my little Atsentma decides to go for a swim in the stream without permission.

Atsentma has always wanted to impress me with his hunting skills, and after all, his name means "wild animal," and this time he decides to chase the ground squirrel out into the open in the falling rain.

The squirrel probably wanted to find a new place to dig a burrow to keep safe from the heavy, pouring rain from the sky, but all it does is attract our attention in the daytime as we watch the stream washing away its banks from the comforts of our snug burrow entrance.

Atsentma is out of the entrance after it before I realize what he is doing. Still it is good that he is showing me he can chase prey in the falling rain also, and I approve while watching unconcerned.

Of course he will have to be cleaned off when he gets back with it, and I dread having to clean him; however, he chases well in falling rain, and I am proud of him for that.

The ground squirrel sees him coming through the rain. With no direction to run except back toward the stream, now more than a simple stream as it overflows its banks, the squirrel runs toward it to escape, and my Atsentma follows. Suddenly I realize where he is heading!

As the prey runs for the streams rushing waters, Atsentma is far too involved in the chase to bother with thinking as the prey runs for the streams rushing waters, and Atsentma with his larger heavier body follows.

I scream before I am even out of the burrow entrance, warning to him and running hard for him through the rain falling from the sky, when the squirrel remembers that it can't swim in all of the rushing water and turns quickly. Doubling back frantically as my Atsentma turns also at the edge of the stream to chase and slips on the muddy stream bank as it gives way beneath his feet and plunges him into the water.

We can swim but not in this!

Atsentma is already crying for me as he washes downstream, trying to keep his head above the water, as the stream drives him underwater. I run frantically along the muddy stream bank in the falling rain, trying to keep up with him as he comes back up. He goes under again, and there is no hesitation as I jump, hit the water near enough to grab him by the scruff of the neck, and try to keep us both above the surface.

The water shoves me under as I push him above me with my mouth. The stream will not have my Atsentma!

The water rushes us both downstream, and I frantically try to reach the bottom with my rear feet to help push us ashore, but there is no bottom!

Scrambling frantically as the water throws us both under the surface again, and then as we come back up I try to see over Atsentma! He is too limp in my mouth. I cry, still holding him. I will not let go. I hope my young behind me are well trained enough to survive on their own as I swim as best possible and am forced under again.

Coming back up, frantically looking past Atsentma. The stream widens out before me the water will be shallower there!

Scrambling furiously, my rear feet touch bottom, pushing hard for the side of the stream and losing it as the rushing water pushes me off my feet again. I feel my rear feet touch again and my front feet touch bottom also, telling me the stream is shallow here.

Clawing frantically, my paws dig under the surface through loose mud and small rocks, as I scramble to stay on my feet, but the muddy, rushing water forces me downstream again and I am running out of shallow area!

The water is pushing too hard against my feet as I scramble for any grip along the muddy bottom, and even though it is only up to my stomach, the stream carries us downstream, narrowing again to faster, deeper water ahead of us!

Pushing, scrambling, crying, I claw my way frantically up the streams muddy bank because I know that Atsentma is dead. Slipping on mud, falling back in, I push frantically up and out!

Atsentma wails his fear, no longer a decent young predator, but now a frightened young one again. I cry with joy, drop him from my mouth, and cuff him hard with my front paw for doing this to me!

He wails again, but at least he is alive since he can wail. I groom him to show him that I still love him no matter how upset I am with him.

I groom him even though the rain falls heavily from the sky over both of us, which makes grooming him foolish. But I do it anyway because he is crying. As I groom his beautiful fur in the rain, I consider the next problem.

I am on the wrong side of the stream.

As far as I can see upstream in falling rain, the stream is running rapidly downstream, making it impossible for us to swim.

I decide we must get back to the burrow, as I turn and toss Atsentma onto my back with my mouth, with strict instructions to hang on.

He thinks he is going to ride home in comfort back there, foolish little one. He does dig his claws into my fur as I have instructed.

I begin to run for the stream, and Atsentma wails from the top of my back as he suddenly realizes what his mother is doing! I run for the bank of shallower part of the stream, the only place where it is shallow enough to fight my way back across while carrying him on my back.

I reach the edge of the muddy bank above the rushing water and, with Atsentma digging claws into my back and wailing

I jump as far as I can, hitting the water as far across the rushing, shallower section as I can get with the jump.

My claws hit muddy bottom underneath the rushing, chest-high water, and my paws scramble for grip, clawing in mud and gravel beneath my feet, clawing water as I slip and recover, then scrambling furiously for a grip in the mud as the water tries to yank me off my feet!

Clawing mud frantically as we start to be pulled downstream, I recover and turn my body upward into the stream. Without the water pushing against my side to force me off my feet and pushing instead against the narrower front of my body, leaning forward into the onrushing water is easier.

Knowing that even turned this way as I fight my way across the rushing water, I must get across before the water can yank me off my feet again, and I am being forced downstream into the deeper area again by the water's force against my legs and lower body! I claw at the bank! It is pure mud. I can't get up it!

Sliding downstream, I turn my head and yank Atsentma off me, ignoring his wails and the claws digging into my back as I toss him.

Wailing, he lands in the mud above us as I frantically manage to claw my way up through mud onto the stream bank.

We have a long, muddy walk back to the burrow in the falling rain, and Atsentma is very careful not to annoy me as we walk. I hope that this is a good lesson for at least this one of my five.

"Do not be careless when you are taking prey, or you may become prey yourself to something else!"

I do not bother teaching the others not to be careless around rapidly running water when I return to the burrow because they have seen all they need to know. It is the fifth set of seasons in my life and they have already managed to wear me out.

I am also starting to seriously reconsider this entire "have more young" thing, but then the rain finally stops as the days pass, and I reconsider again.

They still have not seen the bear, and I am not sure that I want them to. One night, without my young alongside, I found he had killed one of the smaller black bears and had eaten most of it.

If this bear kills other bears, he is truly dangerous. Until they know enough about him, my young are too many and too inclined to wander off on their own for me to take them where he roams now.

For reasons known only to him the bear roamed away from this meadow to the far side of my territory. As long as he is there, and not here, he is not an immediate danger to them, and one less worry for me.

They grow larger, I am not sure how. By the way they get into trouble they all should be dead by now. When I try to herd them together for instruction, every time we are outside they tend to wander off and explore without me.

We go out to hunt after the rain has stopped falling, and I find Akna over by the stream again while it is still too full.

I chase her away from it, only to discover that Alarana and Asiaq have wandered away while I was dealing with Akna.

I find them, herd them back to Akna for instruction with the rest, and discover that Atsentma is trying to impress me by seeking out a new prey, the skunk!

The skunk considers him too small to worry about, and only raises its tail in warning without actually spraying my young one, which is good because if he is sprayed in this new foolishness he would be sleeping outside the burrow for a while.

I get him away from it without being sprayed myself, which is also good because Atsentma will never stop hearing of it if I am sprayed.

Then, when they are finally gathered together, they want to wander off and explore, again, until finally I give up, and we head for the far side of my territory in daylight to find new things to amuse these young ones.

Hopefully it will be possible to teach them what they need to know as we travel there, and it actually is possible to instruct them in all of their curiosity as we move through the trees.

They learn about the new trees in this area as I explain that trees are still small here compared to the truly tall trees of an older forest. I show them how they can find water other than from the stream, and we are lucky enough to find a spring coming from the side of the hill I had found here before when I first marked this area as mine.

The spring flows from a small pond into the main stream in the center of this valley. My young look with wonder at the size of this pond. To them it is much larger than any place of water they have seen before, and all they have known is our stream.

I explain to them that there can be even larger areas of water than this, sometimes so large you can have trouble seeing all the way to the other side.

Aataentsic is the most fascinated of my five as I tell them of the large water I once lived near with my first young.

Then they want to know about my first young and I tell them of the ones before them and how they were trained. I start to cry as I remember Kekuit and my two little huntresses, Cetnenn and Caoineag.

My young are helpless before my tears, and I explain to them that sometimes I get sad for no reason and they should not worry. We roam and I teach them more, until we finally arrive at one of the burrows on the far side of my territory to rest for the night.

At least it was possible to teach them more on this trip, and I relax, until a new scent alerts me just before we go inside the burrow for the night. A rival badger is on the edge of my territory. They may get to see their mother fight now!

I move them with me because they can't be left alone while I confront this new one who makes markings too close to mine.

I move until the sun is almost gone from the sky, and see her roaming too close to the edge of my territory and too close to my young.

She sees me at the same time I see her, and we move to the edges of our territories nearer each other as I prepare to fight, maybe to kill if needed. This new badger is my size and weight, but she will not harm my young.

We move toward each other until she notices for the first time that I have young with me, and we do the thing badgers do from time to time when rivals meet.

This is my territory and marked as mine, giving me advantage in a fight, and she knows that. She also knows, as any creature knows, that a badger with young will fight to the death for them, and she also knows that this fight will no longer be just for territory, it will be to the death.

She turns, pretending to not have seen me and stays inside her own territory. Since that is the way she wants it to be, and she is not actually invading my territory, I turn also, and we simply walk away back into our own territories.

She is not anxious to die, and neither am I and this saves us both face without having to fight. One thing did catch my attention when I saw her: this one's fur was as black as my brother Tigranuhi's fur.

My young could sense my rage, could see my fur becoming erect to make me look larger, could hear my beginning growl of rage, and they want to know why I did not fight her.

Now I must teach again and explain that in any fight you may be injured, and in the wild, any injury can be fatal, even if you are not killed in the fight.

You may be unable to roam or eat, and you may starve to death.

You may be bleeding, and unable to stop the bleeding it if it is where you can't reach, or the bleeding may be too large to stop.

You may have a wound that the flies come to it and lay their eggs, which will hatch and the young flies will eat you alive as more come to eat you, until you are covered with their young, and you are dying in misery.

A fight is the last thing you want to do, and you should avoid it if you can.

They understand, and I breathe relief as we head for the burrow for some needed sleep. I hear her death scream just as we arrive at our burrow entrance!

I run my young inside quickly, rushing them deep into the sleeping chamber, instruct them to not move, and then run back to the entrance.

I know what a death scream sounds like, having heard enough of them in my lifetime, and if it was her death happening I need to know what could kill an adult female badger in her own territory.

I take care not to be exposed while nearing the edge of the territory where I last saw her roaming, and reach a place overlooking the area where we met, where it is possible see into the clearing she had walked back into after deciding not to fight me. He is here, and I sense that something unseen and even more dangerous than he is walking with him again.

The huge brown bear with the white scar on top of his head rips her body apart in the clearing, where he had simply run her down after she turned to leave peacefully and walked too quickly into that clearing without checking for any predators that might be around.

He eats her so quickly, but then she is so small compared to him. Huge and hungry, he finishes her and shambles heavily off to find new prey to kill.

He is here, and my young are not safe! I run for the burrow; we must leave!

I gather them together. He will probably sleep tonight, but we have no time to sleep. I need them to move as soon as it is darkness, for it will not take him long to realize that if one badger was here there may be more. A sound comes from outside. I freeze my young in place, telling them to make no noise.

It sniffs the burrow entrance, and only then do I relax, it is another badger. I can scent it, and there is something familiar about the scent.

I begin walking cautiously up the entrance tunnel, prepared to fight this one if it threatens my young, even if it is another badger.

Then finally I catch its scent fully, and run for the burrow entrance to greet the one that I have not seen in far too long a time, Tigranuhi, my brother!

I hear his growl of joy in front of me outside as he catches my scent also. My beautiful, black-furred brother waits for me to come out to him. He knows the rule about entering the burrow of a badger mother.

We meet outside while my curious young wait anxiously inside, trying to hear if I am fighting for my life through all the snorts and growls coming down to them. Then they come up against my orders to see, and find Tigranuhi and I chasing each other, growling happily together again as we had done when we were young.

Then there is sadness as we tell each other of our lives since we had last seen each other, and the female with the fur as black as his own which had died, was his mate Atida.

Tigranuhi rages because he saw her getting killed, but he could do nothing as he watched his mate get devoured by this monster, the bear that was so much larger than he.

He cries with grief and shame that he could do nothing, and he rages in a desire to kill this one that had killed his mate and knows he can't.

I suddenly remember the monster that now roams this territory, looking for new prey, and my young are far too untrained to avoid him even though they are fierce enough by now. It is dark, and it is time for all of us to leave.

Tigranuhi walks with us, and he will stay with us for a while as he grieves, then I know he will leave again. We are solitary creatures, and my brother must find his new life with a new mate somewhere, but for now, we leave together in the dark.

I know that bears normally sleep in the dark, but that is not comforting to me. The black bears I once knew did that, but I do not know what this huge brown monster does.

Tigranuhi's dark body blends so well into shadows and darkness I have trouble seeing him from time to time in the darkness around us, but I know that he is there roaming with us, and it is comforting to know that another fighter is with me on our journey. The darkness of the night covers us well as we go, and only the uneasy feeling I have about how my life seems to be so joined now with the life of this huge brown monster of a bear that worries me.

Suddenly I notice that Alarana and Asiaq have wandered off from us in the darkness as they tend to do when we roam anywhere. I hear the roar, he hunts in the darkness also, and this monster has my young!

I scream my rage, running past trees and through brush, knowing already that the advantage may still be ours in darkness, despite his size. Although able to hunt in darkness or not, all bears still have poor night eyes compared to ours, we are meant to hunt darkness, and he will be clumsier!

I scream my rage and hear a smaller, return scream of rage from Asiaq somewhere in front of me, and then I wonder where Tigranuhi is. Suddenly I hear the bear's roar of hunger turn into a roar of pain, and I reach the place where the monster is trying to take my young. In the darkness, a fast, black shadow rips the bear and runs!

Tigranuhi is here, slashing and running, as little Asiaq stands in front of that huge brown bear of death, and dares it to take little Alarana behind him!

The bear stands to avoid the claws of Tigranuhi on its body as it screams rage and turns to slash with a massive paw where Tigranuhi was! But he is far too slow as Tigranuhi rips his leg from the other side and runs before the bear can react.

The bear is still turning to react to Tigranuhi's attack as I scream for its death, and rip past the bear on the opposite side, taking both fur and blood from its other leg with my claws, and then run as I have seen Tigranuhi run! The bear turns to slash at me as Tigranuhi rips it again from the other side and runs before it can react to him.

We slash him from both sides, running, ripping, and slashing at him faster than he can react, as I scream for Asiaq to run with Alarana. Tigranuhi rips again, running away before the bear can see him.

I rip and run from the other side again, as the bear stands erect and roars rage at these smaller prey creatures hurting him in the darkness!

The bear might actually see me in this darkness with my lighter fur, but Tigranuhi with his black fur is darkness in the darkness of night and rips him again as he roars and tries to move toward me. I scream again for Asiaq and Alarana to run!

Asiaq screams his own tiny rage at the monster that wants his sister and threatens his own attack, but I scream for him not to be foolish, to take his sister and run with her!

I rip the bear from one side as Tigranuhi rips it from another, and we run in different directions to confuse it. Turning, slashing, ripping the bear again, and then running as its huge paw sweeps down at us!

Screaming for Asiaq and Alarana to run, I notice Asiaq is still standing in front of Alarana to protect her from this monster that can kill both of them so easily! I scream for him to run with her again, and they finally do!

As much as I admire my little Asiaq's determination to die fighting for his sister, I still think he is an idiot who needs far more training from me to survive on his own, and I run behind them while Tigranuhi takes advantage of his black fur in the darkness to harass the bear and to give us time.

Slashing and ripping the bear in quick, running attacks as it roars behind us, trying to see him in the night, Tigranuhi rages, rips at it, and runs!

Suddenly as we run from where Tigranuhi fights the bear alone, the bear becomes strangely silent behind us, no longer raging at Tigranuhi.

Then I hear it running, all four paws pounding on the ground as it comes in the direction it last saw us go, raging again at the ones who hurt it instead of being its prey, and the thought comes to me instantly. *It runs on all four paws, and it is low to the ground now, I can take its face!*

I scream for my young to run! As they run onward, I turn to fight and die for them as the bear runs blindly toward us in the blackness of this night, hitting trees, shaking them with its massive body in the darkness as it comes for the small prey that got away from it and comes for the larger prey that hurt it. The bear runs, low to the ground, and I jump upward, aiming for the side of its face with my claws!

Our claws are long indeed, they are almost the lengths of the paws that hold them, and mine have all the power of my foreleg, the weight of my body, the speed of my jump, and the fury of my anger behind them as they rip through the side of his face!

He screams as four bloody claw tracks tear across the side of his huge face, and moving too quickly to stop in the darkness crashes headfirst into the tree in front of him!

I bounce off the side of the huge body passing me and hit the ground running, hearing him crash, and lie stunned behind me as I run for where I last saw my young running. I find them and run behind them!

I run my young! I run my young! I run them as I hear him screaming rage and pain behind us.

I run them until we are sure that he is far more concerned with stopping from the pain now on one side of his face than to worry about us anymore, and only then do we slow to a walk, while still moving away in the dark cover of night forest around us. Finally we stop to wait for Tigranuhi to join us, but he does not come.

I move my young until it is daylight, find them a secure burrow and tell them not to leave unless I fail to return in a day, and if I do not, then they must survive without me. Beginning the trip back alone, I have to know if my brother is alive.

I notice with great satisfaction that the bear bled very nicely as I pass the place where my claws ruined his pretty face, moving cautiously from there onward just in case the bear is still here, although his blood trial leads away from the place.

The bear is gone and Tigranuhi is gone. I find no blood from Tigranuhi, only the bear's blood where he bled from our slashing attacks. There is no sign that Tigranuhi is dead, he is just gone.

I wonder if he went back to the place where his mate had died to stay there. I wonder if he was hurt in his fight to save us while he stayed behind to distract it, and he wandered off to die. I wonder if the bear took him.

My young do not see me cry when I return, and then we roam back to the burrow in the little hillock. I will never see my beautiful, black-furred brother alive again.

They continue to grow, and I teach them, these last lessons they need before they are almost fully grown to the point that they will soon leave. They grow impatient to find what is in the rest of this forest. They grow and begin to roam more on their own after I teach them. They grow to adulthood, and the teaching is over, and they are ready.

We go out at dusk.

My now-grown little Aataentsic leaves first, heading south, and looks back at me before he enters the too young, too small forest.

He has heard my tales of the burrow overlooking the large water and wants to see it himself, and to see if any place of water can truly be that large, and to mark his own territory there. I hope he reaches it, and settles there and has a safe and long life as I watch him go.

We go out at dusk.

Atsentma is next. He does not look back as he enters the forest on the other side of the meadow.

I do not want him going in the direction we last saw the bear in, but he is a proud hunter, and my little wild animal. He has had enough warnings from me about safety around this monster. Atsentma has to leave, and he has to leave in the direction he wants to go, and that is the way of all our young leaving. I cry for him alone, where the last three of my young can't see me, then return to them.

We go out at dusk.

Alarana and Asiaq leave together, as I thought they would.

They will travel as one throughout their lives, and we sometimes do that, rarely, but sometimes. I know that he will protect her with his life. That was in him when we fought the monster, and he refused to leave her to save himself in the darkness.

I do not bother to hide my tears from the last of these young who once were so many, the many I have had to clean the burrow up after so many times, who have often driven me to distraction, who I have had to rescue more than once, and who I loved so much.

We go out at dusk.

My shy, little Akna kisses me once with a brief grooming sweep of her tongue over my face, then turns and leaves, entering the surrounding, young forest. I cry behind her, as my own mother had once cried behind me. And then they are gone, my five are gone.

Thamuatz will return in this direction to see me again, and I will have yet more young by him. I wait because it is not the end of the warm seasons yet, and I know that he will return, walking through the meadow to find me again, as we are creatures of habit. My young will be just as perfect as the ones he gave to me this last time.

I wait, and though I may have complained about my five from time to time, they were so beautiful and so perfect that I want to have more of them.

I wait, but he does not come. The leaves begin to turn to their many colors on the trees that lose their leaves before winter. The leaves begin to fall at last from the trees, and I begin to roam.

Enough days have passed. I want a mate and want to have more young this next spring when the leaves return. Thamuatz is not coming to me; I will just have to go look for a mate.

I roam and head in the direction Alarana and Asiaq took, for that is where Thamuatz had come from, the one who gave me these many that I loved so much. I roam and find human scent in this direction and my senses go into full alertness! The last time I saw humans was when the fire came, but I still remember my mother's instruction about them being predators that can kill from a distance. True, the ones that I saw back then did not look like good predators, but this one might be.

I roam more cautiously as the humans' scent strengthens, and I find him. I find him stripping the skin from a fox.

I can see that the fox's skull has been crushed, and the fox's leg is still caught in something that has trapped it and bitten almost all the way through the leg; it is something shiny on both sides of one front leg, close to the ground and fastened to the ground.

The fox has bled across the thing that has its front leg and has bled all over the ground around him. We do not bleed after we are dead; we only bleed while we are still alive. My seasons as a predator have taught me this. I know that this fox was trapped in pain with its leg caught until the human came to kill it.

The human takes the shiny thing from the fox's leg and places it inside a large something that he has taken off his human back.

Then using some small shiny thing he holds in his human paw he takes the fox's beautiful fur, leaving the bloody fox on the ground as he places the fur in the thing he fastens on his human back again when he finishes. I wait to watch him eat the fox, hoping he will leave something for me, but he stands up and leaves.

He did not eat it? The human simply walked away with the fox's fur, and wasted all of that meat for just the skin?

"Humans are truly stupid to do this!" I think walking down to feast at the kill. "If he won't eat it, I will!"

Strangely, the fox does not taste that good somehow, it's as if I am eating something not clean, something that should not be. Wasted food for just the fur? The human who has it is either stupid or vain.

I leave the rest of it without filling myself, and roam, following the human. I want to see what other forms of stupidity these vain human creatures engage in.

The human goes through the forest to another of those things that hold creatures and finds another fox trapped by his leg. This fox is also still alive, bleeding over the thing that holds his leg as he whimpers pain and fear, baring his teeth in a last attempt to live as the human simply walks until he is behind it, and then slams something down onto the fox's head.

I hear the crack of its skull from here where I hide and watch as the human takes the same, small, flat thing he used on the last fox to also take this fox's fur.

This fox is still twitching, and I know that it is not fully dead yet as the human strips its skin away from the fox's body, stripping it of all dignity and life, leaving it a bloody, bare, furless thing for the predators to find. He places the fox's fur in the thing he has on his back again with the thing that caught the fox's leg.

I leave, sick. The humans at the fire had tried to save the forest; this human butchers for no reason, for what, the creature's fur only? Again, he wastes the meat, and leaves without eating as I give up watching this thing that takes the fur of others for no good reason, and leave.

Wandering toward the territory of Alarana and Asiaq, their scent is strong in this direction, and I smile for I know that they will be together.

Wandering, I find that they both are still together waiting for me. They are still together just as they had always been together from the time they were born, and when they stayed with me, when they left our burrow together to roam together as one. Now stripped of all their dignity and fur, two bloody bodies, lying together in the forest where the human had left them after he took their fur.

The scent of the human fur taker is all around them, and only then do I see the real horror. We do not bleed after we are dead, the dead do not bleed, but there is blood all around Alarana's bare, stripped body.

Like the second fox, the blow to her head did not kill her; only her leg was caught in the thing that held it, I see where it bit through her leg to the bone.

Asiaq's legs are untouched, and I know that he had stayed to defend his sister from this human when her leg was caught, just as he had stayed to defend her from the huge, brown, monster bear.

He died when the human crushed his skull with the thing he held in his human paw, the thing he used on the foxes, and then the human took their fur. Asiaq's while he was dead, and Alarana's while still alive.

I begin the hunt. My young are dead; the human will be dead.

I will kill him. I do not care how much larger or taller the human is, I will kill him. I do not care what he uses to crush the skulls of the innocent; it will not be good enough to stop me, I will kill him. Rage is inside me as I track him through the forest. I will kill him. The rage makes me shake with fury; my fur is up, my teeth are bared.

I will take him from behind and flatten him with a swift attack from the rear, ripping one of his legs open to drop him as I rush him with weight and claws, and then tear him apart while he is still on the ground. I will kill him. I will follow and track because the human moves ahead of me through my forest, where he will die today!

He moves more quickly this time; not stopping to check more of the things that hold creature's legs, he must be through with that for the day.

It is getting late, and I have the advantage. In the dark he will be blind and helpless. I am a night hunter, but he is not. In the dark I could absolutely kill him!

I smile but shake with fury. I smile and track him as he moves through the darkening forest, unaware of me coming up behind him, closing the distance between us.

He is easy; it is almost dark, and I will kill him. But I do not have the chance to kill him, another does it for me.

I hear his scream of terror and the roar of killing rage at the same time! The monster is here, the huge brown bear!

Even from over here where I watch into the clearing at the edge of the forest, I can see the old, thin, white scar running over the top of its head. I see the newer scars stretching over one side of the bear's face where my claws had ripped it open that night. I see that the human has entered its territory and found the bear's fox kill, which lies before the human. And as he looks up from it, screaming, I see that he is too foolish or too panicked to at least try to run.

The human kneels frozen in fear over the dead fox where he was taking the fur. He had actually stopped to take the fur of a bear's kill, without realizing that the bear might still be around and come back for the food later.

Bears always come back for their food, but his human had no idea that anything as massive as this bear could return this silently; until it was right over him, standing upright on its hind legs, ready to kill the one who dared to touch its kill.

The bear towers above him now, roaring rage as it reaches down and almost casually slaps the much smaller human with a massive front paw.

The human screams as the blow hurls him backward through the air, and the bear is on him as the human scrambles frantically backward, throwing up one of his human paws to stop death.

It is a wasted effort, as the bear simply kills him.

The human dies, screaming, as the bear kills him, ripping the thing off his back that held the fur of others, scattering the fur held in it across the ground around them both. Then the bear finally satisfied that this trespass upon its prey has been avenged, simply turns and leaves.

There is something wrong with that, but I can now see the fur of two young badgers among all the other fur scattered on the ground as the bear leaves the human. I have no pity for this human, only sorrow for my lost Alarana and Asiaq.

I will not kill today, it has already been done for me, there is nothing left for me here, and I am going home. But as I turn back into the forest to leave, there is a thought about something my mother once said, *There is justice in nature, deadly sometimes, but justice.*

I only want to find a mate again and to have new young this next spring season, and then I will teach them of the thing which hold legs that humans use to strip you of your fur and your dignity, sometimes while you are still alive, and how to avoid them.

I will teach them to avoid humans. I am a predator myself, but the actions of this human sicken me, he was not a predator worthy of the name, he was worse than the predator that had killed him.

Still there was that something I sensed about the bear when it first hit the human, and when it was killing him. Not something different about the bear this time, but something I sensed beside the bear again, something I could not see as the bear killed the human.

Although invisible to me, I could still sense that it was somehow growing more powerful with each of the bear's kills, that it had enjoyed the kill as the bear was killing the human, and that it was human.

It is curious that this bear did not even deliver a warning growl or roar at the sight of his food being touched as most bears will do but had crept up quietly on the human instead, nothing that large should be able to move that quietly

There was also something wrong with the bear leaving after he killed the human, as if he had only wanted to kill the human. It was something our mother, Asaseyaa, had told us long ago, but I do not remember what it was.

It was also curious that the bear did not eat the fox as soon as he killed it, almost as if he did not want to kill the fox for food but just wanted to kill it and then leave it untouched in the open where the human fur taker could find it easily.

Almost as if he had known the human fur taker would be coming that way and had deliberately left it there for the human to find it, knowing the human would stop to take the fur, and then he could kill the human.

No bear could be that smart or that dangerously cunning. It would have taken something of higher intelligence to plan that well, and the bear hadn't eaten the fox or the human, he had simply killed them.

Then I realize what was wrong with both of the bear's kills. The bear did not touch the human or the fox after it killed them, the bear left both untouched.

When bears kill they eat or hide the prey for later eating, yet this bear had simply walked away, as if he had wanted only to kill for the sake of killing.

Our mother, Asaseyaa, had told us something important about this, but I simply can't remember what she said. It is not important; at least the bear had a reason for killing, and did not kill just for vanity.

I return to my hillock burrow, alone.

It is later in the season now of the leaves falling from the trees that lose them, the fifth time I have seen this happen in my lifetime. All of my young are gone, and I want to have young again this next season when the trees grow leaves.

I enter my burrow on my little hillock in the middle of my meadow of my forest and cry for my two lost little ones who had died for no reason.

Apparitions

Time here now is spent making sure that all my territory is looked at before I reduce my roaming range this winter to just the area around this primary burrow. After ensuring that my other burrows are also ready, in case I must use one of them instead, I hunt to fill myself for the coming winter. The rest of my time is spent sitting in warming sunlight before I sleep for the daytime, patiently waiting for Thamuatz to return to this territory as he did last year.

He was a good mate then, wonderfully powerful and fierce, with such handsome fur, and he gave me my little Akna who was so shy but grew enough to finally leave proudly on her own. He gave me Alarana and Asiaq who left together and died together, and he gave me Aataentsic who became such a beautiful hunter after so many lessons, and Atsentma who drove me so crazy with his swimming lesson in the flooded stream.

The many that I loved so very much while they were with me, and perhaps this year I will have many more by him.

I wait, watching for him to come again over the meadow to my burrow in the hillock, but he does not come. I even climb on top of the old, burned, fallen tree on top of the hillock above my burrow to look further, and still he does not come.

I wait but he does not come, then I sigh and roam in the same direction Akna had gone as I look for any signs of male badgers.

It is frustrating to have to look for a mate of our kind; they usually seek us out instead, promptly leaving us after we are with their young. Now that I think of it, mates can be really frustrating. Still, I roam because I want new young so badly.

I roam until I scent one in this territory and begin to follow the trail to him. Moving through the forest away from the stream and following him into this area, I hope that this will be the mate because I can already tell several things about him already.

He is young. I can tell by his speed of movement across this territory that he is strong. I can tell by the way he moves through the brush that he is looking for a mate by the number of scent markings he leaves, each one says, "Here I am, a worthy mate for you."

I begin to follow him in earnest; this will be a good mate for me, our young will be strong, powerful hunters in the darkness!

I follow, as it becomes more apparent that he is slowing and looking. I follow until I reach the edge of the forest that overlooks into a clear area.

He is with Akna. My little one has her first mate, which is not at all unusual for one of us. Many mate during their first full set of seasons so they will have young the next spring. But now I feel torn between pride for my little one and disappointment that did not choose to mate with me.

My pride wins, and I turn to leave discreetly. Let her have her first mate and her first young. I leave with a sigh and head back in the direction of my burrow in the hillock again. After hunting for a while to fill myself before I travel again, I will leave from there and head in the other direction.

There are a few days of just relaxing and considering this decision before I leave in the direction the fire came from during my second summer. I am careful, of course, because the huge brown bear also came from that direction.

But if the fire came from that way, then the forest in that area will still be young and small like the forest surrounding the meadow around my burrow in the little hillock.

I have never seen other badgers come from that northern direction before, have never scented any sign of badgers near the far edges of my territory there, and have no idea if there actually are any badgers in that direction, but if I want young, it will be necessary to at least look there. There may very well be some handsome males up there looking for a mate, for the time to mate before winter is growing shorter.

Looking anywhere in the direction I last saw the bear is out. I do not want to see him ever again, although our lives seem to be strangely intertwined with each other.

Aataentsic had gone in that direction when he left and I hope he learned enough of my lessons to survive inside that monster's territory.

To the south Akna has her mate and wants to be happy with him. I will not intrude in that direction. And the only other direction, other than north, has never shown any trace of badgers.

I do not know why there is no trace of badgers in that direction but suspect it may have had something to do with the human who had killed my Alarana and Asiaq.

I did find human scent all over that direction a full season before they died, but thought nothing of it at the time, since that was before I found him trapping and stripping creatures of their fur.

He may have simply killed all the badgers in that direction, and some of the traps he set may still be set there, waiting for the unwary. The only direction left is in the direction the fire came from, north.

By the time the moon is out I start to roam. While not a full moon, it gives more than enough brightness to easily see while I travel northward.

Night is safest now in this too small, young forest that I will be going into. In the daytime I would be exposed in the many open areas in this direction because there is not enough new growth forest to shield me from sight, but at night, even in the full moonlight, the black stripes running down my dark-brown sides will hide me well in the shadows.

The stream serves me well now as a guide and a source of food and water. At night the stream will be easy to follow in the moonlight, and the frogs are still along its banks for food, and the ferns along the stream's banks are thick.

When dawn finally arrives, it is only necessary to find a thick clump of ferns to sleep inside without having to go to all the trouble of digging a full burrow. I am anxious to find a new mate and don't want to waste time digging places to stay.

As the moon grows fuller each night, I move steadily northward over the next two nights, curious as to why larger animals seem to be fewer in number in this direction.

Nevertheless, smaller prey creatures are adequate for food, and the larger ones do not matter unless they are predators that might threaten me, so I do not worry. I am curious about a crack noise in the distance that wakes me during the day, as I seem to remember hearing it somewhere once before.

Still, neither is of real importance on this trip, just curious things to consider, until I reach the cleared area sloping upward in front of me in the moonlight and find the dead deer.

He has not been touched. In fact, he is not even cold, there are no signs of rips or tears from a bear or another big enough to have killed it, and there is no scent of any other around him.

While deer do fight for mates or territory, they seldom kill each other doing so. This one has no antler wounds on him, and no other wound from fight or predator.

I see no reason for him to have died, he is just dead. Still, we will take prey that others provide for us in addition to hunting our own, and this is an incredible find. Deer are a rare treat for me unless I find one already dead, and this is an entire deer to eat, with no bear around to contest it.

I wander over to feast, wondering why anyone would simply kill and then leave prey untouched afterward; then ignore the question to eat, until noticing there is blood on him after all, around a small hole in his side. Suddenly remembering the deer I had found before with the same type of wound and human scent around it. Humans!

The feasting stops instantly, and my alertness is up in the moonlight around me. There is no human noise or scent around, and I start to relax until another thing occurs. There is no human scent around this deer, but "Humans can kill from a distance!"

I recall my mother's words to me, and I run!

I run quickly for the nearest concealing brush, through it, and out the other side for thicker brush, then suddenly remember that it is all shadows and darkness in the moonlight around me, and I remember another thing my mother taught me, "Humans may be able to kill from a distance, but, unlike us, they are not true night hunters as we are and can't see at night as we can."

Even if a human is here he can't be close because there is no scent, and therefore, he won't see me if I blend my dark body and black markings into the shadows.

Food is food, and I return to the kill to fill myself, eating greedily until there is no more room inside me for any more deer.

Waddling happily back to the stream to drink, I find a large enough group of plants to hide me securely during the day. Time for sleep and since this body is far too full of good deer meat to bother digging a quick burrow; the plant cluster will be fine for now.

A loud *"Crack!"* noise awakens me. I stand alert, ready to run or fight, but nothing happens. I relax, then the loud *"Crack!"* comes again, and I jump. Then, it is quiet, except for birds and noisy birdcalls. I wait after a while, nothing happens.

I decide to see what it is, but cautiously. We are curious creatures, but we are also cautious creatures. You do not survive in the wild by making mistakes no matter how strong your claws or teeth happen to be.

I roam in the direction the loud crack came from, trying to stay in concealing brush as much as possible.

The loud *"Crack!"* comes again, and I flinch, wait, and then roam again until I reach the edge of this young forest and look up the sloping ground beyond.

All the northern areas I have been traveling through are almost all the same, new forest still trying to recover from the fire that had killed the old one, and young trees and thick brush growing quickly in the absence of older trees blocking the sunlight.

Some older trees are here and there, a few blackened tree trunks without branches above them, showing the old, faded signs of the fire that had killed them, and other blackened trees, lying burned and rotting on their sides among the newly growing forest.

Here at the edge of this young forest the valley slopes upward between the hills on either distant side, with the stream flowing south through the center.

The grass in front of me is open and wide all the way to the flat area in the distance at the top of the cleared slope. I can see something up there but have no idea what it is.

Somewhere in my memory, I remember something like it, but not exactly like what the humans were riding on. But for now, it is just a thing on a flat area at the top of this upward-sloping land, and then the human moves and I freeze and wait, blending with the shadows of the plants, concealed by the brush around me.

If you are a predator in the wild you quickly learn that the first one who moves is also the first one to give away their position and mark themselves for others, and that is why we learn early to remain still, letting the prey move first while we wait for it. This tactic also keeps us safe from those who would prey on us.

Unless you are actively hunting for prey, you remain still, remain concealed, and do not move first.

He did, and now I have his position and am even more curious. He is not concealed at all. He sits on top of a lower part of a thing on the flat place at top of this rise and makes no attempt to hide.

A badger's eyes are not the best sense by far, but they are good enough to study this new thing. Then I realize I have seen it before when the fire came seasons ago, but it was different.

Humans rode on top of the loud, yellow, clanking things that came into my clearing in the meadow around my burrow on the little hillock. But they were not the same as this one the human is on top of now.

Those were much larger, and this thing does not have the flat things that go around and around its sides that the loud, clanking, yellow things seemed to have as they came through my clearing. There was something else, but I don't remember it.

This thing the human sits on seems to have smaller round things under it. I wonder how this thing moves; if it jumps, or runs, or doesn't move at all and is simply some human thing. I know it, but I can't remember.

He moves again, and I watch carefully as he jumps down from the top of the thing and notice for the first time that the human is holding something. A stick thing, long and slim on the end he holds away from himself and larger on the other end toward him, with something on top of it but much shorter, like a smaller, long, round stick on top of the big stick thing he holds.

Then the smaller stick thing on top of the long stick thing reflects sunlight at me as he turns the longer stick thing my way, and then puts the stick thing back over his human shoulder, and takes something else out from where he was sitting. He puts the smaller something in front of his eyes.

As I watch curiously, he looks back and forth across this area through the thing he put in front of his eyes. And as he turns it toward me, the something in front of his eyes also reflects light at me from its front, just as the thing on top of the long stick thing did.

I feel no real concern; he is much too far away to see me much less hurt me. I simply watch as he looks this way.

He stops looking, puts the thing he was holding in front of his eyes down again, and takes the long, slim stick thing off his shoulder again, placing the larger end against his shoulder while looking through the shorter round thing on top of it at me.

I wait, curious, as he does something with his paws. One of his paws is under the long stick thing near the front middle of it, and the other paw is back under it near his head, where he is looking thorough the thing on top that reflects light at me.

He takes the human paw near his head and lifts something on the side of the long stick thing near his head, pulling it up and back, then sliding it forward and down again. There is a distant "click-click" sound I have never heard before, and then he seems to be really concentrating on where I watch him watch me.

Suddenly there is a small flash of light at the front end of the long stick thing facing me; as an angry hornet traveling far faster than any angry hornet should ever travel passes with a loud *"Crack!"* sound near me.

And the rabbit exposed in the open near me screams as something rips through his body and soars out the other side of his body, dragging his blood with it, as it slams into the ground behind him!

The rabbit flips and falls as a much louder *"Crack!"* comes from where the human is. There was no other flash of light, the first *"Crack"* came as something passed near me, the second

"Crack!" came from where the human was, after the rabbit flipped over and died.

I do not stop to puzzle how one thing can have two loud cracks when the second loud *"Crack!"* echoes off the hillsides, as I turn and run!

Luckily, I am still concealed inside brush all the way and now know exactly what my mother had said when she said that they could kill from a distance!

I do not stop until I am sure the human is still back there, and not anywhere he can see me. I will still go north, but not until it is fully dark tonight. There will be moonlight tonight, and if he is still there, I will carefully blend into the shadows as I pass where he is.

After dark I begin moving cautiously. In case this human can see enough in the moonlight after all to be a threat to me.

After making my way up the sloping ground, I notice the rabbit is still there, untouched and wasted as food. Finally reaching the flat area at the top where the thing he was sitting on was, and find the next puzzle to solve.

The flat area stretches as far as I can see in the moonlight in both directions, and even though it is not that wide across, it is long in both directions, and far too smooth to be natural. Below my paws, the flat area feels as firm as rock should be, but it is not rock. Is it something else?

I give up trying to understand it and just cross it for the other side where there is real ground again and not this strange, long, flat, hard ground that feels like rock but is not.

Finding the next obstacle going north on the other side of the flat area, there is a sunken, hollow area stretching in both directions alongside the flat place. On the other side of that is a tall, stone thing stretching alongside the sunken hollow in both directions, made of stones on top of each other, higher than I can reach on my hind legs.

I turn to follow it and see if there is a way around, but the tall, made-of-stones thing blocks me still, making the decision to turn and try the other way a natural one. Back in the other direction, I find a small hole through the tall, made-of-stones thing, but it is far too small for my body to fit through.

Maybe another smaller creature like a small rabbit could fit through it, but not anything larger than that. At least I can see through the hole to find out what is on the other side of this stone thing.

I look and notice that this tall, made-of-stones thing stretching alongside the flat surface thing is not really that thick, and I can see open land on the other side in the moonlight.

Realization comes instantly. "We are natural diggers; I can simply dig under the stone thing!" I start to dig, and then something happens.

I am a practical predator, and not used to having fears. But in the moonlight around me as I start to dig under the stone thing, I get a sudden sensation of terrible terror, pain, grief, and the sense of someone patiently waiting for prey to arrive. But not the same good feeling I have, when I patiently wait for prey.

This is a different feeling; a terrible, unnatural form of waiting seems to radiate out through the hole at me, which makes me shiver, so I give up the idea of digging here.

I am unable to explain how I know, but I know that something is there on the other side of the hole, waiting patiently for someone, and there will be death when that one arrives, but not from any form of death as I know it.

It raises the hair on my body as I quickly leave this place to look for another way through, speeding my steps up as I leave.

I can't explain what just happened to me, but for the first time in my life, as a predator, I felt truly afraid; even the bear did not make me feel this much fear.

I heard no noise that might tell me some creature was on the other side of the tall stone thing, smelled no scent of any other creature, and saw nothing waiting when I looked through the hole; but I know that something terrible was waiting patiently just on the other side of the hole, and if whatever was on the other side of this stone thing decides to come to this side, I do not want to be here!

For the first time in my life I am not comfortable with darkness around me, and wish it were daylight instead of just moonlight as I find a large clump of brush on the other side of the flat, smooth surface and try to sleep.

Unable to sleep, I sit alert instead for the rest of the night, waiting for something to come walking down the smooth flat surface in the moonlight toward me. Shivering and ready for it with teeth and claws when it comes for me; I already know that it will not be a creature, it will be something other.

Daylight brings death. The human returns in the thing he was sitting on yesterday. This time I see him as he is, and he is not a true predator as I am, he is different, and he makes the human who killed my Alarana and Asiaq look like a prey creature by comparison. I wanted to kill that one. I am afraid that this one will kill me as he brings dogs and another smaller young human with him.

The dogs I would recognize from my mother's descriptions of them, just as I recognize her descriptions of how humans would look told me what I was seeing outside my burrow entrance when the fire came to my meadow.

These human-bred dogs are very much like foxes as she had said they would be, but different and larger, and I can feel the fear radiating from the dogs long before the thing carrying humans and dogs stops near me.

I stay as hidden as possible in the brush patch alongside the flat, not rock surface the human's thing travels on, hoping he does not see me hidden this close because as this human steps out of the thing that carries him, I can sense even from here what radiates from him and surrounds him. I can sense it with a predator's instinct, even before he screams at the other smaller, young human with him, even before he yells at the dogs.

The thing that radiates from him is pure anger, and this anger is natural to him, and there is death in that anger. It is not the anger that we feel when another violates our territory, anger over that is over quickly, or the anger we feel when one of our young is threatened, that anger is justified for all creatures. This is a harder anger radiating from this human, a continuous anger at everything around him, an anger that is as much a part of him as my paws are a part of me.

I do not have to know him to know this. I am predator and huntress. I can sense from where I hide, watching, that this is neither predator nor hunter I am looking at now. This is a killer, and there is a difference.

A true predator kills for food, but this human would kill purely to kill. There is also something strangely familiar about this human, as if I had somehow seen him before, but I have never seen this human before.

The other smaller, young human is afraid of this angry human. What radiates from the smaller human also radiates from the dogs. The angry human curses the dogs and pulls them from the back of the human-carrying thing that brought them here, kicking the dogs and yelling at them, as they cower in fear on the flat, hard surface around them.

The dogs are pathetic prey creatures, unsure of what the human wants them to do as the human yells at them and points down into the valley below us. Then the angry human simply takes the same long, stick thing that he used yesterday to kill the rabbit near me from the inside of his human-carrying thing, puts it to his shoulder, and kills one of the dogs.

It is not simply a loud *"Crack"* this close; it is a roaring *"Crack!"* that makes my ears ring as the long stick thing flashes at the front!

I flinch as something goes through the dog's side, comes out of its other side, and slams into the ground behind it as the dog drops and shakes, screaming pain as the angry human simply makes his killing stick roar again into the dog!

The dog dies, twitching, while I hide and shiver in fear at what humans can do, and the other dogs do what he had wanted them to do all along, they run down the slope away from the flat hard thing that the human-carrying thing arrived on. Running into the brush below as the smaller human makes the mistake of asking the angry one something.

It is not the right thing to do because the angry human screams at the smaller one, and the smaller human cowers; until the angry human, with a smile that I do not want to see again, walks to the dead dog, grabs it, and flings it toward the slope below that leads back into the forest I want to be back inside myself.

I wait hidden as they both climb back into the thing that carries humans and leave in the direction that they came from, and only then, when I am sure that they are truly gone and not returning, do I come out from where I hide, torn between wanting to be far away from here safe inside the forest again and wanting to go north to find a mate.

But now that it is light I can see there is a large hole that passes underneath the flat surface, close to where I am hiding in this brush, with water flowing out of it from the stream I have been following. If the stream is flowing out from it on this side, then the stream must also flow into it on the other side. I go down to look.

Up close, it is larger and wider than I thought, with room to walk alongside the stream.

I go cautiously through it; this is daylight, and darkness will not conceal me from danger in daylight. Pausing to look outward into the valley in front of me, I wait until I am absolutely sure it is safe.

It is safe, and that is another "wrong" I feel while looking out over this new territory. Where are the creatures?

Other creatures should be roaming this valley as in any other place with this much open land, and plentiful grass. Deer should be everywhere this early in the day, but I can see no large creatures, only birds, a chipmunk, and a few smaller mice.

That "wrong" makes me more nervous than if there were a bear standing right outside this hole the stream flows through.

The valley between the hills on either side looks wide and open near the place where I hide, with small trees and brush beyond the area of open space in front of me.

It is still a young forest as in the valley behind me, although there are a few old, dead trees still standing here and there in this valley.

The fire that had reached my hillock burrow had been here, and since it came from this direction, it may have even started here somewhere.

With the youngness of this new, growing forest where the old forest died, there is far too much open space in this valley to hide any of the larger creatures that should be here. There should be larger creatures here, but there is nothing moving other than the few small creatures.

I puzzle this, until I realize that no larger creatures, also means no larger predator creatures.

It is my fifth season of the leaves dropping from trees that lose them in the winter, and it would be nice to have a new territory all my own, with no bears or any other larger predators to compete with. However, I want a mate also, and if I am unable to find one here that will mean a return south to the old territory of my hillock for the winter, which means no mate this season by the time I return there.

I roam cautiously out from my hiding place and enter this new valley, and catch a new "wrong" instantly as soon as my paws step into the valley. There is nothing to see, or hear, or smell, or feel, just the sudden feeling that I am not wanted here. It is a feeling that makes my hair rise again, as I stop with my teeth bared and edge back into where stream drains underneath the flat place above. As I do the feeling disappears.

I step out into the valley, and the "wrong" feeling is there again. I step back into the hole that drains the stream underneath the flat place above it, and the wrong feeling disappears again.

I puzzle it, and then decide to just ignore it and step out to roam in my new valley, trying to think of why I am so nervous here, while reminding myself sternly, "There is nothing to be nervous about. I am a proud predator, not some weak, shivering prey creature!"

But as a true predator, I am also more sensitive to some things than prey creatures, and I still feel the "wrong" inside me of not being wanted here.

I ignore it and walk deeper into the valley. Nothing is here to threaten me, there are no predators here, or anything else of any size to matter in this place, but food is here because the smaller creatures have returned to this valley after it had burned. I can see mice and others are here also.

Curiously, there are no rabbits, and this type of grassy area should have many, but there are none, as if they had been eliminated from this valley and never returned. Still, it might be good territory to find a mate in, and I try to suppress the feeling of wrong while moving northward into my new territory.

The trees that have returned are small indeed, but they do provide some cover and will make good places to dig burrows under the roots, even if they are small.

I hunt, and since there seems to be no predators except for myself, the hunting is good. These squirrels and mice are not wary enough with the lack of predators in this valley, and catching them is almost too easy, then it is time to dig my first burrow here, and that takes up the rest of the daytime.

By nightfall I am too tired to bother hunting and decide to just sleep instead, and by the time I finally do manage to fall asleep, moonlight is coming into my new burrow entrance.

Something rushes past the burrow entrance outside and I awaken instantly. Something else rushes past, and then another, and another, and another, and another, running hard!

It is still dark, but I can see moonlight through the entrance tunnel as I go upward to investigate this new thing, and only then do I realize that it was not real noise I heard, just a sense of something running past the entrance, and it happens again.

More run quickly by outside, more, and more, and then before reaching the entrance to my burrow, I suddenly catch the other feeling from outside.

Pushing backward as fast as I can into the sleeping chamber again, not bothering to turn around to run down into it.

I could not hear them running, only sense it, just as when Kekuit had died in the field I had not actually heard him calling to me, but had only sensed his calling. But that is not what caused me to flee backward into the sleeping chamber. As I neared the entrance there was an overwhelming feeling of terror from those outside fleeing for their lives, a sense of something horrible and deadly coming quickly for the ones fleeing.

The feeling is suddenly gone, and I remind myself that I am not some pitiful prey creature that fears what I cannot see, so I walk back up to the entrance again.

There is nothing outside, and no tracks of running feet in the moonlit ground outside the burrow, no disturbed leaves, or dirt thrown up by panicked paws.

It is light enough with the moon above to show me that I am alone, and there are no other creatures around my burrow, and no tracks of anything that has run past it? I puzzle this before giving up and returning to the sleeping chamber for some sleep.

Light finds me roaming for food and mate. Food is easy again, but the mate is still not here, and I sigh and move further upward into the valley looking for mate, unable to shake the feeling of "wrong" around me.

But there are no predators, or any other larger animals in this valley, either as I travel steadily northward through the day, until I find the curious thing raised above the surrounding not rock.

I discover something flat and wide of something not rock, just as the long flat place I found last night was not rock. But that flat place I had stood on was black, not rock, and this is a gray not rock I stand on now, and is also far too smooth to be natural.

The thing I have found is on the rock, old and burned, with four stepping places going up to it. Two tall things made of stones on top of it stick up the air, obviously broken from the much taller things they once were, since pieces lay around them.

Probably some human thing of no importance, and I do not really have the urge to investigate it, being far more interested in finding a mate than in this new thing as I turn to leave and find the next curious thing near the raised place.

There are bones inside it in rows along the sides and the remains of a dead, burned tree laying from one side to the other through the center of it. But I do not know what this is, and bones are hardly new things to a predator, so I leave this also and roam until darkness.

Digging a quick burrow takes no time at all. I sleep, until the first one rushes past in the night, then the next, the next, the next, the next, as large and small they run in silent terror past the entrance of my burrow in the moonlight above! They flee past where I shiver below in my burrow, as I shake below them with my teeth bared!

Without making noise they run past the burrow, and I sense them running in terror above me, and this night there is a far worse thing I can sense that I do not hear with my ears.

Pain, horrible pain in my head, as the slower ones scream in agony and die above me in my head with no noise in my ears, as the moonlight coming down the entrance suddenly disappears! Then suddenly I no longer sense them above as I shiver below, and the moonlight reappears.

I go slowly up to the entrance. The moon is wider tonight, and soon it will be full, but there is nothing there, nothing dead, nothing above that could have made the moon disappear, no tracks of paws or hooves on disturbed ground, nothing.

I give up. This is all new, but it does not seem to hurt me, and I have not actually seen anything. I go back to sleep.

Morning finds me feasting well again. Hunting here is almost too easy; the smaller prey creatures have been spoiled by the lack of one such as me among them, as I eat and then go to the stream to drink before wandering north again.

The valley is still the same, clumps of brush and grass and no older trees, only younger trees. The ones that have burned in the fire can hardly be called trees anymore because they stick up in trunks with nothing above them, or lay on the ground where I walk among them.

I am bored by all of this and want a mate. Winter will be here soon enough, and I want new young next spring.

There will be no more north; I will go south again tomorrow for my old burrow, and take my chances on Thamuatz showing up late to see me after all. He did give good young to me, and it would be nice to see him again.

Night finds me sitting outside my hastily dug burrow; to-night, I am going to see this thing happen. Nothing does. All night long, nothing new happens, except the moon is a little fuller. No panicked, running creatures inside my head, no fear, no silent death, nothing. I give up in disgust and sleep. I really must have young again this next season!

The day finds me heading back south; there is no one for me here, and I want out of this valley. This time I roam for the hillside and then head south until I find a small stream and stop to drink and feast well on the mice also here for water, then I follow this stream which should lead back to the main stream.

Moving through the brush, I wish I would not have bothered leaving my hillock burrow to come here. With my luck a strong handsome mate might have happened by while I was gone, and moved on, and I missed him!

I roam onward, disgusted with myself and with my bad choice of coming here. Following the smaller stream, I pass through some brush that conceals my view of what lies ahead of me. Suddenly I freeze in place.

Bones, more bones than I can count lay inside and around the edges of a wide, shallow pond of bones; in the pond covered with green, some still showing the old, burn marks of the fire that killed them.

They had run here in panic to try to survive in the water, and it was not good enough, they died here. I shudder and pass the pond to go to the main stream and then reconsider.

They are just bones. It is almost nightfall. The pond is perfectly good to drink from even though it is full of old bones, I do not consider that a threat. Bones are what I make of prey, they can't threaten me.

I dig my burrow near the pond, among the bones around it, and awaken in the night when the silent screaming begins.

They flee, screaming past my burrow in all their different voices, running for their lives, and I feel the screaming inside my head as they run. They run, splashing through the pond as I hear it in my head, and then I hear them all turning and running back into the pond again as something appears in front of them, stopping them from fleeing further, and forcing them backward into the first threat they are trying to flee!

Trapped between deaths in front and behind, they try to shelter in the last hope of safety they have, the water. It is too shallow and too small as they scream in their uncountable numbers and die in agony as the moonlight coming down the entrance suddenly disappears again!

The moonlight reappears, and this time I have had enough. Screaming my rage at this thing, I run upward and out of the burrow to kill!

Nothing is there, and the moon is perfectly normal above me, with nothing to make it disappear. Even the pond surface does not ripple with movement among its bones, and no ground is disturbed among the old bones lying there.

I begin to walk through the bones in the moonlight. It is time to leave this valley, and now I know why no other larger creatures come here. Who wants to? This is a valley of death, and I walk in its moonlit shadows.

The next day finds me moving south, but I have had no sleep, and prey is strangely scarce now as if they finally realized that a predator was among them. They are all hiding. No food for me today.

I sigh in disgust, knowing some fine male badger must have been by my hillock home by now and then left without seeing me. I continue walking south until night finds the moon growing full over the hillside. I decide whether to dig a burrow or keep walking. I keep walking.

The night passes, the moon moves higher in the sky above me, and I am cursing myself for not digging a comfortable burrow when he soars past me in full moonlight, running for his life!

The deer soars silently past in a leap, his foam-flecked mouth wide in a noiseless scream, eyes wide in terror, he runs through a small tree as if it were not there. He simply passes through it!

Another deer runs past, eyes also wide in terror, and I just have time to notice their hooves did not stir the ground or make noise, as his foam-flecked mouth wide in his own noiseless scream, he also soars in a leap through a small tree. Then I sense something huge coming up behind me without noise, and turn to see, and run myself!

Stretched from side to side across the valley behind me in the moonlight and coming toward me in their hundreds large and small, all of the creatures that should be in this valley run toward me, screaming the noiseless screams I can clearly hear in my head, running on hooves and paws that make no noise, as birds fly above them on noiseless wings.

The valley is running, and they all run screaming their fear of what follows them, as large and small, they come running toward me in panic, predator and prey running and flying together to escape the coming death. I run in panic myself now, trying to stay ahead of them!

I do not succeed because many are faster, running past me without seeing me, panicked with fear of the death coming quickly up behind them and outrunning me! Eyes wide with terror, they try to run faster than they can run!

They run alongside and do not see me, or can't see me, as I whimper in fear and run with them, and I now notice as they run silently screaming into my head alongside me, I can see through them!

They run through small trees without touching them as they simply pass through the younger trees! The only trees they dodge around are old, burned ones that still stand, those they avoid in their flight, and I feel death coming up behind us!

I turn to look back while I run, but there is nothing there, only young forest and open areas in the moonlight among the old, burned trees still standing or fallen throughout this valley. But there is something. The slower and weaker ones far behind me are suddenly shrieking in the voices I hear inside my head, writhing in pain and disappearing from my view, and I try to run much faster! For I have seen it, and have not seen it!

There is nothing back there, but the many small lights that are always in the night sky when it is clear are blotting out behind me in rolling patterns above the blackness!

The valley, which should be clearly visible in the moonlight back there, is turning to rolling blackness that covers the smaller, slower, weaker creatures as they scream and disappear!

It is coming. I can't see it, but it is coming! I do not know what it is, but as I look back, more are disappearing into the rolling blackness moving faster than they can run. I hear their screams of agony in my head, not my ears!

I run through a clearing and they lay around me too tired or injured to run anymore. I run onward; looking back as the ones in the clearing scream into my head, writhe in agony, and disappear into the blackness rolling toward me at impossible speed now!

There is nothing there, but it is coming! I run for the stream where it leaves the valley underneath the long, flat place and hope I can make it when a large, unnaturally dark male rabbit runs past me in the moonlight and does something none of the others did. He stops in front of me and turns to look at me with eyes that are terrible to see!

His eyes are burning fire, looking into me, looking through me! And I know that unlike the others, this one can see me just as well as I can see him as I try to run frantically past, while avoiding those eyes of fire!

Suddenly all my muscles stop and I am locked in front of this thing that looks like a rabbit with black fur, but now I can also see that his fur is not the good, sleek black of normal black fur, this is a terrible different black I do not want to look too closely at!

Grief, pain, terror, and terrible unnatural predator patience radiate from this creature that only looks like a rabbit as I hear the voice inside my head!

"See?" he asks. "Leave this place! Predators are not welcome here; there is only one predator who roams here, and justice is coming for him! He killed this valley, and he still kills without mercy in his anger, pride, and foolish belief that he can never be known or touched for what he has done in life! The One who hears the fall of every sparrow knows him well and sends an innocent one and me to touch him together, where I wait patiently for him to come to the wall when the innocent one he will try to kill comes to it with him. You will meet her when death comes for the ones you do not expect to be in your life again, you will care for her in the coldness around you, and you will protect her from others. She will leave you, and then after your own pain, you will bring justice to one and peace to another and see me again in better days."

Then the thing that looks like a rabbit turns and runs in the direction where the hole in the tall stone wall is. Still unable to move, shaking with fear, I watch it go.

Suddenly I can move again. I know what the wall is now and know that it was him I had sensed on the other side of that hole in the stone wall that night, as he runs for where he must be, and I run for where I want to be, out of this valley!

I feel it now, and know it for what it is, as a terrible wave of solid heat washes over me, and my mind hears the roaring cracks of exploding trees behind me!

I look backward, and there is no fire there, just that solid, rolling wave of blackness eating the valley behind me, making the lights in the sky disappear, coming at an impossible speed now toward me, then I run from it!

The wind drives it, but something is happening to the wind. No wind blows the grass I run through, but I still feel a fierce wind that is not there suddenly change from behind and onto my face as I run.

The grass around me does not move in any wind that I can see or feel, but then this terrible wind that isn't there is pulling at me, trying to feeding me back into the fire I can't see behind me!

Near the hole in the stone wall, a small, young female rabbit runs frantically to the stone wall. There is something different about her from all of others I have seen running for their lives, something more solid than the rest of these poor, dead creatures as she jumps desperately against the wall again and again while the roaring, invisible fire soars up behind us!

A lost fawn I can see through soars in panicked leaps past me in the fierce heat from flames that are not there, its mother probably long dead somewhere behind us; and I think this poor long dead creature is the last of this valley's creatures to make it as the fawn easily passes through the solid of younger new trees, only dodging the old burned trees that still stand.

I see it hit the stone wall and fall down, stunned, near where the young female rabbit hurls herself against the solid stone of the wall over and over, trying desperately to hurl her body through it as the thing that is not really a rabbit waits, watching me with those terrible fire eyes beside the hole in the wall.

"See," he says in my head as I run for the stream exit from this valley, and the fawn I know is long since dead gets back up, fleeing again in a noiseless scream, running down the side of the wall it is too panicked to have thought of simply jumping. I hope that we both make it. I know that the fawn did not, and I pity it; for the first time in my life I pity prey and run for my own life!

The young female rabbit trying to hurl herself through the stone of the wall sees the hole in it at last, as she also finally sees the thing that looks like a rabbit but somehow sees him differently than I do. She has no fear of him, only fear of the fire roaring behind her!

Then I realize, "She sees him as he was, not as he is, and she sees him as just another creature trying desperately to flee!"

She scrambles through the hole in the stone wall to safety ahead of him.

Then a realization comes to me. "I did not hear her scream in my mind or see through her; she lived, she survived. This is only a memory or dream to her, and I can still survive!"

I run frantically for the hole the stream passes through as death comes silently, roaring in a wall of invisible, exploding trees from behind me, killing the slow and weak in total silence as they die screaming inside my mind, inside the rolling blackness!

I hear the silent screams, hear all the deafening, roaring, cracking silence of the dying forest, and feel all of the horrible pain and noise of these creatures and this forest dying inside my head not in my ears.

The thing that only looks like a rabbit gives me one last look before I run for the hole the stream goes through, and then he turns to the hole in the stone wall as he had turned to it long ago, and the fire I can't see is here!

I feel terrible wind, heat, and the rolling blackness of death cover me as the valley disappears around me, and I hear a truly horribly loud rabbit's scream of grief, pain, and terror both in my mind and in my ears this time!

"See!" he screams in agony, and I know that he died and waits patiently; for now I have seen, and I almost feel sorry for the one he waits for so patiently for.

I have seen this human as he is, not as other humans may see him. Have seen what he does to others, know who killed this valley, and have seen this one that died in that terrible fire. This one that only looks like a rabbit, who now waits patiently for this angry human to come to this wall again one time too many to kill. The human will die here.

Screaming myself, I burn in the fierce heat of flames that are not there, as rolling blackness covers me in a silent roar of exploding, burning, dying trees. I run through the hole in the wall. And suddenly it all stops.

I stop myself and look back into the valley behind me. I am not burned, and there is no noise behind me inside or outside my head. Nothing is there.

The area I ran from is empty in the moonlight, and no dead, no panicked running creatures, nothing. The night sky above is normal again, with all the little lights in it again, and the entire valley behind me sits silently normal in the moonlight with no more thoughts of "*See?*" from the creature that waits patiently for the human.

I have seen all it wanted me to see in this valley and feel sorrow for this creature that had to come back and live everything over again simply because I entered the valley where it waits.

I know that of the creatures I had seen running for their lives, the young female rabbit that made it through the hole in the stone wall did survive the dying forest, and I hope that she found a burrow again somewhere safe from fire and death.

I am a predator. We simply kill what we need for food and do not think in terms of good or evil, although I now understand it.

For the first time in my life, having seen this angry human as he is, I fully understand the idea of evil, and will never forget the words to me from the creature that only looked like a rabbit.

But I am going home myself and do not want to. "Meet her, care for her, protect her," or anything else to do with "Her," whoever she is, and I am absolutely not coming back up here to see that thing again in "Better days"!

Predators

After leaving the valley, I have a thing about darkness for a while, much preferring to travel in daylight, or to sit in a very well protected burrow at night with my teeth facing the entrance. After a few days, I also find the dogs dumped by that angry human, or at least what is left of one at first. Then I find the others, and realize what that angry human has loosed on this forest.

I scent the blood, becoming wary and excited at the same time. Blood scent means some prey creature is waiting to be my meal, if whatever had killed it has no objections. I am wary of larger predators that might already be there while I follow my nose to the scent, until I find the dead dog.

It is easy to tell what killed him, the scents of other dogs are around him; this one was too weak or too slow for the pack to tolerate, and they killed him. He is torn apart, and I can tell that from the freshness of the kill that the other dogs did it not too long ago.

After I make sure there are no other dogs around to come after me, I eat what's left of this one. Remembering what my mother had said about human's dogs gone wild. "They fear nothing, not even humans and will try to kill everything they meet that they consider to be weaker, including humans."

Finished, I begin to follow the tracks; these dogs may very well be dangerous, but after the things that happened inside that valley, these might as well be pathetic prey creatures for all

I know, and I want to see what they do. They are already fed, even if it was one of their own kind, and I shudder in disgust at the thought of actually eating one's own kind; fighting one's own kind, yes, but not eating them.

They are not true predators; in fact, they are not even good predators. They do not check their own back to see if anyone is following them, and do not even try to place themselves downwind as they move. Their scent, easily available to any that might hunt them, masks the scent of any that might hunt them, and also, they seem to hunt more by chance than by instinct like I do, and they do not even hunt well.

These dogs are making enough noise as they travel to frighten off all the prey around them. I can hear them moving long before I near them; unlike them, I know to stay downwind and move through forest shadows quietly while closing to where it is possible to safely see these famous "Killers" my mother was so careful to warn me about. They are roaming and killing as I follow them, and I watch their actions with growing disgust.

Unlike true forest-bred predators, these wild dogs chase everything and waste most of what they catch. They make far too much noise as they move, howling for no reason, which is a certain way to make the prey in this area hide or move away, or attract larger predators to themselves.

They do not even bother to eat a great deal of what they kill as they move from one creature to another, chasing just for sport, killing if they can, and making a waste of totally good food when they do succeed in killing anything! Mostly they just make too much noise chasing the prey they find, while all the other prey hides from them or runs.

If this group of fools survives, it will be more by luck than good hunting on their part. They might very well even be able to actually kill a human, but from what I have seen of humans so far, that does not impress me very much. These human dogs gone wild will probably all starve this next winter or eat each other, and then the survivor will starve. Or they may just barely manage to survive the winter, after killing all the creatures in this section of the forest and ruining it for decent predators, and then perhaps they will all starve anyway.

Still, I must remind myself that what I am seeing may not be what they will become. These might actually survive, and if they do survive, they might very well become savage hunters without fear of even humans.

They could even become something so vicious that they would be able to kill anything, even creatures as large as bears, although I doubt seriously that they would be able to kill that huge, brown monster that has come to this forest, maybe they could kill the smaller black bears but not him.

For now, except for the one I already mark as the leader, they are pathetic hunters and little better than prey, and all they have going for them is viciousness as I watch their leader control them while teaching them to hunt.

He has obviously been at this for some time out here in the forest. He is the largest and most vicious, and I have a feeling that he is the one who had killed the dog I found. Perhaps he had wanted to impress the others who joined his little pack after the angry human chased them from his own territory, or just because the other dog was not quick enough to decide to accept him as the leader and join his pack.

As the largest and the most vicious, his method of controlling and teaching is not the same as my method of controlling and teaching my young. This one uses his teeth, not his knowledge, to teach the others and does not really have that much knowledge of survival anyway. He bluffs the others into thinking that he does.

As a leader, he does not really teach the dogs that follow him; he simply makes the rest of the pack cower to obey him by force, as they try to understand how to survive in the wild.

They are all hopeless right now, even him because real predators would have sensed me this close to them by now, even if they could not smell or see me. These human dogs gone wild do not have the slightest idea that a better predator is right next to them, following them through the brush and trees.

I could isolate them one at a time and kill them all, especially after it becomes dark tonight, but these are not worth bothering with. Let them starve, after they chase away all of the prey in this area.

I leave, remembering that if I do come back into this area to use caution. Should these dogs manage to survive, they will become very dangerous to meet.

No matter what I think of this pack, my mother's warnings were both stern and clear on this matter, she must have known something about human dogs to have taught me so carefully about their danger, and the importance of avoiding them.

For now, I continue moving south again, heading home, and hoping that there will be someone for me when I get there.

The journey home is not a direct path. While traveling south I move back and forth to see if there is the scent of a male badger. There is not, and I roam more to the sides and less on the direct path home, soon it will be too late for young, and I now want them so badly.

Voices make me instantly aware that humans are here. I know human voices very well by now, and I hide, waiting as they come. They do not make as much noise as the dogs, but it is almost as easy to track these humans without actually seeing them while I wait concealed in my brush for them to pass.

I count two as they make their human-mouth noises to each other, walking through the brush. These two seem quieter than other humans I have seen before. I follow, without them being aware a predator is to their side and slightly behind them, satisfying my curiosity.

The thickness of brush among the trees of this forest makes tracking them easy, this is more a lesson for young badgers to learn these skills than a tracking thing for me. While the humans must fight their way through the surrounding brush or walk around it, I slip quietly through and under.

These two are predators. I can sense that with my instincts, but they are different predators. I follow them cautiously and curiously to see what they do.

There have only been four sets of humans in my life so far, the ones at the fire who tried to save the forest three sets of seasons ago, the one who killed my Alarana and Asiaq, and the angry one who radiated death and taught me the meaning of evil in that valley that I have no intention of ever revisiting, and these two new ones who seem to be different from all of the others humans I have met.

These humans are wearing the coverings that humans put over their bodies, but it's not the same as the humans who came to try to save the forest in the fire, those humans wore all-brown coverings with some things on them.

These two new humans wear strange, new body coverings with what looks like the plants of the forest on them, blending them in with the trees and brush around them almost as easily as my own fur blends into the brush around me.

I sense a purpose in these two. They seem to be predators as I am, in search of prey as I do, but not like the angry human. These two humans do not give the feeling of anger and the need to kill just for killing's sake that the angry human did, or the cold sense of purpose of the other human who had killed my Alarana and Asiaq.

I can already tell from the way they accept each other as they walk together that these two share friendship, not anger or greed, and if they are hunting, then they are simply going about the business of finding prey just as I do.

These two I can understand. We are the same under the fur, or at least we would be if humans had decent fur.

I suddenly remember how delicious the deer was back at entrance to the valley. We badgers seldom get deer to eat, unless the bear or another animal leaves some for us. It would be wonderful to have some more of deer if that is what these humans are about in this forest.

I follow them, trying not to drool with anticipation of fresh deer, and hope it is what they are looking for. Then I sense it before they do.

These humans might be predators also, but I am far better at it than they are when it comes to senses. My ears pick up the sounds of the deer eating and breathing before they are even aware it is near.

They merely continue onward, and if they do, they are never going to see this one. I can hear the sounds of it stopping its eating to listen to their noise, and hear the sounds of its hooves move, shifting itself through the brush to find a clear running direction away from the sounds of the humans coming up near it.

I wait for them to lose it, but they are better predators than I thought. While they may not see it yet, both humans somehow still seem to have some awareness of what is close, as if they have done this before.

Both suddenly stop, making their quiet, human-mouth noises to each other, and both beginning to move more quietly.

Both also have the same type of long, human killing stick the angry human of the valley had, and I watch as they both shift the long, killing sticks they carry from shoulders to human paws, holding the smaller ends upward with paws near the front middle and using their other paws to hold the larger ends back near themselves.

I give both humans credit for alertness as they stop moving and begin watching. At least both of these know enough to let the prey move first while they remain still, and I just have time to think, "These might be competent predators after all!" before the deer makes its decision, the wrong one.

But then that's why deer are only prey creatures instead of competent predators. We predators know "you only get one mistake in nature if you are a prey creature," and he makes his now.

He runs into the open in front of them to escape, as both humans quickly lift the wider ends of the killing sticks to their shoulders, looking through the shorter round thing on top of each killing stick at the fleeing deer, and almost as if they both shared the same thoughts, both killing sticks roar as one solid loud *"Crack!"* with red flashes coming together from the fronts of them. My ears ring from the roar as the deer's head lifts, and he suddenly lurches in mid run from the impact of things that hit him in two places close together, and he drops.

A clean kill; both humans made a clean kill far faster than any other predator could! As my ears try to stop ringing from the noise, the power of those killing sticks awes and frightens me, as it did when the angry human used his to kill for no reason.

I sometimes make an almost clean kill when I kill for food, but very seldom; most prey does not want to die, and fights death, or runs from it. But how do you run from this?

The human killing sticks are something I could not even dream about when out hunting. To be able to have all the meat you could ever eat is a true predator's dream. With one of these killing sticks I wouldn't have to follow bears around, hoping that they would leave something for me when they killed deer. I could have deer every night, or even bear.

Still these humans might be as bad as the rest of them, so I watch from the brush to see if they also waste this meat, as the one who had killed my young did and as the angry human had.

As a true predator, both the angry human and the fur taking human have my contempt; to waste meat you need to fill your body with for the winter is unforgivable!

But now, instead of sharing the meat and leaving some for me, these humans look at each other, and the emotion I sense from here is not the greed of the one who was taking fur, or the anger of the one in the valley. These two seem to share embarrassment, as if they were supposed to choose who took this deer, not kill the same deer at the same time.

I lower my value of humans again. These may be as bad as the other humans were if they can't be practical about this tasty, dead prey making me drool. Deer are deer, stop considering who took it, eat it, and leave some for me!

Amazingly, instead of going for the meat, they are actually making mouth noises to each other that I sense are apologies, then they shake each other's upper paws.

Humans are the stupidest creatures I have ever met. All that food just lying there and these two want to make mouth noises to each other instead.

I wish that they would both leave and let me feast, but they are walking to the deer, and I watch as they fasten something around it and begin to drag the entire deer away.

No! I want some of it!

I begin to follow the two humans as they drag the deer away. Perhaps some will fall off and I can still have a little because a deer is such a rare treat.

We walk through the forest almost together, they in front, dragging the deer, and I to one side slightly behind, tracking them noiselessly.

The humans don't seem aware I am here, but then most humans don't seem to be aware when I track them.

These creatures may be able to kill from a distance, but they have no idea of safety when someone else is tracking them. I lower my opinion of their predatory standards a little more because just their ability to kill from a distance is not impressive enough.

I follow both them and the deer, far more interested in it than them, until something strange happens. As we move I get the impression somehow these two do know I am here.

I consider breaking off following because I am nervous to stay this close to humans deliberately when they have those killing sticks. But they have the deer. I have not had deer since

I entered that valley and am certainly not going back up there for more.

We move until we reach a place I have never seen before, obviously some kind of human place in the middle of this clearing in the forest.

But not a fixed one; the clearing has not been changed by the humans, only occupied by them. There is a large brown thing in the middle of the clearing and one of the human-carrying traveling things like the one the angry human rode inside, with the same lower flat place on it behind the raised enclosed section in front of that.

This human-carrying traveling thing sits beside the brown thing with a new human waiting near it, and I can scent the remains of fire here in a small area near the large brown thing.

I have no idea what that large brown thing is, but there are two long sides to it and two narrow sides. It doesn't look like any animal I have ever seen before, but it may be alive because its sides move in the breeze, and there are small, thin things like trees without limbs holding it up.

I puzzle it until one of the humans simply lifts part of the large brown thing and goes inside, and I stare in awe at this new human thing.

To deliberately let a large brown thing eat you is amazing!

Then, even more amazing; he actually comes back out again, as I understand that it did not actually eat him, it is his above-ground burrow. Strange why those humans would have above-ground burrows, but then they are strange creatures anyway.

I ignore it because I am well hidden and far more interested in the deer. If they leave, it will be mine, and I drool with anticipation of them leaving to go back into the forest to hunt again. I wish they would forget this deer for just a little while, like some foolish black bear forgetting the prey it has just killed to go find other prey.

If they do, I can have some before they return, but the humans turn to the deer after all and take out small, flat shiny things like the other human had used to collect the skins of animals, and begin to take the deer apart.

Putting some kind of covering things around each part of the deer, before loading those covered parts onto the flat back section of the human-carrying traveling thing.

They take most of it as I watch disappointed from my cover at the edge of the forest, as the third human leaves in the human-carrying traveling thing, leaving only a very small part of the deer behind with the two humans who took the deer.

None for me, unless they leave some scraps after eating what is left. But then they wrap what is left, place it in a human holding thing, and fasten that to one of the tree limbs, using something to lift it out of reach of myself or any other forest dweller. I don't think even that huge monster of a brown bear could reach that high.

The two humans go inside the brown thing as I look hopelessly upward at what is now out of my reach.

Hopefully it will be taken down again, and they will forget it. Disturbingly, one said something to the other just before they both looked to where I hide, and both smiled before going inside, but I know I hide well so they can't see me.

Finally, the two humans come out from the inside of the above-ground burrow thing, bringing another human thing out with them.

Nothing for me to eat, and I sigh, preparing to go find my own prey; I watch curiously as the humans do something new.

They gather small branches, placing them together in an area in front of their large brown above-ground burrow, until there is a small pile of branches in one place. Then they make fire!

One of them takes something from the coverings that humans wear on their bodies, and makes fire appear from it as he places it inside the pile of smaller branches.

I watch nervously as the fire grows. I am not too happy with fire, after the fire I went through when I was younger, as well as the fire that was in the valley of the shadows of death.

This fire grows, but the humans seem to be able to keep it contained in the small area that they have it inside. It does not roar out to eat them, and I begin to relax, watching curiously from my place of concealment as they do something strange, but then all things humans do are strange.

They take some white powder from a human holding thing and mix it with water, and form it into small flat round things, then wrap those small flat round things inside something shiny and place them next to the fire.

My interest increases as they take some of the deer down from the holding thing they have it inside, put the holding thing back up out of my reach, put the dear meat on something flat, and place that over the fire. Why? If you are going to eat it, just eat it as it is!

The smell makes me drool, and I want some as they do whatever it is that they are doing while I grow hungrier and hungrier.

Never having had any reason to actually place my prey over a fire after killing it, I find what these humans are doing fascinating, and it smells so good now I wish they would both go back inside for just the little time it would take me to snatch it.

Far too late, I realize that I have been edging forward in my hunger at these delicious smells and am now completely exposed to them.

I scurry backward into my brushy shelter and wait nervously. They do not seem unfriendly; but the human who was taking the fur of others did not seem unfriendly, either, when I first saw him.

I am prepared to run if needed, but the smells are just so irresistible from the deer meat and from the flat white things these humans wrapped in the shiny stuff beside the fire. They really don't seem to be a danger to me, and there is a more practical matter to consider: food.

I come cautiously from shelter again to watch, while both of these human predators watch me, smiling, and it smells so good, I want some so badly.

They make human-mouth words to me that I can't understand, but all of the mouth words seem to tell me it is all right to be here, not to run away. I am still cautious, but it just smells so good.

Finally deciding that these may be predators, for some reason they do not seem to be a threat to me. They are different from the angry human who also had one of those long killing sticks. These two intend to eat the deer meat left here; that I can understand, it's the other humans I couldn't understand.

I wait, hopeful, at the edge of the forest while the two humans continue to turn the deer parts placed over the fire on top of that flat thing holding it, still trying to think of why humans would even bother to do this, as I edge closer cautiously.

They have more than enough for them, and real predators do share; of course, the strong get first choice, but it is not unusual to see several different types of ground and flying predators around one kill.

These human predators with the long killing sticks seem friendly enough, and I am practically dying for some of that food scent by the time they do something else new.

First, the two human predators pull what they have over the fire away and take the shiny wrapped things from the side of the fire, but do not eat or offer me any. Yet they seem to want me to have some, because they are making encouraging mouth noises at me and smiling.

They are not eating, either, and I try to understand the strange behavior of these humans who have food but do not eat it as they put the deer parts they had over the fire onto flat, round things, with some left over they now throw to me.

Not being aware that they intend me to have it, only aware that they are throwing something this direction, I jump instinctively when they do. But then understanding the thrown part is for me, I shamble over eagerly to try this new thing that smells so good.

Only when reaching the piece of deer meat the humans have thrown in my direction do I also understand why they did not just give it to me as soon as it came off the fire or start eating some of it themselves.

It was too hot to eat then, now it's cooled, and the meat is still warm, and I drool all over it, eating greedily as they watch me while eating their own food.

It is delicious, as I finish it far too fast and wait hopefully for more while watching these two humans eat, but they finish without giving me more. I will not beg a human for anything, so I wait to see what these creatures do next.

They begin to uncover the small flat things beside the fire with the shiny covers around them, and the smell is irresistible from here. Now they are no longer flat white things, and they are larger, rounded, and browned.

My interest has not escaped the human's attention as they hold one out to me. The scent is just too good to resist.

I shamble closer, trying not to look like some begging pathetic prey creature as I near these two humans and that delicious, scented round thing.

Seeming to understand my caution, he tosses it to me when I am close, but not too close. I sniff, taste the round brown thing cautiously at first, then fall upon it and devour it. It isn't meat, it is something new, and these new things are delicious!

I eat greedily, and then eat the next one the humans throw to me, this time not even bothering to keep my eyes on the humans while eating it.

Obviously these two are not the same as the humans I have met before as predators in the forest, these two and I understand each other and know the limits. They do almost pass those limits when one of them reaches out to try to touch me.

"I am not some prey creature to be touched by another without my permission!"

I show him my teeth, as he yanks his human paw back from me.

He makes mouth noises at me which I feel are an apology for his mistake, and I am satisfied with his apology. Ignoring him and his friend to sit in the open area with them in front of the fire, I relax after this good meal.

As I relax, I make sure to keep my eyes on them, of course. Predators never really relax; that is a mistake prey creatures make, not us.

Still it is comfortable in front of the fire that warms and soothes me, the food was good, the humans are friendly enough, and they have yet more curious human customs to show me.

Night is here when one of them goes back into the large, brown, above-ground burrow thing to return with some human holding thing like the one they put the rest of the deer meat inside.

The top of it opens as he pulls some tall, rounded things from it, gives one to his friend and keeps one for him, and then both pull at the top end, and there is a popping noise from each of the rounded things they are holding. They put the rounded, long things to their human's mouths and drink from them. I move closer to watch, fascinated by this new human custom as they drink.

Do they not know that the stream is close to here, they could simply go to the stream and drink? But drinking from these rounded things seems to make them happy, and I put it off as another curious human custom when they finish, and each takes another rounded, tall thing to drink from it.

This seems to make them very happy, and the more they drink the happier they become. Until they are making mouth noises that seem to make less sense even to them as they each finish another of the rounded things.

Until finally they are both now saying things to me in a very happy way, and I understand that they both seem to like me very much for some reason.

When the one that tried to touch me before reaches out to touch me again, I let him, he is not being aggressive, just very happy for some reason as he and his friend both belch and take another rounded thing to drink.

He is a little clumsy as he strokes me, but it feels strangely good to let this human run his hands over my fur, and I can always simply walk away if I want to, since both he and his friend also seem to have a problem with coordination.

After a while they both stop stroking me and go very clumsily inside the large brown thing to make loud sleeping noises, actually, they make the loudest sleeping noises I have ever heard any creature make as I go to see what was so good about these tall, rounded things.

One of the tall rounded things they opened had spilled out onto a hollow in the top of a rock before they left to go sleep, and I wander over to see what it is that seems to give these humans so much enjoyment. Pleased to see that almost all of the liquid in the tall, rounded thing is waiting for me in the hollow of the rock it had spilled into.

The liquid looks brown and smells of something I do not know. I sniff it cautiously, and then try some.

It tastes strange, but the taste is kind of nice so I enjoy some more of it, and the taste seems to get better as I drink more and becomes even better as I enjoy more. I lap at it eagerly as the night forest around me grows strange, and the sound of the humans sleeping becomes funny.

I drink as my thoughts seem to grow of greater importance, no matter how silly they are. I drink until all the brown liquid is gone, and then I seem to be a little clumsy while turning to leave as I fall down.

Struggling to get my feet back under me again, I am able to get back up, but now it seems to be hard to think or walk straight.

I manage somehow. It is time to go home, and I stagger through the night forest looking for a bear to punish.

The next morning, I feel strange in a bad way. My head aches, my vision is somehow wrong, and I have trouble walking through the soreness of my body as I debate the wisdom of last night's foolish thought of walking through the forest to find a bear to punish.

Much more likely, if I would have found one in my condition, it would have punished me before eating me. I also need to drink from the stream a lot this morning, but I am on the way home and am not going to let this stop me.

I have learned a lesson from this. The humans were nice, but my head is teaching me that although the liquid brown stuff may have been tasty, it also does things to your head after you drink it, and now I really want my burrow on the little hillock in the center of the meadow, and hopefully a mate before the season becomes too late for new young.

It takes almost another day to arrive and check the territory for any new markings from potential mates or rivals that might have tried to establish territory here while I was gone.

Finishing, I find some delicious prey, and then sleep until the morning finds me resting on top of the fallen fire-burned tree lying on top of my hillock as I enjoy the early morning sunlight, and look for anyone who may be roaming in my territory.

No one I want is here, and I roam to mark my territory, letting any mate know that a female badger is here before making sure all my burrows are cleaned and new again, with fresh new grass inside and loose dirt outside.

Finally I eat some fresh frogs from the stream near darkness and return to my burrow for the night. I want to be up early tomorrow, and not just for the warmth of early morning sunlight. It is time to roam and find a mate quickly before winter is here.

Resting in early morning sunlight before leaving to find a new mate, enjoying sun warmth on top of the fallen tree on top of my hillock, I see him coming from the forest into the meadow . . . Thamuatz!

He is still far away, and I can't be fully sure that it is he, but even if our eyes are not our best sense, my view from up here is good and I would know him anywhere.

Thamuatz has returned and I will have more young this next spring! I fluff my fur with pride, glad to have groomed this morning after I awoke.

He walks strangely slowly through the short grass as he comes this way in little hops, not true walking. Then I realize what he is doing in fun. "Thamuatz knows I will be here waiting and watching him arrive, he is teasing me!"

Thamuatz continues to tease me with his strange little hopping walk while coming this way, and I still can't see all of him as he walks; the grass is too tall for that, but it is Thamuatz, and I go to greet him.

As I get closer I realize that he looks strangely thinner than I remember from the last time I saw him. I remind myself that was a full set of seasons ago and walk toward him eagerly. He could have changed, or I may not remember him as well as I thought.

Only as I grow closer to him do I notice that Thamuatz does not just look strangely thinner, he is strangely thinner, and he looks desperate, and he walks wrong. Thamuatz is not teasing me, he walks wrong!

I see him finally. I see Thamuatz clearly for the first time, and I see all of him or what should be all of him. He walks on three legs, not four!

The fourth leg is missing; one of his front legs is gone, leaving only a short stump and three good legs. Thamuatz can't run down prey or dig with only three legs, and only one of them a front leg. He can't dig a burrow for survival from predators for the coming winter.

Thamuatz hops toward me on three legs, and he is starving. He hops desperately toward me through the short grass, starved, crippled, and dying like my Kekuit, trying to reach the last one he knew who could hunt for him and help him survive.

I Corinthians 13

Watching this crippled, desperate creature coming toward me I shiver, remembering another desperate creature who tried to come to me in another season, crawling desperately across a cold, snow-covered winter field to the only one who he truly knew could hunt, my little Kekuit, who did not learn how to hunt well enough and called to me when he was dying.

I shiver and tremble, looking at this crippled one now also starved and dying. I do not know why he chooses to come back to me, but I only hesitate a moment, it is Thamuatz, the one who gave me the five, and he will not die alone, crippled, starving, and unloved!

His injuries are more than just the missing leg. Thamuatz's sides are torn with old wounds that have scarred.

He has fought, and I will find out how and with what creature or creatures later because right now he needs food, and I turn and run for the meadow, leaving Thamuatz confused behind me as he desperately tries to follow me.

He will finish the job of killing himself if he tries to follow me!

I dig quickly at the first ground squirrel burrow I can find, grateful these ground squirrels never seem to learn to run instead of just staying in their burrows when I am digging for them.

Their bad training is my good luck, as I kill this one and run with it in my mouth back to where Thamuatz is trying to hop to me.

He can't believe I am doing this for him as he eats it desperately quickly. In nature the crippled are often simply left to die; it is not cruel, it is just the way of nature.

Thamuatz will not suffer this way of nature!

I am too busy running for another to watch him, as I dig quickly again and find what I am looking for, as it shivers with fright inside its burrow. I enter from above, kill it, and run back to where Thamuatz is trying to hop toward me again.

He eats again as I run for another, he is starved, but now he understands, waiting for me to return to him instead of trying to follow me.

He eats until full, probably for the first time in a long while from the look of him. Then I try to move him to the burrow, but he is thirsty now, and we go to the stream instead.

Only when Thamuatz has drank enough water is it possible to get him moving in the direction of my burrow on the hillock in the center of this meadow; and then I discover that he is so weak from what has happened to him, he has to be helped to climb the hillock to reach the burrow entrance.

When I finally get him inside into the sleeping chamber, Thamuatz is confused and not sure of where we are; then, as if he had not slept in a long time, he falls over to sleep while I watch.

It would be nice to go hunt for myself. I will need plenty of food stored up inside this body before the winter comes.

Instead, I curl next to Thamuatz to keep him warm as he shivers and cries out in his sleep.

His legs thrash as he cries, and I groom him until he is calm and sleeping peacefully again, as I try to understand what could have happened to the one, that was once such a proud, strong predator, to make him this weak helpless prey creature instead.

It is nightfall by the time he awakens, and then it is with panic as he cries out and thrashes, trying to understand where he is.

I want to know what happened; he tells me after he finally realizes where he is, and that this is not a trap he has stumbled into. It takes me a while and some grooming to get him to tell me about it.

That was exactly what he stumbled into, a trap. He was caught by the front leg in a trap, and could not escape it.

He still shivers at the horror of being trapped like some pathetic prey creature in this sharp thing that sprang up from the ground on each side of his front leg, when he went to investigate a food thing sitting right in front of where the trap lay concealed.

His description matches the thing I saw the human doing, the human leaving these things in the forest that had killed Alarana and Asiaq. But this was after Alarana and Asiaq had died, and the human who had been setting the traps had also died shortly after them, so it could not have been him who did this to Thamuatz.

Then Thamuatz tells me the direction where he was trapped in, and how far away; and I remember now there were no badgers in that direction when I had looked there before, and the human's scent had been all over that area a full set of seasons before Alarana and Asiaq died.

I did not go that direction before roaming north into the valley of the shadows of death because I did not think that there would be any mates there. Now I shudder because it is obvious what happened to Thamuatz, the human was in that area trapping others for their fur, and had set traps in the area before he died.

The human is dead, but the traps he set are still set there, waiting for others. One caught Thamuatz, and since the human was dead, Thamuatz did not even have the chance for release or a quick death as he waited for some creature to come and kill him with his leg trapped helplessly in agony as they came. And they came.

Predators have an instinct for those who are helpless, and the ravens were there first, diving on him while he fought them off as best he could with a front leg, trapped and bleeding.

The foxes came next, two of them, fearfully at first, waiting on the fringe of the forest for Thamuatz to weaken or sleep, but he did not weaken or sleep as his leg bled in pain over the thing holding it.

Only when the foxes were sure the next day did they attack him from both sides at once, and he fought.

He fought, and they bled him, but one was too incautious, and he killed it as the other fox ran from this thing that could kill them even when trapped.

Then Thamuatz waited until he finished eating the fox, with his leg in pain since the trap had worked its way through his leg to the bone by then.

He waited, thirsty beyond belief as there was no chance of water. He waited, fighting the flies off his leg with his teeth, until finally understanding the only way he could escape and survive would be by chewing his trapped leg off with his teeth. And he did.

He could not hunt by chasing prey, he could not dig for prey, but he found water and starved in pain before he came to me. With instinct he came to the last one he had loved, the only one he remembered that was the closest to him.

He came in pain as what was left of his front leg stopped bleeding when he remembered not to try to walk on it.

He came, hopping as best he could, on three legs, as the fourth became more or less a healed stump.

He came in desperation when he saw me, certain that I would reject a crippled one, and tried not to cry like a pathetic prey creature when he saw me coming to him across the meadow, and saw the look on my face at the sight of his missing leg.

Tried not to cry with fear as he tried desperately to follow me when he saw me turn and run away from him, and tried not to cry with relief and gratitude when he saw me catch and bring him prey

As I start to leave, Thamuatz wants to follow me now, but I instruct him fiercely, "Stay!"

He accepts that fierceness, since he has gone from lover to young one now in my eyes, as I roam to find us prey. I do not want him hopping around unless it is to go to the stream for water, and if I had a way to bring it to him he would not even have to do that!

I hunt, kill, and return to him first before going for myself. Returning to him with the next prey after that, he eats gratefully, trying not to appear too grateful.

He does have pride and my having to feed him is embarrassing to him, but hunger is a strong master, and he eats the prey as I bring it.

Finally, he has to go to the stream for water, as I watch him trying to hop out the entrance tunnel and understand that he needs help even in this; walking with my body against his side, so he will not fall as I guide him down the side of the hillock to the stream.

Thamuatz drinks long in the stream, until he suddenly stops his drinking to look at me. I stop grooming myself by the streamside to look at him. And in that look to each other, we both understand.

While our kind is normally solitary, we will now be living together for as long as we live. I will care for him because that is the only way he can live, and he will care for me because I need new young.

It does not take any words, we both know, and Thamuatz comes to me from the stream where he has filled his thirst.

Even ragged and thin with only three good legs, he is still handsome and has survived where others would have lain down and died, he has pride and strength and he will be a good mate. I know this as he comes to me in that strange hopping walk that I know will be his for the rest of his life.

We do not even bother with the fur fluffing to show how beautiful and large we are, or the growling to show we have pride and are strong predators, or the circling to see each other, we simply mate.

We mate and return to our burrow, and then I decide that the trail leading up the side of our little hillock to the entrance of our burrow, will simply have to be made a little less steep the next time I am out here working on improving this burrow. But for now we just mate again, often and well.

I change the trail to make it less steep and do some work on the entrance tunnel to make it less difficult for him.

Over the next few days as we roam to feed, I catch prey, and he eats it with some shame that he can't hunt for himself. Then I remember the frogs and realize that Thamuatz can catch these by himself.

The frogs will not be here much longer because winter is coming quickly now, but for this brief time, Thamuatz can have some pride and not depend on me to do his hunting for him. We both need all we can get now to put enough winter fat layers on our bodies.

We hunt together to build our body fat for the winter as the always-green trees which make up most of the forest do not change colors, while the other trees turn their leaves to colors and drop them.

My territory shrinks in size again as the winter comes, as we both sit outside in the sunlight warming ourselves while we can, watching the things that move across the sky above darken and become thicker.

The first snow falls as we watch, and then we simply go inside, cuddle together, and sleep. It is my fifth winter and for the first time I share it with another, which is unusual for our kind; but we are happy together, and who cares what our kind does normally, as long as we are happy together.

The snow is thick when we awaken in the daytime, and I take Thamuatz outside for some fun.

He has never done this before and considers winter to be just a cold bother, but I have something new to show him as I push through the snow with him following, until I find the deeper layers and throw myself through them while he watches, puzzled.

I rung and dive through the winter white, throwing it up in arcs above my head with my nose, until Thamuatz finally realizes that this is fun, and I have not lost my mind. He joins me, rushing through mock fight and chase games that he has not played since a young one.

He grunts satisfaction at being able to use his body for fun again as we bury ourselves, while I remember not to outrun him or outplay him; without being obvious about it, of course, as he begins to realize that he can have fun again, even without four legs.

In the snow his missing leg is less of a challenge to him than he thought would be when I first led him from the burrow. The snow supports his body, and soon Thamuatz is snarling in mock challenge as he chases me as we mock fight, rolling through the drifts until both of us are covered.

Then we head to the stream. As I had hoped, it is not water anymore but is the clear, see-through stuff that the water becomes when it is cold.

Thamuatz is aware of this thing of course, but he has never tried to play with it before. Now he looks with alarm again as I simply rush the side of the stream and slide across it, plowing my body into the snow on the other side, scrambling for a grip with my paws as I rush over it again and let myself slide back to him.

He sniffs at it, not sure if he wants to risk a cold-water thing if the clear, cold, see-through part breaks through. Like me, he has had that experience before, but I learned how to tell when it was thick enough with the clear, cold cover to support me, how to see the thin areas, and how to avoid them.

He simply gives up, accepts my latest insanity, and rushes onto it himself to chase me, discovering quickly that he can't control his legs, but enjoying himself anyway as he slides all out of control into me.

He learns quickly, learns that he can slide with his chest down on the clear, cold stuff while using his rear legs to push, and soon is all over me as we play our out-of-control chase and catch, and slide, and chase again games with each other. We play and run and slide all over the top of the cold solid water thing until Thamuatz realizes that he is hurting.

I walk him back to the burrow, and he limps on his three good legs, trying not to show me his pain, but I can tell that he suffers.

His fourth leg stump is hurting in the cold, and as soon as he is back inside the burrow, I wrap around him instinctively, tucking the stump of his leg into my body to warm it again until he is happy and no longer hurting.

I did not realize cold would do this to him; from now on, until the winter is over, our play times outside will be over when I see him starting to hurt, not when he thinks he should come back inside the burrow.

He does not have his winter fat layer built up yet, so I hunt for two, but mostly for him. I can sense his shame at being unable to hunt on his own. We are proud creatures, but Thamuatz depends on me to seek prey this winter, and when I come back into the burrow now with prey, he sometimes has trouble looking at me while he eats.

Fortunately, this winter is not as hard as the one I went through before and there is more prey out roaming.

By now I am a master of ambush and chase, and finding prey is easy, but getting Thamuatz to eat becomes more difficult as the winter moves onward.

He was so proud of being strong and free, and now that he needs me to feed him, he suffers inside when I bring him prey.

He eats, but more reluctantly each time and sometimes just lets the food stay in front of him until I wander out of the burrow. It is gone when I return, and I say nothing as we both accept that the prey disappeared without him having to eat it.

He also still shakes and shivers in his sleep from the memory of the trap and having to gnaw his leg off to escape.

But when the bad dreams come I groom him as he sleeps, and warm him with my body, comforting him until the bad dreams stop.

Then only when he is sleeping peacefully again do I sleep myself, cuddled next to him so he will be warm, and his leg will not hurt from the cold. I can certainly understand bad dreams after my experience in the valley of the dead.

When awake during the daytime, we play in the snow and on the cold, hard surface of the stream, as he enjoys forgetting about his leg and lack of pride at no longer being a true predator or at being dependent on me for his survival now as we play.

We slide around on the cold, hard stream surface together, diving in and out of the snow until his leg hurts again in the cold, and then we come back to the burrow and I wrap him tightly against me to comfort him, until the pain is gone, and he is sighing in satisfaction of being here.

The winter moves onward as we sleep and play, and I go for prey for the two of us in the daytime.

We do not go out at night now, even if that is the normal hunting time for our kind. It is too cold for Thamuatz at night, and his leg hurts too quickly in the coldness of winter dark if we are outside. So we become day hunting creatures instead, and Thamuatz gets to have pride by pointing out where prey is to me as we hunt together.

He always says, "So you can catch it for us," when we hunt, and I let him have pride again by catching the prey he "finds." I do not tell him that most of the time I have already spotted the prey by the time he sees it.

We hunt, we play, we share the burrow, and we love each other. Spring will be here soon, and I already suspect our mating was successful, and the problem then will be having an adult male badger in the burrow, I must think of the safety of my young and may have to move Thamuatz to another burrow.

Adult male badgers are never in the burrows with young among our kind, but there is a problem in that also; it will break Thamuatz's heart to leave me because we have bonded totally in our winter together and he will be lonely.

I also know that the fear of starving will be with him again as soon as he moves out, even if he is one of my other burrows nearby, and even if Thamuatz knows that I will not forget to bring him prey each day at that new burrow.

His pride will suffer more to know that he is being fed by me at the same time I have to feed my own young. However, it is not springtime yet and there will be plenty of time before any young arrive to decide when the time comes, and, if possible, Thamuatz might stay here with the young and me, even if it is not what our kind commonly does.

But I will make it work all out somehow; after all, since when has my life last had anything in common with our kind?

Passing

Spring roams brightly into the meadow as we roam from our burrow.

The sound of birds celebrating the arrival of new warmth and growth awakened us this morning. The last of the snow is melting, and the meadow will turn green soon as we watch the stream do its yearly thing of overflowing its banks and running away with them, but water for us is not a problem because there are plenty of puddles near us to drink from.

Most importantly, I know that I am going to have more young. It is far too early to be sure, we badgers only begin the young inside us after spring returns, even though we mate from the time of the warm season until the leaves begin to change colors and fall.

But I know that they are in there and will begin soon, especially since Thamuatz is so frisky while we roam in the new warmth to see our territory together.

I must still consider this moving Thamuatz out of my burrow thing, and know he also thinks of it as we roam. He tries not to show his hopping movements to me while we travel together, tries so hard to walk as if he still had four good legs, and looks ashamed as he stumbles along with me.

Thamuatz knows that he will be provided for, but it is not the same as being able to hunt on his own. He does not want to have to wait each day and hope I show up, or that I am not sick or injured or dead; that I actually will bring him something, while taking the time out from feeding my own young and myself to do it for him.

He has no pride left and I know that hurts him, so I put off the moving him out to another burrow thing as he tries to pretend that he can hunt on his own, trying so hard to convince me that he will be all right without me.

But we both know he will not be all right ever again, and we both also know that I can't move him out.

He even goes so far as to linger near one of my other burrows close to the primary one as we roam, to let me know that this will be a good one and he would be happy to stay here.

But I move him back to our burrow again, and he returns with obvious relief even though he tries to hide that relief, grateful I did not insist he stay there. When he came here to find me, Thamuatz had judged me well; I have seen through five full sets of seasons in my life now, and Thamuatz will not be left alone.

He stays, and we do not bring it up again. I will make this work somehow as my body grows larger.

My body grows larger until it is time, and Thamuatz knows that he will have to leave. I do not ask him to, but he leaves and waits near. I can sense him outside as I begin to bring my young out of my body. I can also sense he knows he has to go to that nearby burrow now.

Two this time, females, and so perfect, and I love them so much as I groom their wet, little bodies and clean them and bring them close to me so they can be warm and fed by my body.

They will be named Ankusha and Ammavaru. Both will be proud huntresses after I have trained them, and I already regret the thought of them leaving me, even if that is some time from now. But for now, I have something else to do after both my new little huntresses are fed and comfortable.

It is not natural for a female badger of our kind to do this thing, but it is something I will do anyway, and besides, since when has my life been natural to our kind?

I go from the burrow on our little hillock and see Thamuatz already hopping as best he can for the other close burrow. I sigh and go to him, turning his confused body around.

Turning him is not too difficult, for Thamuatz has three legs and I have four. What is he going to do, fight me?

I turn him around and push my poor, confused Thamuatz, until he finally understands that he is to come back to the burrow.

Trying to walk in front as we travel there, so I can very carefully not notice him crying while we return to where we will live together with my young. He has the right to have pride, and I will be careful about my young. When I leave the burrow each day or night, he will have to leave it with me.

He is a male badger and they can be a danger to young, but he will not live alone in some other burrow always wondering if I will be there with food he can't chase or dig for with one missing front paw. He will not starve, and he will not fear, and he will not be alone.

Thamuatz is fascinated by the young but remembers to keep his distance on the other side of the sleeping chamber. There is still worry about this thing of him being in here with my young, but the worry goes away slowly as Thamuatz always remembers that these are mine, and I will fight him to the death for them, even if I do love him.

I simply sleep with them on the inside between the burrow wall and my body, while Thamuatz tucks himself against me on the outside position as we sleep.

When I have to go outside Thamuatz knows that we go out together, and he understands this and obeys the understanding we have together.

My young grow as they feed from me, and they sleep as Thamuatz and I go out together to hunt and drink from the stream.

They awaken, and I hurry back with Thamuatz hopping along behind me, to see what new thing that my young need from me now with their little cries for attention, probably more feeding!

They grow, their eyes open, and they stare in wonder at the two large, warm things resting beside them who look so much like them, but so much larger!

I trust Thamuatz now, and he is allowed to see them closely. He fascinates them as they begin to play the fierce little games our young play with each other, although they are still much too small to do more than paw at each other in their play, and promptly forget what they are doing to feed from me again. Then sleep as Thamuatz and I begin the hunting again to provide for them and us.

We hunt, and I give Thamuatz pride by not noticing prey until he does, and then on his urging, find the prey and hunt it for all of us.

We return for my two little, starving young who just know I am never ever returning again to feed them as they cry pathetically for me.

I feed them as Thamuatz watches patiently, and then we go outside, where we eat the prey ourselves, if we have not done so already.

It is harder to feed another adult, these two young, and myself, but I do it. There is no question of Thamuatz leaving, and my young have grown to consider him a part of the burrow as they chase each other and mock fight in here while I try to sleep.

He would no more harm them now than he would harm me. He adores them as they roll and fight all over him, pulling his fur with their teeth, and scratching at him with their tiny little claws while he simply watches, and then grooms them when they are finally too tired and dirty after their mock fights.

They grow, my little Ankusha and Ammavaru.

They grow until the day I bring them prey inside the burrow, and Thamuatz stays behind to watch them patiently for me while I am gone.

He is now the large, warm thing that looks like them and cares for them when I am out hunting for all of us, and I trust him totally now. Thamuatz would fight to the death any other that came into the burrow to hurt them, and they adore him as someone who will always be there to play with when I am gone from the burrow.

I return this time, and they are just as amazed as I once was at this strange, new thing mother has brought back to the burrow for them to play with. And they do play with it until little is left for them to eat, while I simply go for another as they try to finish off what is left.

I find them more and watch them eat greedily, as they finally realize there is something besides mother that tastes good! I find them more, and they grow to love it as they grow larger, until Ankusha and Ammavaru both prefer prey to food from my body.

Then it is time to go outside and we all move together to the entrance as Thamuatz leads proudly, showing them by being in the front that he is the adult who will be teaching them, while I smile behind them all and lead from the rear.

Ankusha and Ammavaru are lost to all instruction as they stare in wonder at the meadow around our burrow from the burrow entrance. So much largeness and so many new things had never occurred to them while in the smallness of their burrow.

The sky above, the meadow, and the forest beyond the meadow, all so large for such small little badgers, until Thamuatz and I finally manage to get our two little huntresses actually moving as they follow us, stumbling all over the short grass of the meadow while we try to teach them the things they will need to know to survive when they finally do leave us.

They are as confused at that as I once was. Ankusha asks, "Leave?" Ammavaru simply tells me, "We will never leave, we will always be together." I do not instruct them further in this for now, when they grow larger they will understand. Now is too early to teach this thing.

Thamuatz teaches them of the plants they may need to know, and they want to know why he has only three legs while I have four as they do.

This has come up before in the burrow, but Thamuatz and I have avoided it, and they have not really noticed it since it was only on entering or leaving that they saw how differently Thamuatz and I moved when we walked.

Thamuatz does not mind; he uses it for instruction as he tries to make them understand the idea of traps, and how to avoid them.

They try to understand, but it is difficult without being able to show them one, and I may have to take them to see what those human things look like so our young can learn to look for, recognize, and avoid human traps.

It is necessary to teach them of the humans I have known, and what those humans can do. I teach them of the angry human of the valley who had killed in the arrogant belief that he was the greatest predator of all.

That human now has something that once was prey, waiting patiently for him as a predator beside a stone wall.

I teach them of the human who had taken the fur of others for no good reason, other than human vanity. We both teach these lessons of humans to avoid, and then return to the burrow with them.

Our little ones are still too small; the day was short for them, and both are tired as they snuggle all over Thamuatz to sleep as I go for food while he lets them sleep cuddled against him like they usually do.

I return, and we quietly share the prey together before I remove the remains from the burrow without waking Ankusha or Ammavaru. We will go out at darkness for their first night hunt and I want both of them ready for it.

I snuggle beside Thamuatz with our young between us, and we all sleep until night finds us out roaming again when it is time to hunt and show the young ones new burrows.

Our two little ones are just as amazed as they were earlier today when they saw their first daylight.

It is a night of full moon, and they want to know why the thing I called the sun earlier today is now so dim and so much larger, and why they can look at it without hurting their eyes.

Thamuatz explains the difference to them as I look for prey, then we all rejoin again, and they watch fascinated by how fast their mother can dig, as I tear quickly down into the burrow and kill.

Returning to them, I drop what I have in front of Ankusha and Ammavaru, then wait for them to finish playing with it and eat.

We roam, I hunt, Thamuatz explains, and we all feast in the darkness, until it is time to return again, but this time not to the same burrow.

I want them to understand why we need many burrows, and they are fascinated by the idea that their mother has more than one place to live as they follow along to visit a few of my nearby burrows, while Thamuatz explains that the creature they hear hooting in the trees is a danger to them.

This makes our two little ones come closer as we travel, and Thamuatz explains that the owl by night may be a danger now, but will not be a danger as they grow older and larger.

He teaches them about the hawk by daytime and some of our other enemies while I tell them of the huge, brown monster of a bear as we travel in the darkness, which makes Thamuatz look at me strangely.

I had not bothered to tell him of this creature before or my experiences with it; not wanting to worry him about this thing that is so much larger than the normal black bears that are our natural enemies, now he wants to know of it also.

I tell him of its size and power above the normal bears we are used to, and tell him of some of the things it has done that I have seen myself, including how it kills the smaller black bears that we used to consider our greatest danger for its food, and how it had actually killed a human while I watched, and how easily it killed that human.

We pass the rest of the traveling in silence, and I wonder when my life will again tangle with the life of this huge, brown monster that hunts the forest for all inside it. Ankusha and Ammavaru wonder if the bear is near us while we travel, trying to be right next to Thamuatz or myself as we walk the rest of the way to the burrow. Until we reach the burrow where we will stay for the day, and go inside, and then my young scramble into the safety of the burrow, and have trouble sleeping until Thamuatz lets them curl up between us.

I did not want that new fear to be there, but I did want them to understand and fear this new huge, brown bear as I fear him.

We travel out the next night after I come back from catching prey for all of us, and, as usual, now when I return with prey, the first thing I hear is the happy, playful growls of my two little huntresses as they take terrible advantage of Thamuatz, scrambling over him with their mock fighting.

He sits patiently waiting for my return to bring him some food, and then sort this out as Ankusha and Ammavaru run all over and around him.

I force them to eat first, and scramble all over him second, for which I think that he is grateful to me, as he manages to eat without them wanting to play instead. Then we all head back to the burrow entrance for some more lessons in how to survive.

The frogs are back and easy for Thamuatz to catch, and he has pride again as he hunts them alone near us.

My own two young are far too eager and make this easy prey hop away too often without food for themselves. Until I instruct them to come slowly, and from behind, and then the frog will wait for you because it is too late for it to hop into the water safety.

Thamuatz is proud as we return to our main burrow on the little hillock; he hunted for himself tonight without my help, and hunted well.

My two little ones are sleepy, but I know that they will be all over Thamuatz again just as soon as they awake, and I watch, amused by my adult male acting like a young one once again with them.

He adores them as they adore him, and he is their protection when I am hunting for all of us, I will find a treat for all three of them before we go out tomorrow, and then we will do some daytime instruction on hunting.

They sleep through the dawn and into the morning; the three of them snuggled together, with my two little huntresses sleeping on top of Thamuatz again as usual. I ease myself out past them to get some food, knowing already that there will be three hungry badgers to feed by the time they awaken.

Hunting is good as I feed myself and bring prey back for my three. I hear the sounds of little badgers playing with Thamuatz before I even enter the tunnel to the sleeping chamber, hoping Ankusha and Ammavaru at least let Thamuatz get some sleep when they awakened, knowing that they probably did not, and he is playing with them now as they roll all over him in the fierce games that train them to hunt and fight.

By the time I enter the sleeping chamber with our meal, Ankusha and Ammavaru have stopped playing to rest, cuddled against Thamuatz as always, and both want to know why Thamuatz stopped playing with them.

Thamuatz does not greet me, he only smiles softly at me with his eyes open, as he lies there peacefully with the two little ones he grew to love so much resting with him as they love to do.

Once my own mother, Asaseyaa, had wept beside me next to the body of my sister, Shareesa, while I tried to understand this new thing, one of us dying, and so now do my own two young try to understand what has happened to Thamuatz, and understand why I am sad as I weep openly in front of them while standing next to his body.

I do not have to check him to be sure, I know death by now. He passed peacefully, smiling in contentment, and content that he would be cared for and fed, not helpless and starving, content that I loved him and would always keep him close and warm in this burrow, and content that Ankusha and Ammavaru would love him when they awoke and tried to get him to play with them again.

He had learned how to play again in his life, but they will never play with him again. As I drag him gently from the burrow, they want to know, "Why are you sad? Where is Thamuatz going, and when will he be back to play again?"

The trip up the tunnel with his body is long, and I cry without stopping as I drag him.

I can't leave him in the burrow, and there is only the one other place, the close burrow he showed me, the burrow he lingered near when we were traveling together in that time before our Ankusha and Ammavaru were born, letting me know he would be happy to just be near my primary burrow if I would accept him staying in that close by burrow after my young arrived. I take him there.

Normally we would simply drag a dead one from our burrow and out into the open for the predators to find and take away, but predators will not take Thamuatz.

I drag him to that burrow where he thought he might have to stay, and drag him inside deep into the sleeping chamber, groom him one last time so he will be beautiful again, and cry, and leave, beginning the trip back to the burrow on the hillock.

I have to care for our young; Ankusha and Ammavaru will be strong, proud, beautiful little huntresses, and if they are lucky they will both find their own Thamuatz when older, but it is still impossible to stop crying all the way on the lonely trip back to them.

I try to stop before I enter, but then they both want to know where Thamuatz is, and when he will come back, and I start crying again.

I cry not just because he had the courage to stay alive when he should have starved and died, not just because he was the finest strongest most beautiful mate that I have ever had, I cry because I was not there when he died.

I was not there when Kekuit needed me and died alone and starving on a frozen white field.

I was not there when my two little huntresses Cetnenn and Caoineag needed me and died alone in the burrow overlooking the large water.

I was not there when Tigranuhi fought the bear to defend my young and me and may have died alone, and I still do not know if Tigranuhi had died there that night.

If ever again the ones I love die, I want to be beside them, helping them fight death!

My young huddle next to me, helpless at my tears as I try to explain the idea of the death to Ankusha and Ammavaru; just as my own mother had to explain it to me, when my sister, Shareesa, died in our burrow long ago.

"Remember, we are predators!" I tell Ankusha and Ammavaru fiercely. "Death is always with us!" They stare at me solemnly, trying to understand that we can die like the prey creatures.

I feel a change inside me, a new fierceness even for me. I groom them, cuddle them, and take them fiercely from the burrow. To learn the lessons they must know, to hunt, to kill, and to survive.

Huntresses

There is much to teach Ankusha and Ammavaru. I must teach them all the knowledge of survival and hunting I have ever learned in this, my sixth season of spring forest growth. They are going to learn in ways they will never have trouble remembering, and they are going to learn about humans, and why humans should always be avoided. I am going to take them on a roam.

Ankusha and Ammavaru think that they are only going out to hunt again and will meet Thamuatz soon. They will meet part of him when we arrive where I am taking them, but first they must see that we can die.

We begin roaming, first to where Thamuatz is; they must understand the death of one of us no matter how much I hate to disturb where he rests, they must understand why I hate some humans now.

The burrow is close, and when we reach it they do not want to go inside, as if they finally know. I make them.

It has only been a short while since I left him, and Thamuatz still looks as if he is only asleep and smiling.

"This is what humans do!" I tell my young. "This is the waste they make in the forest. Look closely at his paw on the front, the missing one; we are going to find it."

My young shrink before me, but look closely at him, see that he is not sleeping, feel his body's new stiffness, and now know certainly that he will never play with them ever again, and they cry as I had cried.

I do not cry now, rage rolls inside me as we leave. I will never return to this burrow holding his body. I want to remember Thamuatz as this smiling creature waiting to awaken and play again, not as some dead creature that is just bones.

I seal the burrow entrance up with dirt behind me so no predator will find Thamuatz; and we begin roaming in the direction Thamuatz had come painfully from.

The area we are going to is dangerous, there may still be traps set there not yet tripped by others. But I know the human's scent and know the way he laid those traps when I had watched him catch and kill others, and this gives me advantage over his traps. I also know that he is dead, and that removes him as threat.

We roam to the territory where no badgers live, the direction I did not go in because I did not think that there were any badgers there; going into the valley of the shadows of the dead instead.

I will teach my two huntresses there about human traps, and about the humans who set those; the lessons will never leave Ankusha and Ammavaru, and one more way of dying in this forest will not harm them.

We travel until nightfall to find one of my many burrows, but my two little ones do not sleep as they wish. First I teach them how to wait in ambush beside the stream, and wait until a rabbit comes to the flowing stream to drink, as the sound of the flowing stream masks our breathing.

We eat beside the stream, and for the first time ever, Ankusha and Ammavaru are strangely silent as they watch me. Usually they do not pay attention to me while they take prey apart. This time they keep the prey they are eating between them and myself, so they can watch me as I eat my share of the rabbit fiercely.

I sense their fear, sigh and go to Ankusha and Ammavaru as they look at me with worry at the new thing they sense their mother has become.

I go to them, approaching carefully as they flinch, and then groom them. Both sighing relief while I explain that I am not going to eat them, and things happen sometimes that make you become different from the one you once were.

I groom and soothe until Ankusha and Ammavaru both understand that I am only trying to fiercely teach them, not endanger them.

We sleep until dawn before leaving, and they want to know why I am roaming with them in the daytime since both Thamuatz and I told them so often that we are creatures of darkness during our hunting.

I explain that some things are better taught in the daytime, hiding my worry about how hard it might be to see any hidden human traps in darkness, looking more carefully as we enter the area I do not want to be entering with them.

Any traps in the darkness that take my front paw, as the one that took Thamuatz's front paw, would leave my young far too small, far too untrained, and far too helpless to survive. This entire area is too dangerous, but they must know, and they must understand.

We find, and they are only bones, but I can tell by the shape of the bones that this was a fox at one time, and on the front leg bone of the fox are two things clamped together, still holding the leg bone.

He was not as lucky or as brave as Thamuatz was. The fox did not chew his leg off to survive, he either died of hunger or thirst, or predators had taken him when he was too weak to fight while his leg was trapped. The bones are partially scattered, but there are enough still there to tell me what had happened to him.

My young stare curiously while I explain of the human things that spring up from hiding, bite on your leg, and hold until you have the choices of starving, dying of predators, taking your leg off with your own teeth to survive, or simply waiting for a human to come take your fur even if you are still alive. They understand, and we leave.

No living badger has a burrow here in this territory, and I do not care to share the burrow of a dead one. With the human dead, some of us will again return here, but for now there is only my young and myself in this territory.

I dig a burrow, and after my young are groomed and I am turned to face the entrance, with Ankusha and Ammavaru behind me, we sleep. I fear this territory, they will not.

We are out of the burrow by morning to hunt food; my young will need a great amount of body weight to survive the winter, as I drive them to hunt. We ambush and kill, and I am proud of them. We roam, looking, and roam again until I find the trap.

He has hidden it cleverly, the human I hated, and he has made another kill of a creature by its leg again. Only bones are left scattered again, but the leg bones are still in the trap, and I force my young to see, and to see how the human placed and concealed his trap.

A rabbit was caught in this one. Again, I can tell by the shapes of the bones, and this rabbit did not have the courage to eat its leg off to have a chance for survival. But then prey does not have good survival instincts in the first place, that's why they are prey.

I show my young, and we continue in this direction to find that the unlucky have found all his concealed traps, and the unlucky have died in those human traps.

Except for one, the one human trap I hate to find, the one my young must see no matter how much they hate to see, the one with the gnawed off lower front leg bones of an adult badger still in the trap.

My young understand without my having to tell them, and no matter how hard this lesson, they cry now as they realize that this was Thamuatz. They will not die in one of these.

That was my idea, as I hide my own tears from them while they cry until it is enough. We leave; there is another harder and more dangerous lesson to provide in another territory, and we are going there.

Traveling all day, I try to teach them while roaming that you are only as safe as other predators think that you are fierce.

I teach them you must take your territory and keep it safe from rivals by making the job of taking that territory from you too deadly for any rivals to consider taking it from you.

I teach them even more ways to kill.

I teach them we are the eaters of meat, and we kill to live.

I teach them of hiding and ambushing, and make them practice with me. I am not gentle with them because if they make mistakes, that can get them killed or make them miss prey and starve.

I teach them the ways of death, as they learn those ways.

We sleep at night and roam by day, until we are clear of the area of the human's traps in case anymore have not been found already by the unlucky.

Then we sleep by day and roam by night as I teach of killing in darkness. They learn, and I congratulate Ankusha and Ammavaru only when they kill quickly and successfully, and then I warn them of the dangers of failing to keep watch while you eat your prey.

I tell them what happens when you fail to be aware of everything around you when you enter an open area. I tell them of a female badger that had been ripped apart and eaten in the territory we are going to because she had left the boundaries of her territory and entered an open field inside her territory too quickly and too confidently.

Tigranuhi's mate, black-furred Atida, had been satisfied her territory was not going to be violated by me, she failed to look around her and smell from downwind before entering that open field.

We roam, and Ankusha and Ammavaru share the fierce pride of the kill with me as we stop and feed together, becoming as I am in fierceness, despite their still small sizes.

Thamuatz had loved them and had played with them; but their playtime is over, and I must now teach them to survive.

We again cross the stream that is the center of our world, and roam for the territory of the monster. We find one of my burrows by night and sleep, then wake, kill our food, eat, and roam in daylight; until we find the kill of the other, the monster bear.

The time for caution is here, and I am grateful for the finding of this kill because this is the best way there is to impress my two with the danger in front of us now.

Before, the black bear was our most dangerous enemy in the forest, if you do not consider the dogs of humans, or the humans themselves.

This black bear is not a threat to them any longer, it lies dead, torn apart and eaten, and the claw marks high on the sides of trees around this dead bear marking the territory tell me all I need to know of what creature did it.

The black bear may have once been our most dangerous enemy, but this huge brown monster of bear catches, kills, and eats those smaller black bears as easily as I catch and kill and eat a ground squirrel. The monster is here.

Strangely, I do not fear him now. I respect his size and power and the danger of him, but I no longer fear this monster.

I had ripped one side of his pretty face open once in the darkness while defending other young, and I would be happy to rip the other side of his face open in the daylight, defending these two. Caution is what I feel here in his territory, not the fear of him.

We move deeper into his territory, and I teach Ankusha and Ammavaru about him as we roam slowly and cautiously forward until I find his hiding place, and then we stop our roaming from the downwind side of it.

My teeth are out, and my fur is up, as I realize with pride that Ankusha and Ammavaru have their own teeth out and their own fur up.

We move as three moving as one, softly through the brush with no sound. Sliding smoothly into shadows of brush in the daylight around us, and using the dark stripes running through the darkness of our brown fur to blend and hide in shadows as we move.

Ankusha and Ammavaru have learned well in the last few days and nights as they slide, shadow streaked, through the brush beside me while we close in on his hiding place.

He is not there.

I can detect no fresh scent of him; scent, yes, the scent of him, and the scent of death. But all from a few days ago, nothing new, the huge brown bear is out looking for others to kill and feed on, and there is no trace that he was here recently. Still I respect his power and stop before the entrance to his den to consider.

The entrance is in the side of the hill and is not his; he has taken advantage of some natural entrance into the hillside to make a den.

It is a larger entrance than even he needs with his large size, and I lose some respect for him. To have an entrance larger than you need, is to have an entrance too large to defend against many, or to defend against one that is larger than you and wants to enter.

It is not too great a danger if he is roaming from here, checking territory, and has recently fed on the black bear we found. He probably sleeps somewhere, and we would be wise to leave now, but he is much different from the other bears, and I want to know how this monster lives.

My young are not too thrilled with this idea and hang back at first when I move forward, but they have found their newfound fierceness from me in our roaming since leaving the body of Thamuatz, and will not display the caution of prey creatures in front of me, as they follow behind me.

I feel their fear behind me, but they follow anyway, and I have pride in them for doing so. I have no more fear.

We blend softly with shadows as we close through the protection of surrounding plants to the open area before the entrance; tracking slowly, not ready to make the mistake some pathetic prey creature would in entering that dark entrance without using all of its senses.

We use all of ours, and especially our noses as we close to the entrance and enter it, and smell the death in there before we enter, and the smell grows stronger as we enter.

Smell mostly toward the rear of his den as we go inside to find death. He has killed well and often, and it is disgusting to me. We badgers clean the dead out of our burrows after we eat, and also if one of us dies in that burrow. So the burrow will be tidy, to prevent the burrow from smelling which could attract unwanted attention from larger predators, and instinctively to prevent sickness.

He does not bother to clean out the dead. Bones are everywhere and despite my new fierceness I shiver for he has found a new prey to kill. Some of the bones are human.

Sometimes when a predator kills a human they discover just how weak these feared humans actually are, and how easy they are to kill because humans are not that strong, are not that large, and can't run that quickly. Their human eyes are also almost worthless in darkness, and they have no claws or teeth that might help them to defend themselves.

When a predator such as this one discovers these things, that predator can develop a taste for new, easy-to-kill human prey, and this one has done so.

I count two human skulls and two sets of broken human bones near the front of this den, without even going to the back of this monster's den. Much more scent of death comes from there to here.

I go there now, with instructions to my young to stay, wait, and watch near the entrance, in case he returns while I roam into the back of the bear's den where the real scent is coming from.

Find the other bones of prey he dragged inside here to eat whenever he felt hungry again and count the number of bones that are human, and they are too many.

I feel no fear of bones. Bones are what I make of prey myself, but it is time to leave before this creature thinks of returning to his den.

"We leave," I say, returning to where Ankusha and Ammavaru nervously wait for me. They want to know why. They want to see what I have found back there, and they want to go look.

"We leave!" I command.

We leave, as I hurry Ankusha and Ammavaru to the entrance again and out into the surrounding forest, not stopping until we are well clear of this monster's den. I wonder how he could have killed so well and often without the humans coming to hunt their missing, and finding both den and bones.

Or maybe they did while hunting for their missing humans, and came in too few numbers, or came without their long killing sticks when they came to hunt their missing humans, and that is how he keeps getting more prey.

He has been busy at his killing. I once considered killing a human; this monster of a bear has done it, and done it to more than just the human fur taker I watched him kill that time. To this bear, humans have become just become another form of prey. If he ever encounters any humans with those long killing sticks he might learn differently, but for now he just kills them.

I do not like humans, but I have seen their long, killing sticks crack loudly and kill at a distance, and have the sense to know that humans can indeed kill from a distance, and I respect that.

This bear has lost his respect for humans, and yet he is smart to hide the bones because he leaves no bones in the forest to attract unwanted attention from humans.

Either this bear has far more intelligence than I gave him credit for, or this may have started when he killed the human fur taker and dragged that one back to hide from other predators, concealing the body more by accident than by thought.

He discovered, then, how easy humans were for him to take, and started going for humans because to him, they were far easier prey than running down deer or wasting time on smaller prey.

He may also have concealed the bodies in his den simply to hide them from competing predators, but I can't think of any predators that would compete with him in anything, or that would be a threat to this huge, brown monster, and it may just be an instinctive thing, much like our own kind's digging.

There is still something wrong with all of that, which worries me. This bear displays far more intelligence than any bear should display, no matter how intelligent, and every time I have seen this bear, there always been a sense of someone unseen walking with him. Someone I know or have met somewhere, and something our mother, Asaseyaa, had said to me once.

I forget it; he is a threat, but I have an instinctive feeling he is returning, and we must make some distance from here.

My senses save us. I feel him returning from somewhere inside me long before I can hear or smell him. I already know that somehow, we are bonded in life, he and I. At my order

Ankusha and Ammavaru move deeper into the brush around us.

There is still nothing, until the smell of death comes softly in the wind, and we move to where that wind is above us, so we can smell him, but where he can't smell us.

Downwind, we listen and track him by scent as he comes walking far too assured that he is the best of all predators.

He comes as we listen, and he comes making far too much noise in his belief that he is the ruler of all this forest around him, as I move my two young again in the concealing brush.

Shadows streak our dark-streaked sides, hiding us well inside that surrounding brush, as we adjust our concealment for his coming; using our sense of smell to guide us, using our sense of hearing to adjust again in our concealment as he comes in a slow, steady heavy walk through cracking branches.

He comes, breathing with power through his nostrils, and as my mother had showed me a smaller, less dangerous black bear, now I show Ankusha and Ammavaru the largest and most dangerous predator of the forest, the one that kills humans.

He has grown larger and plumper since I last saw him. Killing has been good to him, as I shiver at the wrong I see! He should not have grown larger; plumper maybe, but not larger!

His legs are now longer than before, his body is also much larger, his nose is flatter in a larger head, and his teeth and claws are longer.

This should not be, it is not possible for an adult of any kind to grow larger, or change its shape, but he is changing. His body is changing, and he is already an adult and should not grow any larger or different in shape, but he has!

Changing or not, he is still somehow the same, huge brown bear, and sizes larger than the black bears, which used to be the only bears in this forest. He has the claw scars down the side of his face, where I had ripped his pretty face and made it less pretty that night when he dared to threaten my young and he still has that thin, white-furred scar running from front to back over the top center of his head.

Strangely, I also sense again that someone is walking beside him, and it is a human, but no one is there, and he passes, unaware that we are even near as we watch him.

I can sense the fear of my two young beside me at the size of him, the power of him, and the rage that seems to radiate outwards from him.

"And," I think savagely, "the foolishness of him!"

In his arrogance he is too confident he can kill anything and that nothing can kill him, and that confidence will kill him someday, when he takes on something that can kill him.

In nature there is always something that can kill even the strongest. He is a fool, and a powerful, supremely dangerous one, but still a fool! Someday I will see him dead, but for now, we simply watch him pass, and then leave.

We roam, and I sense the new respect my young have for me. I did not shiver or think of leaving this monster's den until I had seen all I wanted to see.

They still want to know what I had found back in the deepness of his den, but I refuse to tell them, and they respect me and do not ask again. We roam until I sense someone else is here, in the forest ahead of us.

My teeth show fiercely again as I move to the side of my young that this new one is on. We continue roaming through the shadows of the brush while my young look at me curiously, wondering if this is another strange lesson in killing, and it might well be a new lesson in killing for them if this new one thinks it can harm my young.

They still sense nothing, but I know that there is someone there in the forest, and know that it is a he now, and know that he is heading this way.

Ankusha and Ammavaru will need more training before they are ready to leave on their own. The wind is wrong for me, his scent is still masked by it, but I know he is there. This comes from experience and instinct, not from any training or senses. Ankusha and Ammavaru will learn this experience and instinct now as I prepare to kill.

They sense him now also. My two huntresses have learned well in this roaming and I am proud of them. We hunt him as he hunts us, for he knows we are here in his territory.

I have his scent fully and begin to run. It is one of my five, my Atsentma!

Ankusha and Ammavaru run beside me, sure by now that I am showing them some new way to hunt, and very interested in why I now seem to have forgotten all about having my teeth out for kill as we run.

We three break free of the brush as he snarls a happy greeting. Atsentma recognizes his mother from the last set of seasons in his life, rushing to see me also in his new territory, the territory of the monster bear also, but Atsentma has remembered my lessons to him and somehow has managed to survive in it!

We growl fierce joy at each other and circle, as my Atsentma shows me how beautiful and strong he has become in only one full set of seasons since leaving me. He fluffs his fur with pride and shows me how long his claws and teeth are.

My young one has done well, he is fierce, strong, and fully grown now, and he has the true pride of one who has survived the danger of the bear.

My Atsentma, my perfect, little, wild animal walks with us as we roam together with Ankusha and Ammavaru and head back for my own territory again. Atsentma tells me how he has survived.

My young Atsentma has cheated the bear on more than one occasion. He had already learned that this big monster has trouble seeing in the darkness on the night I scarred its pretty face forever with my claws, and Atsentma hunts only at night, coming out in the daylight when he has made all of the checks for scent and sound before leaving the burrow.

He also remembers to dig his burrows under strong tree roots as I had taught him, and sleeps in a secure burrow every night. He also switches that burrow for another burrow often, so the bear can't become used to finding him in just one place.

He has learned the lesson I taught all my five after the run we made that night, and the lesson poor Atida, Tigranuhi's mate, did not understand well enough, the lesson of checking carefully before entering any open areas. Open areas are dangerous, day or night, and Atsentma has seen the bear waiting for prey to wander into open meadows while it remained concealed near the forest edge.

"The bear has become an absolute master of ambush and stalking!" Atsentma tells me as we travel. "And he seems to hate humans most of all. To him, all other prey is just prey, but for some reason he does not just hunt humans as prey, he hunts them simply to kill them."

Atsentma also tells me how he watched this monster stalk two humans through the forest once.

The huge brown bear is good at stalking humans, but the two humans somehow seemed to become aware he was near as he moved closer, and as Atsentma watched, he had a strange feeling that a human was walking beside the bear as it stalked them, but he couldn't see any human there.

Atsentma watched, following in awe, from the correct downwind side as I had taught him while the bear stalked the two humans, awed at how quietly this monster has learned to move through the forest, at how well it could hide in spite of its size as it stalked.

He was puzzled by that strange feeling of an unseen human walking with the bear and the stranger feeling that the bear was not actually controlling the stalking of the two humans, the unseen human walking with it was.

The description of the two humans sounds somehow familiar, but only when Atsentma describes what the humans wore, what they fully looked like, and what they had with them do I understand.

It was the same two humans wearing the coverings of the colors and shapes of the forest I met this last season of the leaves falling from the trees before winter.

It was the two humans who had treated me to some of their deer; and to some of the little round good tasting things from their fire, and to that brown liquid I do not intend to drink again because of what it does to my head and body.

They are back in the forest this season, and the bear was stalking them as they stalked deer through the forest, and the bear knows about human killing sticks.

Atsentma mentions this so casually that he himself does not know what he says even as he continues. "The two humans each took some kind of long stick thing from off their shoulders and brought a wide end up to their shoulders, with a slim end pointing away from them when they seemed to sense him around."

"He did not make any noise or show himself as he got closer to them, but both these humans seemed to know he was near anyway, and as soon as the bear saw the humans knew he was near and were ready with their long stick things, he turned away and disappeared back into the forest moving away from the humans. And the bear seemed to be even more enraged after he saw both humans had long stick things, as if he had been sure of them and wanted them, but now knew they were safe from him."

I did not teach Atsentma of what these human killing sticks could do, and now I must.

He does not understand what he saw, but I do, and somewhere before, this bear has met a human with one of those long killing sticks and learned of what it can do, or somehow, he has learned about killing sticks from another . . . suddenly I remember that each time I also sensed the unseen human walking beside him. He could have learned from the human!

I do not know how this could be, a human can't instruct a bear just as a bear can't instruct a human, but now the bear simply avoids humans who have the killing sticks and goes after the humans who do not have them, or the humans who have them but are not prepared.

That is how he gets away with it so often, and it has been very often if the human remains I found in his den are any indicators. This makes him far too dangerous for us to remain in this area; even Atsentma will not be able to avoid this monster forever here.

No bear should be able to move this quietly through the forest, certainly not this huge one, and few creatures, even bears, will deliberately stalk humans. Humans have the power of the killing sticks.

He is more than just a simple bear now, this bear has learned too much about humans somehow or somewhere, and he no longer fears them. He hates them, and he stalks them, and he will bring humans into this forest to stalk us all if he continues.

I have seen the humans who fought the fire and have seen how they protected each other when they ran from the fire.

I have seen how the two humans who hunted here and gave me some of their food hunted with each other.

Except for the human who was taking fur alone and the angry one of the valley, humans seem to care for each other and the humans this one killed will be missed someday, and then other humans will come searching for the missing ones. No matter how little the missing ones have been missed, they will be looked for eventually; and when humans do come searching for their missing ones, the den of this monster will be found, and then there will be more humans, and then more, until the entire forest is searched for him.

There will be humans with those long killing sticks all over this forest, and I do not have the power to kill this monster of a bear. I only have the power to get my young safely away from the territory of this monster, and to tell Atsentma of what these humans killing sticks can do.

Then until it is safe we roam back toward my territory, and Atsentma does what I hate most of all, he bids me goodbye and turns again to head back into his territory, the territory of the monster.

It is his wish, it is his territory, and I can't say no, for this is where he has a right to go and he wants to go back there. I do not let Ankusha or Ammavaru see my tears as he looks back at me once and then disappears into the forest.

I turn them fiercely away and we roam the other way, and there are other lessons to teach and they have more to grow before they are ready to leave by themselves. They will survive!

They survive, and they grow as we roam, never staying in one burrow too long while traveling through the forest, as I teach them all the ways to kill, and of the humans they must avoid.

I teach them of the one who was taking fur over and over until they can repeat back to me from memory what the traps they saw in the territory where he trapped creatures for their fur look like, and all the ways they had seen those traps concealed.

I teach them again of the angry one of the valley, and how to avoid ones like him, to stay concealed, looking for others who might also be concealed, until you are sure it is safe to enter open areas.

I teach them of the killing sticks and how those killing sticks can reach long distances in the open areas, but humans can see only so far, and you are safe if you are concealed in thick brush that makes your stripes blend well with the brush.

As days pass, the season changes into the hot one, and I know that they may leave me soon. They know of the bear already, and know how to dig strong, safe burrows under tree roots or rocks to avoid him or any others that would dig you out from your burrow.

They do not need any further instruction from me as to why they should avoid him and his territory, having seen all that they needed to know when he passed close to us.

I remind Ankusha and Ammavaru that the bear did not know we were there when he passed close to us, and by using our senses as we should and concealing ourselves as he passed, we avoided his threat to us. He might be a good predator, but we are better.

I point out to both of my now-grown hunting sisters, "We may not be the largest of creatures in the forest, but we are among the fiercest, and the forest knows this. Most predators will simply leave us alone when we are grown. The bear and the wolf are the exceptions, but there are no more wolves in this forest because the humans killed them all."

Red Fur had told me that seasons ago and I believe him. I have seen the human's dogs gone wild but never a wolf.

Ankusha and Ammavaru also learn of the human's dogs gone wild as I now teach that to them. They must know of these creatures and how I have seen them myself, roaming the forest as they kill far more than they need to kill among its creatures.

I teach, and they listen while we roam, and the hot season is upon us fully as we travel back to the home we started from, the little hillock in our meadow. The humans are there already in numbers!

We become shadows in the brush, blending our bodies into shadow in daylight. My daughters and I are no longer mother and daughters now; we are three huntresses and fighters together as we study the humans.

Ankusha and Ammavaru have become as I am, and I have become death. I know death in all its forms. I know how to give it to others and how to avoid it myself, and alongside me, the huntresses Ankusha and Ammavaru know all that I know.

We three live by death, knowing of killing for food, knowing of killing to survive; we three know death and we three avoid death ourselves. We do not fear the humans as we study them from our sheltering brush; we only look to see what purpose they have in our meadow.

Many are there, many more coming in human-carrying things with much noise. They all have a purpose that we can feel from where we hide, concealed, watching, and the purpose is not good for the forest.

They all carry killing sticks, and some of them do not have those long killing sticks over their shoulders; they carry their killing sticks nervously in human paws instead, facing outward from the edges of where all the other humans have gathered.

We can sense fear and anger, and we can hear it in the nervousness of their voices as they argue among themselves, as we can sense the coming death for what they seek.

Something large flies in overhead. I sense fear between Ankusha and Ammavaru as it comes into the air above us, and then there is another, and another.

I caution the two hunting sisters that were my daughters, "Do not move and do not fear; I have seen something like this before."

But these are not the same as the flying things that I saw when the fire came. Those flying things had long, large bodies and long wings like birds that never flapped as they flew above me.

These are smaller flying things with no wings. Instead, something revolves around the top of them very quickly like the wings of a hummingbird as it flies, and these make a different noise and do not continue flying. They stop overhead like a hummingbird does to stay in one place.

The humans on the ground talk to things in their hands, just as I once saw the humans talk to things they held in their hands outside my burrow when the fire came.

Then the flying things stop staying in the air overhead like giant hummingbirds, go in different directions, and begin flying back and forth as the humans begin to move outward away from the thing on the ground they had all been gathered around. Now I can see it clearly and I have seen this before in the bear's den.

The bear is an arrogant fool. I knew that it would come to this!

The body is torn apart, the humans have been looking at it, and they know, and they have missed the other humans after all, and now they know why.

He did not bother to hide this one, or even bother to eat much of it, as if he did not have time to hide it or did not want to drag it all the way to his den.

He left it in my meadow, near my hillock, and they have found it here and come in their numbers for revenge with killing sticks, and anything that even looks like a predator will die here today, or tomorrow, or the next day.

We watch and wait as the humans begin moving into the forest in numbers of no less than three in each group, and we can sense the fear among these creatures as they begin the search for him.

I have actually seen him and can understand their fear of what they are seeking, if they are not careful he might seek a few of them.

This one is huge and powerful and crafty, and he knows very well how to stalk them while they stalk him, he has learned from others of their kind. Humans may die here today also.

The burrow is out of the question for now. The humans will use those long killing sticks on anything that startles them in their fear, and they may not stop to notice the difference between one of us and a bear before they use them. Creatures that fear like this when they hunt make mistakes, and in the forest, mistakes can kill.

We blend into the brush until only a few humans are left in the meadow.

The fear radiates from the ones that remain now that the others have gone. They look nervously outward, with their killing sticks up against their shoulders.

There are others here, carrying strange, large things on their shoulders, with lights on those things.

They point the things at other humans as they talk, and at the ones that went away from here with the killing sticks, and then try to point them at the body.

As soon as some of the other humans notice them doing it, they do not allow them to point the things on their shoulders with the lights on them at what is left of the body of the human.

There is argument about this among these with the things on their shoulders and the other ones wearing brown coverings like the ones that were outside my burrow when the fire came, but the ones in brown seem to be more powerful and win the argument.

Instead, the others do something else as one of the flying things, a differently colored one lands in our meadow. The humans with the things on their shoulders climb into it, and it flies away.

But the time for watching is over as we blend and move while shadows streak and hide us in the brush as we roam. We are going in the safest direction, the one the humans moved in.

They are searching the forest in front of them and around them, not in the forest they have already passed. They will check every burrow and every den, and every possible hiding place they find large enough to hold the one they seek, but they will not expect us to be traveling behind them, so we follow them.

I also have curiosity as to whether or not they will actually be able to kill this monster, no matter how many killing sticks the humans have among them.

I do not feel they quite understand just how large he really is now, and how much his body has changed even though he was already an adult bear. At least they are going in the right direction.

The humans move as we move cautiously behind them, and these humans are fools, they do not ever think to check their back trail as I knew they would not check it after watching how they left the meadow on this hunt. The bear could circle them and kill them before they were even aware that he was behind them.

Now I understand how he was able to kill so many of them. These humans here today are not very good at this, unlike the two hunting humans that fed me some of their food.

Those two humans were true hunters with the forest instincts of our kind, and I respected them, remembering Atsentma telling me how he watched while this monster tried to track them, and the two human hunters knew without seeing or hearing him that this monster was tracking them from somewhere around them. Then they prepared for him with their killing sticks, and when this monster of a bear saw that they were prepared for him with those killing sticks, he left.

He does not attack those who are prepared for him, but these humans tracking him now may not be so lucky, and these are not true hunters as the two humans I had met were, also, these new humans fear as they track their prey; in the forest, fear leads to mistakes, and mistakes lead to death.

The fear of this bear may make these humans too cautious, which may also make them dead. Atsentma had said that the other two human hunters I knew were not afraid when they sensed this monster bear around them.

This bear can sense fear just as we sense it, and if this group of humans runs instead of using their killing sticks when they find him, or he finds them first, he will kill them. We follow, and the loud cracks of the killing sticks begin. Death is here, and it is busy.

The direction is right, but the distance is wrong. We are not near the bear's den yet.

We find the first kill, and it is human. They have gathered around him, and he was wearing the wrong colors, it is one of the ones in brown that was guiding them, and someone has made a mistake.

One of the other humans is crying as they stand around the fallen one. The crying one has obviously panicked in fear and used the killing stick too quickly without seeing what he was using it on.

This is obvious from what we see as we watch without emotion. After all, what is one human more or less to us? They are a plague upon the forest.

We forget this one and follow the rest of the humans as they travel; while the humans remaining behind us take the fallen one and the crying one away to one of the arriving human-carrying traveling things.

We follow the others who hunt, listening to the sounds of killing sticks from time to time as fear-driven humans use them on things they do not need to, without seeing the thing they do need to use them on.

We roam, and a loud crack comes again. Humans scream and yell at each other in front of us, and we find.

We find that this time they at least did not kill each other, but two of them are fighting until the others pull them apart. One human who was fighting another human seems to be very excited and angry about the other human's use of his killing stick.

We roam away from this as a single loud *"Crack!"* comes in front of us and someone calls to me, desperately wanting me.

He calls again in pain for me to come, and I realize with a chill that I hear the call not with my ears but inside me. Then the call that can't be heard with ears is suddenly gone, and there is the feeling of someone standing alongside, desperately wanting me to see him.

But as I look up no one is there, and I cry pain and grief, for I know already what call comes into the head and not into the ears, and know what the sense of someone that can't be seen standing alongside, desperately wanting me to see them means!

I know the voice of the one that called to me, know the one alongside trying desperately for me to see him one last time!

I begin to run as Ankusha and Ammavaru run alongside. They are curious, they do not understand, but they are fellow huntresses and they run with me now.

They did not hear the call, but then they would not, and they did not know him as I knew him.

I run past trees, through the brush and clear areas, knowing the direction to go without knowing it, see the brown lump with the black stripes mixed with the brown of its bloody side laying in the forest among the fallen leaves, and wail my grief before I am even close enough to be sure it is Atsentma!

He was not a bear. He could not do the things the bear did. He could not have done that to a human. He survived here, unhurt, in the territory of the bear. He did not do anything, but they have killed him!

I promised myself once to never again cry over the deaths of the ones I loved, but I lied to myself. I wail my grief while trying desperately to clean Atsentma's bloody body and groom him back to life. He only grows colder, and I hate.

We roam away, and I can't help him, I can only hate!

We roam for the den of the bear, following the foolish humans I hate. We roam and hear the cracks again. One at first, then many more, as the humans hidden from our view by the forest suddenly begin to scream.

But not in fear or pain, they scream in triumph. We follow the sounds of foolish humans who kill what they do not need to kill in fear and rage until we watch from a sheltered place to see that they have killed very well indeed.

I was wrong. The humans did bring enough killing sticks with them after all, and they have killed a bear as they intended to kill a bear when they began this hunt for him.

The bear lies in front of the den, the same den that we had roamed before, and this bear is very dead, the humans have used their killing sticks to kill far more than they needed just to kill one simple bear.

There are many bloody holes in this poor bear that had the bad luck to be in the wrong place at the wrong time. It is the wrong bear.

I remember briefly that I always sensed a human I could not see walking with the huge brown bear. I always sensed something with the monster bear when it killed and sensed the bear had more killing rage than any normal bear should.

But that huge, brown monster bear has outwitted the humans again and is not here; this is some poor, simple, smaller black bear that found a den not in use, moved inside to make it his den, came out in curiosity to see what humans wanted outside his new den, and then died in the monster's place.

The humans seem to be happy, the humans are fools!

But now the humans gather around this poor bear that had died for no reason and are happy as the flying thing that carried the humans with the large things on their shoulders lands near them. Other flying things that carry humans gather above, but there is no more room for them to land also and they simply stay above.

They all seem to want to see this dead bear that had nothing to do with what they are now carrying out of the den; the bones that the real bear had taken inside there.

They carry much out of this den of the monster, and all the things that I already knew were in the back of that den when I roamed there.

None of the bones are the work of this poor bear, but the humans are happy with finding both the bones and the dead one. They celebrate around the dead bear, while the real bear roams somewhere else looking for fresh humans to kill.

There is nothing more for us here, and I turn with my two fellow huntresses to leave. I had ripped him one dark night by myself with only claws, while these humans have missed him in this bright daylight, with all of their numbers and all of their killing sticks. These fools will see more dead humans before they kill the real bear. We leave in disgust.

We are three huntresses together, and roam as three huntresses through the forest around us, shielding ourselves easily in shadow and brush, moving silently, finding distance from this place, avoiding the humans as we listen to the killing sticks cracking loud from other humans who still do not know of the death of the bear behind us, where humans celebrate far too early.

I wonder briefly if they will meet him with all their noise and his desire to see more humans again, and then dismiss that thought.

He is far too clever for that now. He will roam far from all this noise and find a new place for territory, probably avoiding humans for a while until it is safe for him to begin killing again. Then he will not make the mistake he made this time of leaving a body for humans to find, and I know now that our lives are actually joined somehow, and I will see him again.

My sisters that were once my daughters follow as I lead them to safety, as we roam for the area near our burrow but not too near.

I want all the humans long gone before we return to the hillock in our meadow, so we simply hunt at night and hide by day without a burrow.

The only creature that contests this, and assumes we are helpless outside of a secure burrow, is the smaller, young black bear that thinks foolishly that we are prey for him.

He finds us roaming by day, and we three see the hope light up in his eyes at the thought of three female badgers to help fatten him up for the winter.

"We have seen too much. We are sisters in death, we do not think so!"

He roams slowly and carefully toward us, trying to get closer without scaring us away so he can make three quick kills, feast, and fatten more.

We only smile as we walk toward him without changing our direction as the light of hope for extra winter fat turns to confusion instead in his eyes and becomes even more confusion as we come to him deliberately.

Other predators in the forest are larger, and some like this bear, will commonly feast on us if we are alone, but we are not alone, we are three, and we are three huntresses.

The two hunting sisters Ankusha and Ammavaru, who used to be my daughters, and I come to him together, smiling, as the light of hope in his eyes becomes nervousness.

We begin to separate as we move toward him. I come down the center, Ankusha to one side, and Ammavaru to the other side as we approach. He stops stalking us as his confusion is slowly replaced by another emotion that no good predator should ever have, fear.

We do not even bother to growl a warning as we come toward him, stalking him as three creatures that are one, smiling prettily for him as the distance closes, showing him our teeth as the emotion that no good predator should ever have grows inside him.

We see the fear, and as we come closer it increases in him as he remembers now the lessons his own mother must have taught him before he left her den for his own life in the forest.

He remembers as he begins to back away from us that the badger, while not the largest, is one of the fiercest creatures of the forest. The female badger is the fiercest of badgers, and we are three female badgers, and we are not stopping.

He backs and the growl that is intended to frighten us into becoming prey again betrays him, it is the growl of the weaker, not the growl of the superior predator.

We stop smiling for him, open our mouths wide to show him all our pretty teeth because he can already see how long our claws are, and we rush him!

He forgets this foolishness of trying to take all of us on at once, turns and runs as we rush. Bears may not be known for their superior speed except in quick rushes for close prey or charges for more distant enemies they really want to kill, but this bear is very good at running.

We chase for a little while and then have to stop. His legs are too long for us to really catch him at the speed he is running, laughter is getting the better of us, and we have to breathe while trying to run after the bear and laugh at him at the same time.

It is too difficult to do both at once, and so we stop to groom each other while making unkindly remarks about his present and future abilities as a predator.

Then we simply resume our roaming, but he will probably be nervous about badgers for the rest of his hunting life.

We roam for the territory, where I last saw the two hunters, to see if any male badgers have entered it yet. I want to have young again next spring season and that is the best place I have found for more badgers, if any have returned.

We scent the humans before coming near to them, and hear them before coming nearer, closing with them cautiously until I smile and realize that there are only two humans and I know both of these humans from scent and sound.

These are the two that Atsentma said the monster bear stalked before giving up on them, the two that shared deer with me before when we met in this forest.

It is not surprising to find both humans here again this season as we enter this territory, this is obviously where they hunt, as around the burrow on the hillock is where I hunt.

I respect these two humans, even if they are predators in the forest competing with me for food. These two only take what they need and nothing else, as we do, and I hope that they have another deer. It has been a while since I had deer, and they have already shown me that they are willing to share.

We find them by scent and sound, even humans who are as good at stalking as these two seem to be, they still make far more noise than we do in the forest.

Smiling again at how easy it is, I show Ankusha and Ammavaru how to track humans through the forest without being seen as we drift through the brush, becoming shadows in sunlight, closing the distance between them and us.

This is the best lesson I could give Ankusha and Ammavaru before they leave me. Humans are obviously now our worst enemy in this forest instead of wolves that no longer exist in this forest, or bears.

However, unlike the last humans with killing sticks Ankusha and Ammavaru saw at work in the forest when the monster bear was being hunted, these two human hunters do not try to use their killing sticks on things they can't even see.

Ankusha and Ammavaru are cautious because they have seen little good in humans to recommend going anywhere near a human, but I reassure both of them that I know these two humans already as we move close to where they stay.

My mouth and stomach are both ready before we get there, I scent deer and both of my humans are there, sitting in the clearing with that strange above-ground burrow I saw before, in that other clearing where we met before. They have deer, and it smells delicious!

As I prepare to leave this brushy shelter for food, Ankusha and Ammavaru want to know why I want to enter the clearing at all, after what we have seen of other humans.

I explain, "There are humans, and there are humans, and some humans are often different from each other, just as we are."

They have food, they have been generous with that food, and I am practical about this; walking into the open to greet the humans, and to have some of that food.

Both humans have good memories; they look as I enter the clearing. Remaining where they are sitting, and making friendly noises, and noises of knowing me from the last set of seasons they were here.

One of them, the one who had stroked me before, wants me to come closer and makes friendly motions at me with his paws as he sits with the other.

However, I am not some creature to just go forward and be stroked before I am ready to be stroked, not even from someone I have allowed to touch me before. There is something more important than that anyway . . . food!

Scent says they have already had deer over the fire, and scent also says that they have some of those small round things, which turn brown and tastes so good when placed near fire wrapped in the shiny stuff.

The smells are overpowering; I want some so badly, and I can tell from the drooling, hungry noises behind me in the brush that Ankusha and Ammavaru have the same idea.

However, I have pride, and wait until the humans get the idea themselves while I look politely at what they have on the round things they eat from.

Why they do not just put it on the ground and eat off the ground like decent predators is beyond me, but humans are humans, and these two humans have what I want.

They do get the idea, as food comes off the round things and is thrown to me. I eat greedily as Ankusha and Ammavaru forget their caution and come out from shelter to get some also.

Their appearance with me brings more noise from the two humans, but it is friendly noise as they keep throwing us deer and the little, round, good tasting things, and they both have sense enough not to try to touch us or interrupt us while we feast.

We feast well until they finally give us the last of what they had on the round things humans eat from, and then we allow them to show us proper respect by admiring us as we sit and watch them.

From the way they make mouth noises to each other, I gather that badgers do not often show themselves to humans, seldom return to see them again in the next set of seasons if they do, and do not simply wander into human's places to sit patiently and watch.

They do not understand how fascinating we think humans are.

When humans, like these two, respect us, and do not try to touch us without our permission, we do not mind sharing some of our time with them, and when they share food with us, that makes them one of us.

The badger who gathers food for young or for others is the most important badger in the burrow, and they have just gathered and shared their food with us.

They do not understand that by the act of giving us all they had to eat, they have just become the most important badgers in the group inside this clearing where we sit with them.

I hear the happy sighs of Ankusha and Ammavaru from beside me while I sit digesting my food and watching the humans with my fellow huntresses, listening to the two humans talk in wonder at how we sit with them.

It is surprising that they even bother to wonder why we sit with them around this fire thing of theirs; of course, we are content to sit with them, they fed us, and they know the rules of dealing with us, and about not touching us without our permission.

These two seem to be what I have found them to be before in this forest, predators as we are, hunting for food as we do. I explain this to my two fellow huntresses without the humans even being aware that I am talking to Ankusha and Ammavaru.

Then we watch curiously as they take the long killing sticks and do something to those killing sticks.

But it is not a threat to us, so we only watch as they take each killing stick and lift something small that sticks out of the side near the top back when the stick is against their shoulders.

They lift the small thing, and then pull it backward and it comes out of the backs of the sticks. They set this aside and begin pushing small white things on the end of a long something through the killing sticks with a strange smell on those white things that comes from a little thing of liquid they have with them.

The things come out of the front ends, dirty at first, then cleaner as they do it again, until they finally take another small white thing and coat it with liquid from another small thing of liquid, push that thing through the backs of the sticks, then wipe the things they pulled out of the backs of the killing sticks and finish.

Pushing the thing they lifted up and backward to remove from the sticks, forward and down again, with a "click" noise as we watch this strange human's thing curiously.

It is a human thing and when this human foolishness is finished, we simply sit with them around the fire.

We sit as night comes to the forest, and the day creatures are replaced by night ones as we enjoy the warmth of the fire soaking into our bodies.

Sitting in contentment along with them as the humans find food again for us, we watch as they talk to each other and to us, although we do not have the slightest idea what they are talking to us about.

We do not speak human talk, and I hardly think that they speak badger; still they have fed us and fed us well, so we sit with them until they go inside the large brown thing that humans have for an above-ground burrow in the forest, and then we leave.

It is the season to mate, and we leave to find mates. Both of my young should be gone by now, and Ankusha and Ammavaru are fully grown, but we still travel and hunt together, and now we hunt for a mate.

I am not too particular about what mine looks like, just as long as he is male, and can give me young this next spring. We roam, we hunt, and at last we find scent.

Just as I was starting to think that there were no more males left after Thamuatz died, there is the slightest of trace of male badger scent in the air.

I change direction through the forest while Ankusha and Ammavaru follow and scent becomes stronger as we near him.

He has a surprise coming, and this one is probably only looking for a single mate, instead here comes three female badgers, and as we close with him I can tell that behind me Ankusha and Ammavaru are starting to become interested also.

Their natural instincts have emerged, and they are following more eagerly even if they are not quite sure yet where we are going and why. I explain to them as we follow his markings.

We roam, and we find him, a fine, strong male. I know this even before we break through the brush into the open to see what our new lover looks like.

He makes a strong pathway through the brush as we follow his trail, telling me he is strong, and probably a younger male. He leaves strong scent markings, so he is interested in finding a mate. He can hear us coming and knows that a female is near, so he is alert.

He waits in an open area to begin the mating ceremony; probably confused as to why the approaching female badger he can hear makes far more noise than for just one female.

He has no idea how lucky he is as the three of us emerge from the surrounding brush to smile at him. He looks at us confused. He expected one female, and there are three instead, and all three apparently interested in him.

He is still confused as he tries to decide which of us the suitable mate is; he has obviously never met more than one female at a time before, unless it is female escorting her young.

Badgers almost never travel together, but now there are three and we three huntresses ruffle our fur to show him how beautiful we are, how splendid our markings are, and he still hesitates in confusion trying to decide.

"He is handsome, with fine dark markings on his brown fur!"

We three huntresses smile at each other as we wordlessly agree that we are going to take terrible advantage of him. We give him the mating growl together, then smile at each other again, and advance on him as he starts to back off.

He can't run quickly enough to escape, and we catch him, take terrible advantage of him, and mate often and well, until he is finally able to escape a few days later. We watch him leave, pleased with ourselves.

His name was Sesondowah; he has probably had enough mating this season and will probably be more careful next season when he tries to mate again.

My Ankusha and Ammavaru will have their very own young this next spring and I will have more young.

We leave to roam again, this time for home. We roam back to our burrow on the little hillock overlooking our meadow.

The humans have returned to human places, leaving us the forest again, and it is once more safe to be in that meadow together, but I know that we will not be together for very long now. I can feel the call coming to them.

I have told them what to expect when they have young this next spring, how to make their burrow or burrows perfect for those young, and how to be safe, and there is nothing left to teach or show them.

I will have young this next spring and am already eager to see what it will be this time and how many, and please not five again.

The time comes that I always dread as the leaves begin to turn colors before they fall, and the time to leave is here and Ankusha and Ammavaru are ready.

They are grown enough and have learned to be more than fierce, and the bear was proof of that. Like me, both have been fattening for the coming winter, and now they want to find their own burrows and mates and lives.

We three look like sisters in size and coloring now, even if I am the older by five full sets of seasons, and they know all the ways to hunt and defend themselves that I can teach them, then is time to go at dusk, which always seems to be when my young leave me.

We go out at dusk.

Ankusha and Ammavaru will leave together, and I know that they will leave this dusk, as they both also know. Once, two sets of seasons ago I knew this for Cetnenn and Caoineag also; but they died in the burrow overlooking the large water before they could leave. Ankusha and Ammavaru will live; they have been trained in all the ways of death for hunting and defense, these two will not die.

We roam from the burrow together for the last time, cross our meadow together for the last time, kill and feed together for the last time, and then it is time.

I groom Ankusha and Ammavaru fiercely before sending them off in the safest direction, the direction the monster bear's den was in, the direction that my dead Atsentma had claimed as territory.

It is probably the safest of all the areas in this forest for them to go to because the last foolish human has left it by now, and there are no other badgers there I know of that could have claimed it yet.

The monster bear is too smart to come back into it, and he chased all the other bears away just by being there, so there will be no larger predators that might threaten my daughters or their young.

No one owns that territory, it is Ankusha's and Ammavaru's to have, and they will have it all and can share it with each other or make adjoining territories of it as they wish when they get there.

I am happy with whatever they decide, as long as they are close enough to each other to defend against common enemies. It may be the last dusk we ever see together, and parting with my two huntresses is hard, but it is the way of our lives.

One last fierce grooming for both of them, one last kiss across the top of each now full-grown heads of the fellow huntress that once was only my young, and then Ankusha and Ammavaru turn to leave together into the dark forest, and I share a final instruction with both as they leave. "Survive!" They go, and I am lonely again.

Lonely

I am lonely and I am sick. The cold rain came early, and I let myself be out in it for too long while chasing extra prey for the winter, and had failed to get back to my burrow in time to dry off, and now I sit sneezing inside that burrow.

Winter will be here soon, and I do not want to pass it like this as I sneeze loud enough to wake all the prey in the meadow outside.

It is cool outside as the rain continues to fall from the sky, but I am warm, far too warm. I should feel cooler. I am warm and miserable, and, sneezing again, as I wish to die and just sneeze instead.

My body aches too much to move, but when the sun finally emerges from the dark mass that is the sky overhead, I edge to the entrance of the burrow anyway to sit in the sunlight for warmth. It seems to help to do this.

Still sneezing, I try to decide if I want to go hunt prey, or just sit here in the emerging sunlight and die instead. Since it makes more sense to go hunt, I force myself out into the field to find the food I need for the rapidly approaching winter.

Fortunately, worms are out. Even though it is not dark yet, there was enough rain for that and I eat without feeling like eating for the first time ever. Then the sun leaves the meadow as the sky above darkens again, and I try to make it back to the burrow before rain falls again.

Too late, the rain falls on me again as I drag myself miserably back to my burrow, down the entrance tunnel, and into the sleeping chamber to suffer and sneeze, and they come to annoy me as I suffer.

The sun is finally out again, and I am outside the burrow entrance in sunlight, absorbing warmth to help myself when the large human-carrying traveling thing enters my meadow. Far larger than they need to carry them; but I suspect this is common with these four humans who come into my meadow, while

The two large humans and their two smaller ones making more noise than I need to hear right now, as I try to sleep in the sun; until finally giving up on the sleep idea to go see what these noisy humans are doing.

I notice other humans are also near, but they stopped outside the meadow in the forest nearby, as if they had followed these new, noisy humans here, but didn't want to join them.

I know the humans that stopped in the forest; they are not a threat to me, and if they choose not to enter my meadow as these noisy humans did, then that is their choice. I am sure they will enter it anyway after these noisy humans leave. They come to see me from time to time.

However, these new ones in my meadow are much more annoying because they have brought young ones that run around with no control from the two larger ones.

They make far too much noise. Any predator that is around here could probably eat these two smaller humans before the adults were even aware it was nearby, since they seem to pay no attention at all to their own young.

By the time I move closer, I am unkindly hoping that one does, both young ones are throwing rocks at the ground squirrels which are my food, and the adults are not much better as they try to set up one of those outdoors above-ground dens humans use when they stay in the forest.

But unlike the two human friends I stayed with, these two apparently have no idea how to set up the above-ground things, which brings many loud angry mouth noises from the male human to his mate and brings back other loud angry mouth noises from his mate to him.

For mates, they seem to spend a lot of time disagreeing with each other on how to do simple things. I wonder if the two larger humans really are mated, and if these really are their young or if the two adult humans just happened to find these two small ones somewhere and brought them here to eat.

I will eat them if they do not stop throwing rocks at my food! I still ache, but my sneezing is less and I do not feel as warm now. All I want to do is sleep, and these humans are annoying me.

I blend with the nearest brush to watch as they finally get the larger-than-they-need human's forest-dwelling up after dropping it a few times.

The two youngest are finally brought under some kind of control, and then they all sit to make loud mouth noises at each other.

Not angry mouth noises, just far too loud ones, as they babble happily away at one another, apparently without actually listening to each other at the same time.

I do not have to be able to speak human to understand that, and only after a long time at this, they do something that makes my mouth water.

Food has been something I did not really want while I was sick. Now that I am a little better, the hunger is there, and these humans are preparing food.

They bring out the round things humans seem to like to eat from. Instead of eating off the ground like decent creatures would, as I wait for them to build a fire.

But these humans do not even build a fire. Instead, they bring out a large holding thing from the large humans carrying traveling thing they arrived in, and take food out of it. Even from here the food does not look that good, or even something that I would really want to hunt and eat, but they seem to like it, and I am hungry.

They also do not have any of the long human killing sticks with them, either, which makes it safer to come out.

I wonder briefly what the four of them would do if the monster bear who hates humans appeared in this meadow?

Answering my own question, "They would die."

If he does, I hope he eats the small ones first because they are again making too much noise and again throwing things at my ground squirrels.

Then, as they take the covers off the things they are eating, these four humans simply throw those covers on the ground around them and leave them there. My meadow is becoming a mess, but they have food, and I come out for some.

They do not even notice me. If the monster bear were here he would eat them easily. As I walk carefully toward them they fail to look around, not even noticing a predator has entered their territory. Unlike the two human hunters I admired as good predators, these humans have less survival sense than the average ground squirrel, and I certainly have eaten enough of those over the last few sets of seasons.

I walk toward them until they finally do notice me, too close for their safety if I would have been a larger predator. Then the high-pitched squeal of one of the small ones that brings their attention to me, and they all want to touch me!

Not feed me, to touch me!

I have not shared friendship or food with these, as I had with the two human hunters who were unlike these fools. Those two humans earned my friendship, but these are four fools in my forest, and they draw a quick, angry snarl as they try to reach for me. I am not some simple prey creature to be mauled by squealing, young humans!

They jump back, and I hear angry words from the male human.

I snarl at him also because he is breaking all the rules of dealing with my kind. I did not invite him here into my territory and am not his to touch or yell at. I snarl again, and he tries to bluff!

This one likes to bluff, he must live by bluff among his fellow humans, but I am not one of his fellow humans. I am a proud predator.

He picks up something small to throw at me when I do not move away from what is my territory, and he is a fool to do so. I do not bluff, and this time the snarl that rips from my throat is pure rage!

He stops the silly idea of throwing that small thing at me and backs off with the rest of his kind. They have been in my meadow long enough, and I am angry as he and the rest of his kind begin to move for their far too large human-carrying traveling thing until they are close enough to run for it, and safely inside it again.

I do not pursue because they are leaving, and this failure to pursue and keep them away from my territory almost kills me.

I underestimated how low this human one who likes to bluff was in terms of being a creature, the worms crawling upon the ground after the rain falls are above him. He tries to run over me!

He screams at me for calling his bluff; and screams at me as the round things the human-carrying traveling thing ride on spin in the too soft grassy ground of the meadow, get a grip on it at last, and it comes straight for me!

His fellow fool of a mate and squealing young scream what I can only feel is encouragement from inside the safety of the human-carrying traveling thing as he comes for me. He is a coward, too cowardly to fight me as a good predator would on the ground, one to one.

The grassy ground is soft after the rain has fallen so steadily for the last few days, and even though I am still sick, I can run fast enough to dodge the first pass as his too large carrying traveling thing spins around at high speed, sliding in the soft rain grass, as he comes for me again!

I barely dodge it this time, and he almost has me as he screams triumph! His young laugh from inside their cowardly safety, and that makes him more of a fool than he already is.

In his frenzy to show me who the real predator is, this bluffing fool turns his human-carrying traveling thing far too tightly at the speed it is moving now. As he spins again on the soft grass to come for me, the traveling thing slides sideways across that soft grass at high speed. The old, fallen burned tree of the fire from seasons ago is waiting for his human-carrying traveling thing, and for him.

I watch as the round spinning things on his sliding human-carrying traveling thing hit and dig into the fallen tree sideways.

I watch his face change from cowardly triumph to fear as he tries to turn it away, but obviously it is already too late to turn.

Fascinated, I watch as the bottoms of the round things it moves on bend inward from the high-speed impact with a loud crunching sound that does not sound good for them, as the still moving human-carrying traveling thing leans sideways over the fallen tree.

Watch fascinated as it continues leaning further across the fallen tree at its speed as the round things collapse inwards completely across the fallen tree with a much worse noise.

Watch as the lean becomes a fall to that side, and the tree fails to slow it down.

I listen to pathetic humans scream inside the human-carrying traveling thing, as it continues rolling sideways over the old fallen tree.

Watch as the sideways roll across the fallen tree finishes, and it hits the ground hard, sliding on its side.

I have never seen one of these things actually fall over something before. It is fascinating and just a little exciting to watch.

It also makes for a great deal of strange noises, and all the pathetic human wailing from inside is hard to listen to as I try to concentrate on watching this thing slide across my meadow now that it is all the way across the fallen burned tree, still sliding on the wet grass, leaving the round things it once rode upon and other pieces of itself behind, until it stops, and all the pathetic human crying becomes still.

I watch as they climb out of what was once a too large human-carrying traveling thing, and he begins yelling at me.

I am not sure why he yells at me. He and his own bluffing foolishness started this, but then I guess he does not consider that in life and perhaps gets away with it far too often to even consider that.

He and his foolish young did all the wrong things, and I guess that in his human world, this bluffing human coward is always right, and everyone else is always wrong no matter what he does.

He is still yelling at me with the rest of his pathetic humans, and still too cowardly to come over here to actually do something about it, when the brown human-carrying traveling thing enters the meadow with its colored light things flashing above it.

These human-carrying traveling things come through this meadow from time to time looking at the forest and visiting me, with humans wearing the brown coverings on their bodies riding in them.

I know these two humans, they were the same humans, who were outside my burrow seasons ago during the fire, trying to get me to leave, and the same two that then watched me walk out of all the burned area to go find new territory.

For some reason they come to visit me from time to time now that I have reclaimed my meadow and always seem excited to see me again every time they do, but I have never seen colored lights flashing above their traveling thing before.

The bluffing, cowardly human apparently feels that they are there to help him because he runs to them when they stop, points to me, and begins yelling at the two inside.

They do not like him for some reason. I can sense this from here. But he does not as he continues to yell. Then the two wearing the brown coverings on their bodies climb out of it and point to me, point to where his human-carrying traveling thing had left its tracks across the meadow where he tried to run over me with it twice, point to the mess he and his kind left in my meadow, and then point back into the forest from where they were watching all of this happen.

I saw them watching this meadow, waiting in the edge of the forest, inside their brown human-carrying traveling thing before I came over to these four fools. But the bluffing, cowardly human obviously did not see them waiting there and watching when he entered my meadow, made a mess of it, and then tried to run over me.

The two in brown put him against their brown carrying traveling thing, place his upper human paws behind his back in spite of his yelling and struggling, and fasten his human paws together with some shiny things.

When his mate yells at them and tries to stop them, they do her the same favor.

They then place him, his human mate, and the two loud-voiced, squealing young humans in the brown human-carrying traveling thing and take them away from the meadow.

He is still yelling, as is she, but I do not think the two humans wearing the brown coverings on their body really care. I just hope the two humans in brown who watch over this forest will come back later and get his broken human-carrying traveling thing out of my meadow. It ruins my view and frightens the ground squirrels I need for food.

They do, and with much more noise than I like, but at least they are removing it as another large human-carrying traveling thing finally manages to lift it after hooking something on to it and pulling it upright.

The side where it hit the ground and slid does not look the same as before, and the round things that hit the fallen tree have been left behind in the meadow, along with some other large things once connected to them.

This seems to give the people removing it some problems, until they finally give up and drop it, and bring in another larger human-carrying traveling thing with a large flat back and drag what is left, still on its side, on top of that to take it away.

It is in much worse shape after this, but at least it is gone, and my meadow is peaceful again.

I relax in the sunlight. Winter will be here soon, and then it will be time to play and have fun in the snow and time to think of the young that will arrive in springtime.

Names are already planned for them, and now is the last time to get grass from the meadow and make this burrow well lined and snug.

The grass of my meadow turns brown. The last of the trees that lose their leaves in winter drops its last leaf, and the sky overhead turns to darkness in daylight.

The first snow is falling as I finish making sure that this burrow will be the best ever for my arriving young when winter is over, and then go inside my snug well-lined sleeping chamber to rest and wait for spring to come again, as the first snow begins to fall outside.

It is the same as the many winters, not as harsh as the bad one or as mild as a good one, just a winter.

I play in the snow, throwing it around me joyfully with nose and paws, play on the top of the stream after it becomes clear and hard, sliding back and forth, shrieking like some pathetic prey!

I hunt for food, making my body nice and plump for my arriving young. I sleep more and more as the winter moves onward, until it becomes warmer and the snow begins to melt as the stream does its yearly thing of becoming a roaring, dangerous place to be around, and I drink from the melting snow instead.

I go out to hunt, and then stay in the burrow to wait for the first signs of movement inside my body, and wait.

The days pass into warmer ones and I wait. There is nothing.

The days pass and I wait, there is still nothing. I do not grow as plump as I should.

There is no movement, there is nothing.

Instead of gaining weight I begin to lose it as I would do every season after the winter was gone, and my young were grown past my needing to feed them from my body.

I wait, and finally realize that it did not happen. I mated, but there are no young, and no young to use the names I selected, no young to admire, feed, groom, and love. This set of seasons there will be nothing until next spring, if I even find a mate this set of seasons.

I feel disappointed and still hope, but it still does not happen as days and nights pass, and I do not know what to do in the days or the nights. After my first set of seasons alone, there were always young to care for in this season. Now what is there to do each new day? I am so bored.

The season passes into the hot one with no young to share it with, and it is certain by now that there will be no young this set of seasons. Just going through the nights hunting and the days relaxing or sleeping is lonely.

I have never been this bored before, and then I give up and begin roaming to find the two fellow huntresses that were once my daughters, Ankusha and Ammavaru.

Since they probably did not have young either, they will be lonely also. We will hunt together for a while if they do not object to me entering their territory, the territory that once was the territory of the monster bear.

The monster is gone, I check very carefully on that while entering this dangerous territory. Deer have returned and roam in large groups, so the monster bear is not hunting here as he did before. He is not here, but the faint scent of Ankusha and Ammavaru is, and I roam eagerly through the forest to find them. As I had hoped, they have stayed together and are roaming together.

While there is happiness that Ankusha and Ammavaru are both here together and safe, there is also a growing sense of sadness inside as I seek them, and there are other scents with the two of them now, small scents.

They have young, Ankusha or Ammavaru, or both have young with them. The mating worked for at least one of them, but not for me.

There is a feeling of sadness as I realize that they will expect me to show them my young also when we meet.

They have young, but I do not, and it is strange to know that my two huntresses did better than their mother did this season. They will be able to show me their young, but I have nothing to show them.

I try to decide whether to turn back and leave instead, but I want to see Ankusha and Ammavaru again so much, so continue anyway with a feeling of almost shame as I near them.

The feeling of shame grows more uncomfortable as I greet them where they wait, their teeth and claws ready for the one they hear moving through the brush toward them and their young.

I have trained them well. Despite my quietness in the forest, Ankusha and Ammavaru both heard me coming, and stand ready to protect their young. They move to keep their bodies between their young and the sounds they hear approaching, moving also to get the wind in the right place so they will have the advantage of having my scent before any predator could scent them fully with young alongside.

I move slightly as I approach to give them the downwind scent so they will know before I come too close, and sense them relaxing in front of me as they remember who their mother is.

Smiling at that thought and coming out into the open through the brush, I notice approvingly that they still have their teeth and claws ready to fight just in case the scent they have is a trick of some predator.

They see me fully, and we all greet joyfully together, to see fellow huntresses after our too long absence from each other, and I feel jealous. Ankusha and Ammavaru both have young, and those young are so beautiful and perfect!

As they had left me together, so they have done this together, but so differently at the same time, Ankusha has two perfect young females while Ammavaru has two perfect young males.

We greet and roam together, as they tell of the season since they had left to take this territory for theirs.

They have survived well here indeed; the bear has not returned, and the foolish humans in their fear of him probably killed all the other smaller black bears that might have been here. Ankusha and Ammavaru now have all of this area to themselves.

Prey is plentiful without other competing predators, except for hawks, and owls, and an occasional fox roaming through.

They both remembered what I had told them about having their first young: fattening themselves up nicely before winter came, to be ready for the spring and birth, staying together in the same burrow to have them, enlarging the sleeping chamber as necessary.

When I had to leave to hunt for myself and my young, I always worried about leaving them alone back in the burrow, but Ankusha and Ammavaru take turns hunting, so their young will always have one to care for and protect them when the other one is gone from the burrow.

I wish I had young to show them, but do not and will not this season, maybe next year. For now I am content to roam with my two very adult huntresses as we seek new things in the forest to train their young.

There is pride in my two huntresses. Both Ankusha and Ammavaru have remembered their lessons well, and train perfectly as we roam. Their young have passed the stumbling-all-over-their-own-paws stage of life already, as they follow us, listening to each instruction.

Only then do I realize how little I am needed here as I try to introduce new instructions to their young ones, showing those young the trees and plants with instruction on each, and getting the uncomfortable feeling that what I am telling these young is something that Ankusha and Ammavaru have already covered.

Ankusha and Ammavaru look embarrassed more and more often as their young pay less and less attention to the new one among them and more attention to their own mothers.

These young ones almost ignore me as we walk, and I love them so much because they are the young of my young, and I want to walk with them, to watch them grow, to teach them new things.

Then I realize that I am invading the territory of my own young to do this. I am not needed here.

The day is not nearly over when I make my excuses to go. They do love me, and we did enjoy meeting again, but they need to teach their own young how to survive without me around because I am only in their way. Neither Ankusha nor Ammavaru said as much while we walked together, but that is the way it is.

I leave, trying not to feel sad as I look back one last time in farewell before entering the forest again.

Ankusha and Ammavaru are already roaming to another lesson with their young as they go their own way away from me, and I wish that I had not bothered to come here. Now I am even lonelier than before. My own young do not need me to help them teach their young.

I shake it off. A true predator does not think like this. They are adults and must roam their own lives, teach their own young, and survive on their own without me. It does not help the sad feeling that my young have young, and I do not.

My first thought is to roam back to the hillock burrow to stay there until a mate can find me, or I can find a mate this season, but the thought of maybe seeing another of my young comes. My Akna has territory not too far from here with a handsome mate attending to her the last time I saw her.

I turn toward shy little Akna's territory, remembering that it has been almost two full sets of seasons since we last saw each other.

Akna is not so little anymore, and the last time I saw her she didn't look that shy with her new chosen mate either. Her territory will have to be approached cautiously if she has forgotten me, or I may look like a rival for that territory.

I roam and enter her territory, scenting approvingly that she has remembered to mark it well to protect it from rivals or other intruders, and then feel sad again.

From the scents Akna has young also and out is roaming with them. I wish that I could have had young again, and I wonder if she will have no use for me either as I close the distance between us, downwind, while moving toward her.

Maybe I should just turn, return to my own territory, and give up the idea of seeing any former young again, but that thought only increases the lonely feeling inside me. I will follow Akna's scent trail for a little while, just to see her from the shelter of the brush.

She does not even have to know that I am here. Just a look at her and her young is enough to see how she and they are doing, and then I will leave.

I follow the scent of my once little Akna, hoping that she will want to see me again and maybe let me play with her young and teach them a little. It would be so nice to be able to teach again.

The distance between us closes, until anger suddenly rides into me as my teeth show and claws make ready to kill! I speed up; another roams here, he roams behind them, and he is not good!

He is also downwind from them as my Akna roams with her young, and he has the advantage. Akna will not be able to smell him until he makes his attack.

He follows her quietly as I run as quietly as possible to where they will be when he meets them.

Many seasons of being a predator and avoiding other predators have taught me well. I know what he will try, and roughly where he will try it. I have met this one before and he will die here today. This is the angry human's dog that had been dumped on our forest and gone wild.

This was the dog I saw after leaving the valley of death, the savage one that had killed one of his own before I found both him and the rest of his poorly trained pack, the one who was trying to teach those more by force than by experienced training.

He will find his own valley of death here today, as I wonder briefly where the rest of his pack is, but that is not important, the only thing that is important now is that this is the most vicious of them.

Then I know where the rest of pack is. I have their scents at last. They run to the sides of him. He has trained them well after all. He has trained them to circle; they will attack from the sides, at the same time he will deliberately show himself to her. Seeing only him she will turn to face him, unaware that others run with him.

I feel sick as I run, dropping the need for caution to just run, not caring if I make noise now, I must get to her before they do.

They are too many. I count at least five scents to my sides and his scent in front as I run frantically to where they will all meet.

"The wind is wrong! The wind is wrong! Turn and find the wind, Akna!"

She can't smell them coming with the wind blowing the wrong way, and she roams in the open with her young!

There are more than six. Someone is coming up behind me!

I run faster. I will distract all of them and give her the time to find a burrow. I may die, but she will not!

I hope that she remembers what I had taught her about digging under tree roots or large rocks, she can have a chance there. They won't be able to dig her out, and as they stick their ugly noses unto her burrow, she can bite them off!

Someone is still coming up faster behind me, at least two, running as fast as myself. No, even faster than me; they will close the distance too quickly, and the wind is wrong for me also. I can't count how many more dogs are behind me, but I will die distracting them, so she can run with her young!

The ones behind me run wrong for long-legged human dogs gone wild. The noises of their running are wrong, and they have dropped all caution like me to close the distance as rapidly as possible. They run wrong, and they are not dogs!

Twin growls of rage come from behind me to identify themselves before they come too close and a mistake is made. I suddenly realize that we three hunt as three huntresses again. Ankusha and Ammavaru have come to kill with me!

They have scented these that do not belong here from the edges of their territory and came to find where and what this thing is. I have told them of dogs gone wild and they have both my scent and the scents of the dogs in their noses, but do not know who is in front, and think the dogs are after me!

They catch me, and do not question as we three run where the scents of badger and badger young lead. We run to kill those that threaten our kind!

They do tell me of their own young being sent deep into a burrow for safety as they came to find their mother.

They came to find me because they were sorry for being impatient with me being there, remembering guiltily that I had trained them and that we were three huntresses together until they left for their own lives.

They found my scent, and the others', and did not know who was in front, but came to see who threatened their mother.

Now we three huntresses run without fear as we come together into the trail of the dogs gone wild. We run to kill them, and the dogs are not well trained by their vicious leader. He forgets to check his back trail from time to time. We have surprise.

He thinks that he and his kind run for a single adult badger and her young, but he will find four adult badger huntresses ready to protect those young with their lives, and ready to kill for those young instead.

We three huntresses run for him as in front of us he finds her, and I hear Akna's scream of rage as she puts her young behind her, and the dogs attack as we break through the edge of the forest.

I notice approvingly through my rage that Akna is doing a good job for only one. My full-grown, no-longer-shy Akna rages and rips at the air with her claws as the dog's leader stands in front of her bluffing attack.

He had not taken enough time to train them how to rush. They should all have rushed as soon as he distracted her from in front and not waited to see if he was ready for them to rush.

These are very poorly trained predators, indeed, as they come from the sides too late. Akna tries to turn from where he stands in front of her. And my Akna suddenly realizes that there are too many dogs to fight, and she and her young are dead.

I note approvingly again that Akna does not flee in spite of this. She tries to take all of them instead, ripping her body from side to side as they all rush, trying to turn at least some of them from her young as she fights the rest to the death.

She does not have to fight to the death for them or herself. Screaming rage and running hard, Ankusha, Ammavaru, and I rush them together!

The dogs only have time to look up and realize that a terrible mistake has been made by them, not us. Then they also suddenly realize that they no longer fight just a single young female badger with her young to defend.

They now face four enraged female badgers, and the badger is one of the fiercest creatures in the forest, as we run for them, not from them. They are larger and taller, six to our four, and we do not care, we are female badgers, and they are dead!

I hunt for the leader, rushing him across this clearing. Seven full sets of seasons hunting, and all my instincts tell me that if the leader of these dies quickly, the others may run.

I do not have to kill him or them, and he has already realized the mistake. For a leader he is also a coward as he breaks and runs while the others also realize that the one they chose as leader is in full run to be anywhere we four are not, and the others also decide that a badger's young are not worth dying for today.

They should have thought of that before they tried to kill one of us or one of our young. None of these are true forest predators, they are just poorly trained human dogs dumped on my forest and gone wild.

We chase anyway, in hopes of having one of them for food, but only as far as we need to before we return where Akna comforts her young beside her and waits for us. And now we are four huntresses together.

We four huntresses are exhausted and did not realize it until now, yet we four huntresses are also extremely proud of ourselves. We came to fight four against six and won in spite of the six being larger and taller.

I have a feeling that my fellow huntresses will never stop telling their young of this day, especially not Ankusha, who reminds me that I did not actually kill mine, only frightened him away. Then I remind her that he may still die from fright in the forest.

Still she is right in a way. I am older now, and the speed was not there when I tried to claw him, I should have had him, but he escaped. Also, I was out of breath more than I should have been when we finished the run to this place. I used to be able to run longer and not be out of breath like this.

There is a little worry in this, but Akna has such beautiful young that the worry is quickly forgotten as we admire her two little ones.

One is a beautiful little female, and the other a perfect male. My formerly shy little Akna grooms her two perfect young ones to comfort them, and they try to understand where these other adult badgers came from, and who they are.

Akna tells them of the only one of us she knows.

I wonder, "Do all of my young have two each time they have young?"

My Akna has grown well, and her young have finally gotten over their curiosity about me being their mother's mother and are rolling all over me in a fierce game of trying to show us how they too could have fought the dogs by themselves without our help.

Akna tries to get them back into some kind of listening order, and then tells us proudly of them.

They hunt already, under her supervision, of course, for their own prey, and dig well for their age. The fact that they showed no fear in front of the dogs and stayed with their mother tells us already that these will be perfect little predators when they grow into adults.

No other predator will touch these when they are grown, although I do remind them to beware of the huge brown bear if he comes back into this territory. Akna has already told them of him, but I remind them anyway.

Somehow our lives seem linked, the monster bear's and mine, and if he can always find me, and roam back to where I am now, he will be far too close to the ones I love.

We roam for a while as a group, until Ankusha and Ammavaru have to return to their own young who sit waiting deep inside a snug burrow under the roots of a tree.

Their young are well trained and will still be in that burrow when Ankusha and Ammavaru return, but there is always worry when leaving young alone, and they want to go home.

I see them both off with the same instruction I gave them when they left me to roam on their own for their own lives, "Survive!"

Then give them each a last grooming, and a softer "I am proud of you," as they turn to leave.

They leave, and I am lonely again as they both enter the forest to return to their own territory.

Still, I have Akna and her young to admire, and she seems reluctant to see me leave, so we roam together and teach her young together as the season moves into the hotter one.

Her young grow larger under both our instruction, and I am no longer lonely as I stay to roam with the ones I love.

Seasons

We roam as Akna's young learn all the things they should watch out for in the forest, and the predators that might take them, the plants they should not taste for they might be sick if they do, and as we return from our nightly hunts, they learn of frogs and other easy-to-catch things that might taste good in the hunt.

We roam as they learn of the hard-to-catch prey things, and how to find and hunt those hard-to-catch prey things.

They learn of how to ambush beside the stream when prey comes to drink, and how to blend our bodies into the shadows, using the shadows of darker stripes mixed into our fur, and to both hide from predators and to ambush prey from other shadows.

We return to the burrow from training them, and rest as Akna's young listen, fascinated, to the stories of Akna's life since leaving me, and stories that teach from experience, one of the best things to train from.

Her young also listen to the stories of my experiences. Some of those stories make Akna look at me strangely as she listens with her young. I tell them of the huge brown bear, of roaming into his actual den with Ankusha and Ammavaru, and how I escaped him from the burrow when he tried to dig me out of so many seasons ago.

Akna already knows of him, and tells them of the night we ran from him and how Asiaq stood in front of Alarana to defend her even if he had no chance to defend her from one as large as this, and that teaches them of courage in the face of death.

They have already seen their mother Akna stand in front of the six dogs, and without fear to defend them, even if she thought there was no real chance to survive. That teaches them to defend their own young.

I tell them of the valley of the angry human, and of the prey-creature rabbit that was not really a prey-creature rabbit, with black fur that was not good to look upon too closely, and eyes of fire.

I tell them of the ones in that valley of the shadows of death, who ran in moonlight from something long gone into the past, as they themselves were long gone into the past.

I tell them of the small young female rabbit that threw herself against the stone of the wall over and over as the fire came for her, until she found a hole in it large enough to fit through. And I know that of all the creatures I saw that night she lived, and it was only a dream or memory to her. If she relived it again in her dreams after that, someday she might be able to use it in her own fight.

I wonder if she found a safe burrow to live in again, free from fire and death and fear, and wonder if the black-furred rabbit of the black fur and terrible fire eyes still waits patiently at the hole he could not fit thorough.

I am certain he does wait and is still watching by the wall for vengeance, for who can kill that which is already dead?

I still shiver as I remember that former prey creature, which is now a more terrible predator than I will ever be. As a predator myself I have known patience while waiting for prey, but never that type of endless, unnatural, lethal patience, waiting to bring vengeance for all the dead of that valley.

Then I dismiss these memories after telling Akna's young of them. I do not want to remember that night or that valley too clearly.

Instead, I tell them of the other four who were brothers and sisters alongside Akna, and of Asiaq and Alarana, how they grew alongside Akna, and how they died for no good reason, just so some human could have their fur for vanity.

I tell them how I loved Asiaq and Alarana as much as their own mother Akna loves them, and how I mourned the untimely deaths, and how the human who took the fur of my young died before I could kill him.

I tell them how I lived in the burrow overlooking the large water, how large it was, and of the sunsets that passed over the green hills on the other side.

I tell of the things that arced up into the sky when it rained into sunshine over the large water, the curving things of bands of colors, and how I loved to sit with my other young and watch this happen. I tell of hunting in the area around the large water, and how easy it was to find food there.

But then I also have to tell Akna's young of my poor starved Kekuit who did not learn how to hunt well enough to survive a harsh winter, and how I found Kekuit dead in the snow after he called with a voice that came into my head, not my ears.

I tell how Kekuit tried to crawl through a barren field of snow to return to the only one he truly knew could hunt, the only one who might have been able to find him the food to allow him to live for more seasons.

This is a harsh tale for them, but a valuable lesson in why their mother and I spend so much time teaching them to hunt.

I tell Akna's young of my two huntresses Cetnenn and Caoineag who are still inside that burrow overlooking the large water where I told them to wait for my return before they could leave the burrow.

It is a lesson to these two young of Akna, of why they should always let their mother know at once if they feel the slightest bit sick in the burrow, so she can stay to care for them and keep them warm and safe from the death that sneaks into the burrow without warning to take the ones you love away from you.

This is a lesson for Akna also. We die too often and too easily in the forest, and I do not want this for the young of my young Akna.

Akna's young listen as I teach through the stories of life in the forest before we sleep.

I have seen the seventh spring of my life now, and the seventh summer of it is now here. Akna's young grow larger as they listen while we hunt.

We hunt, and I teach them how to survive in this forest and how to avoid the humans, for while some humans are good, others are bad and a danger to us and our kind.

I tell them of the two humans who hunt the forest like we do, the ones who wore the human body coverings that resembled the shapes and colors of things in the forest, and how these two humans understand the forest as we do, and do not take more than they need from it when they hunt in our forest.

I teach the young of Akna that these two had been good to me when I met them, but others with the same killing sticks that kill from a distance may not be good, and humans should be avoided unless you are sure of them.

These young of my young understand the instruction clearly, and they understand that the angry human of the valley was not like the two humans I knew.

They also understand that the human who killed my Alarana and Asiaq was not like the two who understood the forest as they hunted, and shared with me each time we met when we crossed trails in our hunting. The humans who do not kill simply to kill like the angry human of the valley.

The angry human of the valley hunted everything out of anger, pride, and the arrogant belief that he was the master of all with the power to kill from a distance, and who intended to use that power, without worrying about the consequences.

One of those consequences is patiently waiting for him to come to the wall again, when an innocent one arrives there at the same time.

I tell them of the fearful humans who tried to kill the monster brown bear, and who made too many mistakes in judgment because they feared, and because they also did not know the forest and its creatures well enough not to fear what they hunted.

Those humans in fear, and the bad judgment caused by fear; killed the wrong bear then went away foolishly, satisfied that they had killed the right bear while the right bear still roams to kill again.

I told them how humans like these should also be avoided because they kill what they do not need to kill.

Only when the young of Akna fully understand that some humans kill without reason from anger, foolish pride, and vanity am I satisfied about finishing this lesson, but then I also have to tell the young of Akna's brother who died because of this.

I tell her for the first time about her brother Atsentma and how he died, and she sorrows with me as she had sorrowed when I told her of her other sister and brother, Alarana and Asiaq.

Her young wait for us to begin again, and then we tell them of how they will find a place of few badgers, in the direction that was empty of badgers, when they leave her.

It will be a good direction to go in, and there they will find new territory not claimed by other badgers.

Some badgers will wander there eventually to reclaim it for our kind, and why not Akna's. That territory had plenty of prey inside it because of the few predators left inside it by the human who took the fur of others and upset the balance of forest by killing all the predators there, which would mean that prey creatures, unchecked by the natural balance of predators, would eventually eat their way to starvation.

These young of Akna's will not starve there as my poor Kekuit had starved. Instead, they will help restore the balance inside that territory, along with the other predators that will find their way back.

They are almost grown now as the hot season moves toward the time of leaving, and it will be soon, as they listen while I tell of Akna's other brother Aataentsic and how he went to find the place of the large water for himself because he loved water so much and was fascinated by my stories of that place.

I hope that he found it and now lives in peace, where I could no longer live after my two little huntresses died there.

I teach until the season to leave is here.

We go out at dusk.

Akna's young female looks back at us, turns and leaves to find her own trail in the forest and her own territory, and I sense the sadness from Akna.

We go out at dusk.

Akna's young male leaves in the same direction, to find the territory of no badgers his sister had left for, and to claim that territory with her.

The young of my young are now gone as Akna cries her loss softly, and I try to console her with the reminder that there will be more young to train again in her life.

It is not consolation to her, as it was never a consolation to me every time my own young left me to find their own way inside the forest.

We return to the burrow together, it seems pointless to remain out and hunt tonight.

We go out at dusk.

I groom my daughter with pride at how strong and adult she has become and leave while she stays to wait for her mate to return in this season, to find her again, and give her more young to love in the next springtime.

I wish to find my own mate without intruding on either her mate or her territory; it is time to roam again, as I begin roaming toward the area where the two hunters had roamed.

I am lonely again, and they were very generous with deer the last two times we met, and perhaps this time there will be something to share again, if they are in the woods and hunting again.

Deer is a rare treat for one such as I, who can't ambush a creature that large or run them down with speed, and even if there was the speed to do it, the size is still something to think of, and the fighting ability of deer is often misjudged by those who do not know them.

Deer have those antlers if they are male, and I have seen them fighting for mates in the season of mating.

They fight with power when they use those antlers, and my mother, Asaseyaa, once taught me that during each new mating season in the forest, male deer hurt foolish humans who misjudge them as creatures.

In the mating season, the males will often stand to fight anything they think to be a threat to territory or rival in dominance for mate. Humans approach what they think is a magnificent creature, just waiting for them to pet it, because the male deer stands without fear of humans. Without bothering to ask themselves why any wild creature of the forest would simply be standing and waiting for a human to come near it.

In all the sets of seasons, it is the only season when the male deer fears nothing and sees everything as potential rivals for mates or power.

Humans approach without thinking, and then wonder why they have a set of deer antlers newly planted inside their human bodies.

Both males and females of deer also weigh far more than humans would think. Although the deer's looks are delicate, the hooves of a deer are strong, sharp, and deadly.

My mother, Asaseyaa, once told me those hooves can kill a wolf, and male or female, all deer use their hooves for survival against enemies.

They can easily drive those hooves into a human body if they are panicked by a human, or if they think that a human traps them.

Still the two humans who I know have the power of the killing sticks, know deer, and have already shown that they will share with me if they have taken deer, so I roam hopefully to where they hunt in the forest.

It is the right season and they might have something to share this season. I roam to find them and hear the crack sound in front of me. Smiling with satisfaction, I know there will be deer to share tonight.

But it is not the two humans that I know by scent, it is another, and he and his friends are already working on the deer he has taken.

I sigh with disappointment, watching them take all of it away in some human-carrying traveling thing. I do not even get the parts humans throw away this time. I roam again, still looking for the ones I know.

It simply didn't occur to me to show myself to these other humans as they were working on this deer. These are new humans, and I do not know if they are bad or good humans.

I only know that they have the power of the killing sticks with them, and I will not show myself to humans I do not know, remembering what happened with the frightened humans hunting the bear that had killed my Atsentma.

Other humans are in the forest hunting also this season, but I do not know them either, and drift silently through the shadows near them without their awareness, seeking the two that I look forward to seeing again.

Until suddenly, I realize that what I really want is not the deer meat they had given me, I just want to see them again.

I miss Akna and her young already, and it will be spring at least before I have my own young, if I even find a mate again this season. There may not be a mate for me, and that will mean no new young this next spring, and I am lonely already.

I want to see someone I know again, even if they are only humans. I roam, and they find me instead.

The crack comes as I move cautiously to near where it came from is and find scent. The scent is the right one this time and I close in, until someone beside me in the brush coughs and they smile as I jump defensively to the side!

They fooled me; they hid after taking the deer and waited for me as if they both knew I would be here again this year, and wanted to have fun with me.

I snarl at both of them where they sit concealed downwind, after backtracking from the deer I see on the ground in front of me.

While this is fun to them, it is deadly serious to me. If they had been predators, they would have had me!

They both make comforting mouth noises to me as if they realize what they had done was not fun for me, and they also move slowly enough when they come out from concealment.

But I am still upset with them, until one of them throws me one of those small, round, delicious things again, and the desire to eat it overrides the desire to eat both of them.

I eat and watch them as they move back to the deer, and wonder where the human-carrying traveling thing is that will take most of it away like before, as I watch the two humans take this deer apart and wrap it in things.

The large above-ground den humans stay in is not here either. I am curious as to what they can possibly do with this entire deer they are now loading onto a flat thing, until they begin to drag it away on that flat, soft thing together, and then it becomes obvious they have a forest den elsewhere.

I follow. Deer is deer, and I am both hungry and practical about this. If they take it elsewhere, then they will prepare it elsewhere, and I want some of it.

I follow until we reach the place where the large, brown, above-ground den is waiting, and wait curiously to see what new thing these humans will do this time with food, instead of eating it immediately like decent predators would. Until the human-carrying traveling thing arrives with the third human I had seen the first time I met these two.

I drift carefully back into the forest to watch from concealment as they load the larger part of the deer with the head and antlers onto it until they are finished, and then the two humans I know call in the direction I am watching.

I am not some human's thing to be called like that, but they do have the deer, and being practical about this, I finally come out to the amazement of the third one.

He seems to find it strange and somehow exciting that one such as I would be with his friends, but if they have treated me well in the past, why should I not come to see them?

He seems even more amazed when I sit between the two humans I know and wait for all of this to end so we can eat, letting the one who touched me the first time we met carefully touch me again, and then stroke my fur as I sit contentedly, waiting for these foolish humans to stop being amazed over me and get to the food.

That seems to make their friend even more excited as he cautiously reaches out to me from the side, which is nice of him, since reaching from the front is a threat to me, and I allow him to stroke me as his friends do.

This seems to make him really excited at both his friends and myself, and I begin to wonder if I will have to bite someone instead of eating food today. They finally stop stroking me, and he leaves with the rest of the deer in the human-carrying traveling thing, looking back as he leaves, as if still unable to believe I came to find his friends again.

Humans seem to be easily amazed, but then they are only humans after all, and I have already learned that they often do not have good sense in the forest. These two who remain do have good sense in the forest, and now they have the good sense to prepare the important part, my food.

We eat, and it is as good as the last time I met these two, and then we simply sit together by the fire as I let them both stroke me from either side because it pleases me to do so, and it feels good.

We sleep at last, and they go into the strange, above-ground den to sleep, while I stay outside listening to the sounds of the night forest, full and happy, then I decide to see just how these humans sleep in the forest, wander inside to look.

The strangeness of entering a human den makes me cautious, but they both sleep soundly and are not a threat.

It is even stranger that, unlike us, they do not simply sleep on the ground, and these two sleep on either side of this strange above-ground den, wrapped in some kinds of thing that go around them as far up as their heads.

I investigate first one then the other as they snore, unaware that I am inside with them. Then moving around in curiosity to see the rest of this den, I find some nice food things they neglected to tell me about.

Eating those nice food things while the humans sleep, before remembering to groom each of them for the consideration they have shown me, but stop when it becomes obvious that my tongue across their faces is beginning to awaken them. Then I simply plop my full body down below them to sleep myself.

When they wake, they seem to be very surprised to find me there, but yesterday proved that humans can surprise easily, and sometimes for no understandable reason, so I simply wander out to wait for them to eat again.

We eat, and then spend the day roaming the forest together, eating again at the end of the day. They watch this time after they go into the above-ground human den and are less surprised when I wander inside, and then after nicer stroking from these two, we sleep with me near them again.

Just before it is light outside I groom them again as they sleep and leave to roam for home. There are enough badgers returning to this area now for a mate to roam through my territory soon, and the best place to see a new mate roaming will be from on top the fallen tree on my little hillock in my meadow.

I have been away too long, and there are things to do if it is to be a good burrow for new young this coming spring. Old, dry grass has to be pulled out and replaced with fresh thick layers of new grass to make a comfortable sleeping chamber, and the entrance needs more work.

My territory also has to be re-marked with new scent to say, "This is mine." I work on the burrow, hunt in the meadow, and wait for a mate to arrive.

It shouldn't be necessary to roam for a mate, at least one should find this meadow by himself, and after all, it is on the stream that flows from north to south, a perfectly good path to roam.

I wait patiently, watching from on top of my little hillock in my meadow, and wait more, and wait more, and sigh impatiently, wondering if I made a mistake in returning here . . . until I see him coming through the meadow in the fresh light of the new day.

Checking the scents I have left for him, I follow them, trying to see if he can find his new mate for this season.

I smile as I recognize him from on top my fallen tree, on top of this little hillock, in the center of what is mine. He has a poor memory. It is Sesondowah, the one that I took terrible advantage of with Ankusha and Ammavaru.

I go to meet him in the meadow sunlight. Sesondowah was good the last time I met him, but I really have to refresh his memory.

We meet, and he recognizes me again, but still can't outrun me in spite of my greater age. He really needs some more experience, but he will do nicely for now, especially after I manage to convince him that Ankusha and Ammavaru are not with me this time.

That makes him less nervous and we mate in all the growls, fur fluffing, circling, and trying to impress each other that is part of our kind's mating.

He is very nice, and we return to my burrow together to discuss this further as we stay there to mate often and well.

We mate and hunt together, and he is very nice indeed as we share food, sit in the sun outside the burrow before the day ends, and then go to hunt again.

We stay together, until he makes his excuses as the males of our kind do, and I watch him leave through the meadow to return to his own territory.

I am satisfied. There will be young born this next spring, and there is still time to make myself nice and plump for the winter coming before that spring.

The leaves of the trees are already shifting from green to reds and yellows as I hunt and feast. I make myself nice and round while the leaves fall more and more, and then the sky above turns darker, and the first flakes of white begin to fall.

The winter is neither better nor worse than other winters, it is just simply winter.

I wait for the spring and for new young to begin growing inside me after spring comes again. I play in the snow and on top of the frozen stream as the winter and I pass our time together.

Following prey in the moonlight while it shines on the nighttime snow more for fun than for need, I am more than plump enough. Feeding was good this last season.

I roam in sunlight for sun warmth and sleep in darkness, waiting for the first signs of spring to come, until the sun starts to turn the snow into water, and the small plants begin to peek through the melting snow to turn green again. I enjoy the first day of spring one more time.

This is the eighth spring of my life as the stream once again becomes something not good to be too close to while it eats its banks in rushing water and flows south to where I already know it flows over the top of the hill near my burrow there, into the large water in a fall of roaring water, and that reminds me of the home I had there, and that makes me lonely again.

I remember fondly of the time that my little Atsentma tried to go swimming by lack of caution and accident in the stream near this hillock, and how I rescued him. Then remember sadly that Atsentma had died because of a human mistake in judgment.

Then the sad memory passes while I wait happily to begin feeling the first movements of new young inside me.

I wait as both meadow and forest around it turn to green, the spring moves fully into new life, and all the creatures that have young in the spring begin to celebrate the new life they have given to forest and meadow, and their young come forth from inside them, all of them, except myself.

There is no new life inside me and I realize sadly that once again there will be a full set of seasons with no new young. I wonder if I should go to Akna's territory again to see her and share time with her young as I had the last set of seasons.

Then forgetting that idea because Akna will look at me with sorrow, no matter how much she loves me, when she sees I have no young again.

Of course, Akna would let me stay in this season of birth and new growth to help her train and protect her new young, but I can't stand the look of sorrow she will give me. It is better to stay here than to see that look in my daughter's eyes.

My Ankusha and Ammavaru would let me come see them and their young, but the looks would be there also, and so I stay in my own burrow. I am barren, and there may never be young for me ever again.

The spring moves into a deeper green while I watch the fawns play with their kind in the meadow, watch the ground squirrels emerge from their burrows with their own young. They are only prey, but I am still jealous of them as they roam not too far from the burrows to explore and play with their young.

I watch the birds returning to their nests in the trees around my meadow as their young lift little mouths to receive the food brought back to them. I watch the foxes drift through the meadow in sunlight with their young, teaching those young the hunting of prey, as I had taught my own young. I watch the owls drift silently overhead in the darkness while roaming at night for food, watch them find their own food and bring it back to their young in the trees.

The days consist of sleeping and sometimes catching the sunlight before roaming at night, and the nights are for roaming and finding food.

The spring passes while all those that have young to care for and love move around me in daylight and darkness, and I simply roam among them, trying not to be too bored by the alone, looking for a mate far too early in the season, and hoping that the next spring will bring me more small ones to care for again, and suspecting that it will not matter how many mates I take this season.

The season passes into the hot one, and I miss seeing my own young grow while watching the young deer begin to fight with each other. Not seriously yet, just the same learning games my own small young would play in the burrow around me, the games that will allow them to learn how to survive and have their own territory someday.

But soon what is now only playful cracking of small antlers in mock fighting fun will turn to the solid cracks of antlers for real as they fight to have mates, and have their own young in the next full sets of seasons.

The plants brown around me in the full heat of the hot season, and the stream dries but is still there for us as we roam to hunt and feed. The forest dries and browns more in heat and lack of rain from the sky, and the stream becomes less in the heat until we all search for water in the stream together.

Predator and prey alike, we all need the water. As the stream dries we form an uneasy truce with each other to get the last of what used to be a stream.

Predator and prey alike, we thirst together as the stream dries and becomes nothing in the heat.

As both predator and prey, some of the creatures begin to drift away to find a new source of life before they die of thirst at what used to be the old one, our stream.

Until one day when the white things that drift across the sky turn darker overhead, turn darker still, and mass into one dark mass, blocking the sunlight and the rain falls heavily in daylight as I watch from my entrance tunnel.

I watch and see grass, ground, and forest soak it up as all the creatures of forest and meadow celebrate the coolness of it falling on them, and the return of the green that follows falling rain as the stream comes to life again for all of us.

The stream grows larger with more rain from the sky, and the rain continues to fall steadily, until the stream roars from the runoff as the rain continues to fall, and begins to eat its banks again.

I watch as the small chipmunk that was too careless falls into the stream as the stream bank collapses beneath him, when he should have been going to the rain's runoff to drink instead.

I watch as he is driven downstream by the force of the water and see him go under the force of that water.

I watch as he comes up again, screaming in the rushing water around his helpless body, and he goes under again, comes up screaming less, goes under again, and then does not come up again.

I watch his mother stand watching in sorrow at the stream bank as she sees him go away from her, and I remember the time Atsentma had fallen into it.

I could kill the chipmunk's mother easily; her attention is totally distracted from any danger around her as she watches downstream for him to swim out of it. But both of us know that he will never come out ever again.

I could catch her, but I will not. I sit in my entrance instead watching and sorrowing with her. She has lost what I could not have this season. She will die someday when her attention to danger wanders when it should not; but it will not be today, and it will not be from me.

The summer changes into the season of leaves on trees that lose their leaves each year. Only reds and yellows so far in the leaf colors, but those will soon fall and turn browns on the floor of the forest around my meadow.

The season of winter death is coming, and except the trees that are green all the seasons in this forest, most of the other plants will die for the winter, but most will come back to green again in the spring.

It is beautiful to see as it always is, but I have no young to share it with, and the season passes alone.

The seasons seem to pass so quickly now that I lose track and wonder where they have gone, and wonder where my former young are. But I do have a lover again, the same lover as this last set of seasons and the set of seasons before that.

Sesondowah has returned, more experienced this time, and fully aware I am here waiting for him to arrive.

This time there is no chase involved, and we simply share our burrow together and mate, and I hope each time we mate that it will give me young again.

Then he makes his excuses, as the males of our kind do, and I see him off again as Sesondowah roams away from me, moving south in the meadow for another territory.

This is the third time that he and I have been companions in mating, and I know that we are comfortable with each other, and he will return in this next set of seasons so we can mate again.

And if I cannot have young by him this next spring, then perhaps the spring after that will work for us, and I am comforted by that thought while Sesondowah roams south into the forest at the edge of the meadow.

I never see him alive again.

The leaves of the trees turn to darker colors and begin to drop as I roam to fatten myself for the coming winter, and for some reason the memory of my dead little Kekuit keeps returning, along with a strange feeling that he will return to me again after all.

But that is impossible. He died seasons ago, and it has been seasons since, and he could not possibly return. I try to shrug the feeling off, but it persists.

Still the reminder of how he died is good in a way, and it helps me focus on preparing for what is coming. While this may be a mild winter, it is always good to be prepared because those that do not prepare starve in the cold as my Kekuit had during the season of death.

Winter will be here soon enough, and all I can hope for is that this time the mating worked, that I will have young this next spring. I am certainly plump enough for it, and there is now more time to simply relax and enjoy the warmth of sunlight at the burrow entrance in daytime.

Or for just sitting in the coolness of night at that entrance before going to hunt; until the thing I cannot understand happens one night in the moonlight, and I see her for the first time.

The night is clear with the full moon lighting everything in my meadow perfectly, as the trees drop their leaves softly in the night breeze.

I could be out hunting tonight but there is more than enough winter plumpness on my bones, and so I simply sit in the entrance of this burrow on the little hillock, watching the grass of the meadow and the stream in the moonlight, watching the night creatures roam.

The moon suddenly shifts to a new place in the sky above me, as I wonder, "What?"

Suddenly all the roaming night creatures run to hide, and I wonder, "Why, there is no danger here," as the first human comes from the north edge of the forest into the meadow.

I stiffen instantly. I have already learned the lesson well enough by now that humans are not always good to have around, but there is something different about this one other than the strange body coverings he wears. All humans seem to prefer to wear body coverings, but I have never seen any human in the forest or in my meadow wearing body coverings like this before.

I watch curiously as he stops just inside my meadows edge and looks cautiously around before coming further into the meadow, as if he doesn't want to be exposed in the open.

Then another comes out of the edge of the forest behind him wearing the same new body coverings, and then another, and another, and another, and another, until six of them are exposed in the open in my meadow, all of them carrying strange, long curved things upright in their paws.

They move with a strange wariness for humans who are supposed to be the masters of forest and meadow. As they wait, look around, and then say something I can't hear for some reason, although I see their mouths move.

Only then do the others follow them into the meadow: male and female, old and young. Some females carry human infants in strange pouches on their backs as they come, and for the first time, I notice that these humans are not only wearing body coverings that I have never seen before, they are all wearing body coverings that are alike.

True, the humans who care for this forest all wear body coverings that are alike, and brown like the body coverings these new humans wear, but that was a different brown.

Then as they come closer I realize that I know this brown, these humans seem to wear the colors of the deer, and then I also realize that it is of the deer, they all wear the skin of the deer upon both their bodies and on their lower human paws. I have never seen a group of humans wearing deerskins before.

These are also different from any other humans I have seen in this forest. Some humans who come into the forest and my meadow are white humans, some are black or brown humans, but these humans coming toward my hillock now in the moonlight are all the same brown, and smaller than most humans I have seen before. Their faces also look somehow different from other humans I have seen, not bad or good, just different.

As they come still closer I can now see that the curved things some of the males carry upright have what look like sharp stone tips on sticks held in the middle of those long, curved things, while others among them carry much longer sticks with sharp stone tips also on the ends of them.

The females follow with their young alongside, except for the very young that they carry in pouch things on their backs.

All come silently toward my hillock burrow through the meadow, and I shiver for only then do I realize why all the other night creatures fled when these arrived.

"Wrong" is here, "wrong" has walked into my meadow tonight!

These humans make no noise of walking in the grass, nor do their lower paws move the grass of this meadow as they walk through it.

Their lower human paws pass through the grass they walk through without moving it, or making any noise. The night breeze is blowing toward me, I should hear the noise of their movements by now, and they have no scent, as if they are not really there.

I saw creatures that were not real like this once before, and it was not good.

I begin to shift backward into my burrow. If this is like that valley of the running shadows of death, then it is time to hide no matter how proud a predator I am.

I change my mind because another thing is becoming more obvious as they come closer. They walk in fear. I can see the fear in the way they move, and while the fear is not there to smell, all these humans walk in fear, except for her.

She is still young, but she is an adult and walks proudly with her head up, not looking fearfully from side to side and behind as the rest do.

She does not fear, and she also has a small young human in her arms as she walks. Then she smiles up at me where I sit on the hillock as she approaches, and I suddenly realize that she sees me!

The rest do not see me, or even seem to notice that I am here, and another memory of the valley of the running dead returns with the realization that I am not there for these other humans walking through my meadow in the moonlight, only for her, and somehow she can see me.

I do not know human standards of beauty. She does not have the nice, plump winter body we badgers have, does not have the perfect fur of us, the proud teeth and claws of us, or the pointed head and lovely short legs like of one of us. But I can still somehow sense that in human standards she would be considered beautiful.

She turns to the others as she walks and talks to them, and for the first time I hear her voice, and her voice is not as normal human voices I have heard before, her voice sounds as if it is of the wind as she talks to the ones behind her,

Her voice flows from her mouth as if soothing them, and I am startled to realize that her voice sounds like the warm wind of late fall, as if her voice actually were tonight's warm, late fall breeze before winter comes to kill.

Somehow I know that they all follow her as they all walk south past my hillock, as she continues talking to them in that soothing voice of the wind, and only then do I realize that while the others talk back to her, and they are all close enough to this hillock for me to hear them now, I do not hear voices from them, only her voice can be heard as they pass with her.

They move south through my meadow as she turns her head and smiles at me, and a sudden thought comes into my head: *Life comes from the north and goes south to die.*

I watch, startled, and unsure why that thought came into my head as she looks forward again while her voice shifts and changes, soothing them as she guides them. Fascinated, I listen as her voice shifts and changes into other voices of other winds and breezes.

Until all of these humans wearing the skin of the deer on their body and lower paws pass into the edge of the forest, and as they disappear into the edge of the forest, the thought comes into my head again; *Life comes from the north and goes south to die.* I shiver, it was her voice, and twice she has thought it into my head, not my ears.

Only when I am sure that the last of them have passed from sight do I go to investigate this new thing in my meadow, and find that just as in the valley of shadows of the dead there is no disturbed grass or ground behind these humans.

But unlike that valley where I heard all the screams in my head, these humans made no noise in my head or in my ears except for her, and for some reason I actually want to hear her voice again.

Her voice had soothed me as I listened to her talk to the others before they passed from sight. Her voice was like the strong, spring wind moving the treetops around my beautiful place of large water when I lived there.

Her voice was heated summer wind across the grass of the field above where my burrow overlooked the large water, the warm wind of summer not the wind of the winter when I found my poor starved Kekuit dead in that field.

Her voice was fall wind rippling the surface of my large water when brightly colored leaves were falling into it and the fall breeze of a warm night before winter, but her voice was never the wind of winter

Her voice was beautiful, and I want to hear it again.

There is no scent, no grass pressed down from feet moving through it: nothing to show they were truly here. However, I am not asleep and did not dream that this did happen.

I wander for a while, investigating the entire trail they walked from forest edge to forest edge and find nothing. Giving up, I start wander back to my nearby burrow on the hillock for sleep when he comes into the meadow in the moonlight from the edge of the forest to the north, riding a strange, long-legged animal with a long nose. And I run for the hillock!

I know this one instantly with my predator's instincts, even if I have never seen him before; this is the one who takes fur purely for vanity, this is the angry one of the valley of the shadows of death where I ran from the fire that was not there, this is the cowardly loud bluffing one with his too loud young and mate that tried to run over me with his too large human-carrying traveling thing in my meadow. This is the evil one!

I sense all of this as I run desperately for my hillock burrow, and another comes from the forest edge to the north, and he is the same as the first, then another, and he is the same, and another and he is the same.

Many more come into my meadow from the forest edge, moving south through my meadow, walking on human paws and riding on those strange, long-legged, long-nosed animals.

They all come into my meadow in the moonlight, and I know they come for no good reason. The smaller, darker humans had radiated fear from them in the way that they moved, but these new humans radiate death in their movements!

I do not have to know them to know this. Like the angry human of the valley, death radiates from them as they come with no noise, just as the other smaller, darker people came into this meadow with no noise, and the grass these new ones pass through also does not stir as they pass through it.

Watching from the safety of my burrow entrance as they come silently toward it in the moonlight, I realize that unlike the other smaller, darker ones, these are all white-skinned humans, and are dressed strangely.

I have seen humans wearing many kinds of coverings, but these humans coming now are strangest of all in their body coverings. These new body coverings are looser than any I have ever seen humans wearing before, and in more colors, and covering their chests are strange things that gleam in the moonlight as if being reflected.

On their heads are other things that also gleam in the moonlight, as if they were made of the same things that cover their human chests. The shiny things on their heads rise from side to side above their ears to come into a ridge from front to rear on top of their heads, and they carry killing sticks.

Then I realize the "wrong" of the killing sticks carried by these strangely covered humans who radiate death as they come. These are not the same as the other killing sticks I have seen other humans carry in this forest; these killing sticks seem to be thicker and simpler than any of the killing sticks I have seen other human hunters in this forest carry.

But I can't say how, and I can now see there is something smoking and glowing red in a thin curved something holding it above the top and near the back of each of these killing sticks.

Simpler or not, they are killing sticks, and I stay concealed in my burrow entrance while I watch these humans come, chests and heads gleaming in the moonlight.

Not all carry these strange-looking killing sticks. Like the smaller, darker people before them, some of these white humans walk beside the ones riding and also carry long sticks with pointed tips, and yet there is no sharpened stone like the ones on the ends of the long sticks carried by the smaller, darker people.

On these new longer sticks carried by the ones who have them, there are three things on the upper end of each one. One long point at the top of each stick; a flatter, wider thing on one side near the top point, and another point like the one on top on the other side of that flatter, wider thing. All of them gleam in the moonlight, just like the things the humans wear on their heads and chests.

As the first human passes my burrow, riding on that strange, tall creature with the long legs, long nose, and flowing tail, I can see that they also wear things on their backs that gleam in the moonlight, like the things on their chests and at the top of the long sticks.

Other humans are walking, carrying other things, but I do not know what these are, only that they look somewhat like the curved things carried by the darker people before them. They are shorter curved things, like a short human killing stick, but with a curved thing on top of it and carried sideways, and each has on top what looks like a shorter killing stick held in the curved part.

Two others emerge from the edge of the forest to follow, walking quickly as if they had let the others see that it was safe before entering the meadow themselves. Now they both hurry to catch up with the others, seeming to want to lead, and these new ones are different as they walk among the others in the moonlight. They also wear looser human body coverings, but don't have the shiny things on heads and chests that the others wear.

These two wear long, flowing things of all black on their human bodies, and I sense that while the others carry things to kill with, these two do not need things to kill with because others do it for them. I sense this, and know them, without needing to have met them before.

These two new ones wearing the flowing, all-black body coverings have a harder look to their faces, and radiate more than just death. These two radiate the absolute belief that all should think as they do and believe as they do.

Those who do not think and believe as these two do will not find any mercy from them; these two will not tolerate others believing differently from them, and they will kill those who try.

Somehow I know this; it comes from them just as a deadly sense of anger and greed comes from the ones riding those strange tall creatures, and those who walk beside them.

Somehow, I know in my mind that there are many humans like these, and humans, who are exactly like these, may even hate these humans and what they stand for because of their own human beliefs. But they are still the same as these, and they will not tolerate those who want to have different beliefs.

With no sound, they all pass through my meadow in the moonlight, moving south, and I know what they go for, and the smaller, darker people who passed before are their prey.

These many go as one to find the smaller, darker people and to kill them, driven by anger, greed, and the two in black.

And as they pass my hillock, without noise and without stirring the grass their human paws pass through, a new realization comes. Like the humans they follow, who passed before them; these new humans do not go as now, they go as before.

All of these had passed through this meadow long ago, as in the valley of the shadows of death where creatures that had died many seasons before ran from a fire that was not there.

These and the other smaller, darker people who passed here before them are all shadows that passed here long ago, and for some reason have been forced to repeat their passage here again tonight. They cannot touch me just as I cannot touch them.

I go fearlessly from my burrow, running down the hillock, running after them, and passing among them as they pass through me without touching me.

I no longer fear these; they carry their own fear and their own death inside themselves in their greed and anger at the smaller, darker people they follow. These humans, who are not really here in my meadow, died long ago after they killed the smaller, darker people.

I also remember again the thing my mother, Asaseyaa, had told me many sets of seasons ago, "There is justice in nature, and deadly sometimes, but justice."

I pass among them, as they pass through me without touching me, going long ago to their own justice, and then I simply stop and watch them go onward.

The last of them pass into the edge of the forest, and as they do, the moon suddenly shifts back to where it was before in the sky, and I wish that she had spoken to me more in that gentle voice of the winds as she passed with her people.

She smiled at me, and she alone of all of them, saw me, smiled at me, and showed me her young, infant female in her arms. As I watch the edge of the forest, I know now that she died long ago with them. Then I go back to the burrow to sleep.

Morning finds me roaming for food to fill myself for the coming winter, and for the possibility that this time the mating worked, and I will have young again this next springtime.

But it is not winter yet, and there are still things to do before it arrives. There are burrows to give a last check to before my roaming territory shrinks to the smaller winter one, and prey to be found before I spend time sleeping and hoping for those new young.

A thought suddenly occurs to me about what would really be nice for food to fatten my body out nicely for the coming winter. I decide to go where the two humans I liked had roamed in the seasons before.

Some nice, fresh deer would be good now, and those two always could hunt well, so I roam for where I know they were the last time, and this time they do not surprise me, I surprise them.

They sleep well, these humans, and I note that with satisfaction they sleep comfortably inside their large, above-ground den, unaware that I am outside in the darkness of night's shadows. I scent food things, and it only takes a little bit of effort to quietly get the top off the outside thing they have food inside.

Deer meat is in there, packed in some kind of hard, cold stuff like the top of the stream in winter when I play on its hard surface, and I feast well and quietly. I was hungry, and they are sleeping so nicely, I eat most of it. They will probably not even miss it, and they can always hunt more deer, we will see to that tomorrow.

I feel comfortable around these two now; we are predators, we hunt for food in the forest as predators, and we understand each other as predators.

I know that they understand the limits of dealing with one such as me and will not overstep the boundaries. They also seem to like me coming to visit them, and I am now very well fed on almost all the food things they had in the closed thing, then it is time to sleep.

I enter their above-ground burrow without disturbing them. After making sure to groom each of them for the nice deer I ate inside the human holding thing, and all the other food things I found to eat in here as they slept, I snuggle between them while they sleep on each side of the above-ground-burrow.

There is a great deal of excitement when they awaken, and it annoys me. I am trying to sleep because I hunt at night and sleep in the daytime.

Why would they be so excited to find me sleeping with them anyway? I stayed in here the last time we visited together.

However, they seem excited, and I wander outside to sleep under a nearby bush while they get over their excitement at finding me inside sleeping with them.

I wait for them to emerge from the above-ground den so we can hunt for more food together, but there seems to be some confusion inside as I hear them exploring all the things I opened to find the delicious food inside those things while they slept. So, I sleep and wait for them to come outside and eat.

When they do, there seems to be confusion about that also. They seem a little upset with me and I can't imagine why. All they have to do is go get more deer.

But they don't seem to want to do that. Instead, they take one of those things you hold in your human paw and talk to it, and little voices answer you back if you talk to it. It does not surprise me when a little voice comes from it as they talk to it, and after all, I have seen these things in use before.

Then we wait, and they still seem a little upset with me for some reason, but they upset me when we met before by surprising me from the hiding place as I was approaching the deer they had taken that season, so there is nothing wrong with me surprising them now.

I sleep until the sun is fully in the sky before finally hearing a human-carrying traveling thing coming.

There is no need to drift back deeper into the brush. I recognize the sound from the last season these two shared with me; their friend who was so amazed at me being with these two is coming, and I wonder idly if he will be just as amazed this time when he sees me with them.

He is not amazed, but he seems amused at them for some reason, and laughs when I bring my plump, full body out from the brush to see him.

He brings more deer and other things for them, wrapped in those things the humans wrap things in, and it seems as if we are not going to hunt after all, almost as if these two were only allowed to hunt one deer in this season, and I seem to have eaten most of that, or at least everything left of it here for them to eat.

Still they seem to forgive me for eating all that was theirs, and we sit together as they eat again.

We just sit afterward, and they stroke me as their friend becomes amazed again, and takes a small something from his human-carrying traveling thing and points it at us, while his friends stroke me.

It flashes light as it makes a noise, and then flashes light again, leaving me puzzled by his behavior. Has he never seen a badger stroked by humans before?

But humans amaze easily, and so we roam the forest, and their friend is amazed again at how we walk together while we roam.

He takes the small something out again and points it at us often as I roam with these two, then sits in the forest, stroking me himself as they make the small thing flash at him and me. Then he sets it on a tree stump and it flashes at the three of them and me as we sit together.

They do this many times, until it seems obvious that humans place some kind of special meaning on this thing that flashes.

Then we roam back to the place of the above-ground den to sit by the fire as day becomes darkness, and they remember that I am here to be stroked and talked to.

Of course, I do not understand a word of human, but the sound of their voices is mellow and nice as they talk to each other and to me.

Their friend insists on staying to watch me for some reason and is more amazed as I wander in to sleep with them. He makes the thing flash at us again when I am inside their above-ground burrow, until we all go to sleep.

I awaken early while it is still dark outside and groom them quietly in the dark as they sleep, even softly grooming the amazed friend I still do not understand. .

Winter is here, and it is time to go back to my burrow and sleep. If I am lucky the mating worked this time, and I will have my own young to care for and teach in the spring season of new growth, and then see leave in the season of falling leaves before winter arrives, while I cry behind them as my own mother Asaseyaa cried for me.

The wandering leads back to my little hillock, to the last marking of territory, to the cleaning of the burrow, and then inside to sleep as the sky above begins its winter darkening before the white falls from it.

The winter passes slowly as I wait anxiously for the spring, hunting when needed, sleeping, and watching my white-covered meadow reflect the moonlight brightly around my hillock. Seeing all the beauty of the barren winter forest and meadow around me, I am bored beyond belief as I wait for spring.

Then one day the snow melts in the sunlight as the stream flows faster and faster from the melting snow. The winter dead plants come back to life; and all the creatures of forest and meadow return to spring time as the stream does its seasonal thing of eating its stream banks, and life begins again in my meadow.

This is the season of new, green growth in forest and meadow, the season of life beginning again, and I wait impatiently, but it does not happen. I am barren. It is the ninth spring of my life, and there will be no young. Not now, and probably never again in my life.

I roam because it is important to establish my territory again, and it is important to hunt and keep myself plump, and it is important to make sure that all of the burrows that have been ignored in the winter are once again cleaned and ready if I need them for some reason.

I roam and wait through all of this beautiful spring for summer to arrive when he will return, and then I will try again. I am a predator, not some weakling prey creature, and I will have more young to care for.

All this territory that is mine looks brighter somehow with that thought. It is mine and it will be shared with other young someday. If not this next spring, then the next; badgers do not lie down and die if things do not happen as we wish them to.

For now, I roam to see my fellow huntresses. If they have young and I do not, that does not matter because I will try again and will succeed, and if not, then, I will not quit and lie down to die as a weakling prey would do. I will simply live and go on living.

I roam to Ankusha and Ammavaru, proud of them, and proud of their new young as we play together, those young and me. Ankusha and Ammavaru let me stay to help teach them from my many seasons of experience.

They are both strong, proud huntresses, and their young will be strong and proud. I stay and teach, and then move on to see Akna, staying there to teach from experience also, and her young roll over me in their fierce little hunting, stalking games in her burrow while we talk of the things that have happened since I last saw her.

If there is an occasional look of pity from Akna, I ignore it. These young are the same as my young, and I teach them to survive as I had once taught her to survive. Then I move on as the summer moves onward, roaming back to the little hillock where my much-loved burrow is. I hunt at night and sun in the last part of the day to soak up warmth.

Sometimes when I awaken it is colder, and my legs may be a little stiff, but it is not important. I can still hunt, and if I work my legs back and forth before going outside the burrow they are all right.

While chasing a rabbit I surprised in the open a few nights ago, I had to give up the chase far too early because I had no breath to continue the chase.

Before, I could have caught a rabbit from a chase starting that close, but this time I missed, and still it is of little importance, there are lots of prey I can catch easily in my meadow, and I simply have to find slower prey or let it get closer. But it is a little worrisome.

The summer moves further onwards as I watch the grass dry in the sunlight of this season's heat. The stream remains lower than it should be, but is still there as I wait beside it, hidden in shadows for prey to come seeking water.

There is no uneasy truce this season as there was the last time this happened. My mother, Asaseyaa, once told me predators killing slower, weaker prey isn't cruel, it is simply the way nature makes stronger prey and stronger predators come about.

"You come from me and you return to me," she told us. I do not know exactly what that means, but I am a predator and we hunt, it is what we do to survive.

I survive this summer as it turns into fall and the leaves begin turning yellow on the plants and trees that lose them for winter.

Soon the leaves will turn darker and begin to fall as the wind becomes cooler in the evening when I hunt, and there is more time spent sunning myself to soak up warmth before winter comes drifting white across the meadow and forest.

I go see my two human friends again, remembering this time I should not try to eat everything they have inside the above-ground burrow.

They are there, and neither of us surprises the other this time. I find them hunting again as they find me roaming to them.

They make a quick kill and we walk together back to the above-ground burrow while they drag the deer behind us. We stay, and their friend comes to see us and to pick up the parts of the deer he takes each time in this season, but this time there are others with him.

Somehow, I get the impression that this is not what my two friends wanted to happen, but I am tolerant of the others as they make the things they hold in their paws flash light at me while I sit with the two I know.

Others also arrive, and I do not think these new arrivals are hunters at all. They do not carry the predator way about them, and they actually seem to dislike the fact that my two friends took the deer.

This is foolish, of course, since I want some of that deer when this foolish human thing is over, and everyone goes away again so I can eat.

But the two new ones seem even more excited than the friend of my friends was when he first saw me with the two I have known for five sets of seasons in my life. This is all foolish. I am hungry, and finally I snarl at the two new ones when they try to stroke me. This seems to confuse them even more, but they go away and I can finally eat.

The fire warms me as we watch it burn, and I feel contentment for the first time since leaving the young of Akna, as if I were meant to sit here and watch this fire while these two spent time talking to me and stroking me.

I feel contentment again as we go inside to sleep, noticing they have put some kind of thing around their food things to keep me out of them, which is foolish, since I am already full of good deer meat and those small, brown, round things from the fire.

But they have been nice to me, and I remember to groom each of them as they sleep, then leave before it is light outside.

It is time to roam. Winter will come soon and there are things to do before it arrives: burrows to prepare, territory to check, and also checking Akna's territory to be sure that she is all right.

Her young will be gone by now, but it seems more important lately to check on my young as I roam. I am older, and roaming is less now, and even my own territory is becoming less as I roam it.

This is a long distance from my burrow, and there are too many humans here now. I will not come here to see my two human friends again.

I watch from on top of my little hillock in my meadow, content to be home at last. A mate for me will soon return to this territory around the little hillock and I already know who it will be, Sesondowah.

I wait on top of the fallen tree, on top of the hillock where the view is best as I wait for him to arrive, but Sesondowah does not come.

He promised to return. "Each mating season, I will be your mate as long as we both live." But he does not return.

If Sesondowah were alive he would return, but he does not return.

I finally accept it. Sesondowah is dead, and there will be no mate for me this season, and no young next spring.

He was strong and proud, with beautiful fur. I mourn him, and then return to make my burrow ready for winter.

Winter comes and flows into my meadow while I sleep, covering both meadow and forest around meadow in white. I awaken and stroll outside in the night to see my new playground and play in it. The time for sadness at lack of young is over; it is my life, and I will live as long as I can.

Soaring across the top of the packed snow in the moonlight, I chase mice that can run faster than I on top of snow, but that is not the point, the point is the chase.

Diving in and out of the softer snow, I find enough of the stream's hard, cold top to run toward, and then I spin out of control across its slick surface and fly with the wind in my face.

Then I find other prey that can't outrun me and chase with the thrill of the chase for food I can catch.

It is the same thrill I once felt many seasons ago after had I caught the much faster rabbit just outside its burrow as my mother, Asaseyaa, was training me. My sister, Shareesa, and brother, Tigranuhi, shared the rabbit with me in that first spring of my life.

I roam the night winter when moonlight showers the snow with light, and roam in the darkness of no moon, while night's shadows shower me with cover for the hunt.

Sitting in the opening of my burrow at the last of the day, I watch falling snow covering meadow and forest and try to count the flakes falling near me, swatting at them with my paws on their trip to cover my hillock in whiteness, and then I roam back inside to sleep until it is time to play in winter's deep, white cover again.

Winter passes into spring again, and sunlight warms me as the snow begins to melt, and the stream floods again from that melt and runs away toward the place of large water where my burrow used to be.

I come to the entrance of my burrow to see the sunlight in all of its glory from the clear blue sky of this early morning, to see the first plants begin to show green and push their buds outwards to the sunlight, to see the sun warming forest and meadow, and to watch the grass growing again to feed the planteaters who feed me. And then I see him returning to my meadow.

He is here, and now I know why Sesondowah did not come back to me. He roams into my meadow from the south where my lover went after leaving me.

He comes into my meadow with full confidence that none will tell him not to, for he is the lord of forest and meadow, the killer of humans, the huge brown bear with the old, thin, white scar from front to rear across the top of his head and the thin, white newer scars on the side of his face where I had ripped him the night he tried to take my Alarana and Asiaq.

He is even larger now. He has become to the large brown bear that he used to be, as the large brown bear he used to be was to the smaller black bears I used to know, and his skull is larger and flatter from front to rear now, his body is huge, and his legs are longer, and his teeth and claws have become terrible! He roams into my meadow as I tremble inside the entrance of my burrow. He should not be here; this one should have died long ago!

The humans must have noticed more of their kind missing by now if he is up to his old killing patterns. He should have been hunted to death by now. He can't be killed, this monster can't be killed!

I sense something else besides this one again as he comes closer, the presence of the other that walks with him, the human I can't see walking with him. Anger, hatred of life and greed radiates from the unseen human walking beside this bear, as I tremble, and ease myself backward inside my burrow, trying not to draw the bear's attention with sudden movement, and hoping that he did not see me at my burrow's entrance as he comes this way.

I hide deep in the sleeping chamber.

I do not have to see outside to know he comes this way; we are bonded somehow, he and I, and I know he comes this way.

I wait, but there is no sound of digging and no scent of him.

I wait until I am sure he has gone by, hoping he will go all the way north to that valley of death and that the angry human will kill him.

This bear that changes his shape and grows terribly larger seems to be wherever I am, no matter how I think I have lost him! I go cautiously to the entrance, ready for a trap or the sound of swift paws. I thought I was not afraid of this one after exploring his den with Ankusha and Ammavaru, but I am, and he should not be here!

I cautiously look outside to see if he waits to trick me. But he is not outside the entrance on my little hillock. Instead, he sits in the meadow near the hillock, as if for some reason he can't actually come all the way to this hillock where my burrow is.

I push my head far enough out to be concealed from view while still able to see where he is. He sits in the sunlight, and then turns his head to where I know I am fully concealed from seasons of experience; and then the bear smiles, as he looks up to where he knows I am watching him!

Although the bear is alone in the meadow looking where he can't possibly see me, I sense that the one walking with the bear is still beside him, and he sees me, no matter how well I am concealed, and suddenly, I remember where I sensed all of that anger, hatred for life, and greed, and I know who the unseen human is that keeps this bear company.

Evil is becoming larger and more terrible inside this bear, and changing the bear as it does, and the bear is not the evil.

This bear does nothing of his own will now, the angry human of the valley is the one somehow walking unseen beside the bear, and he owns the bear's will. I know now, as the bear has become larger, the human walking beside him has also somehow become more powerful.

Then the bear stands and simply leaves with the unseen human of the valley walking beside him, and I know who guides the bear to do things he should not do, and why the bear is changing.

It is the tenth spring of my life, and I do not want to die in it. I watch as he goes and wonder how he knows. Not the bear; that one does nothing of his own will now, the angry human of the valley somehow walks with the bear unseen and owns the bear's will.

How did the human of the valley know this is where my primary burrow was, and that I would be here, and how can he see me if I stay concealed inside the burrow entrance? His bear looked right at me, even though I was fully concealed.

Then answer my own questions with a sudden realization; the human who walks with the bear unseen knows somehow.

In the season when I roamed with Ankusha and Ammavaru, this bear did not leave the human's body near my burrow in this meadow by accident. The unseen human made him do it deliberately.

Either this bear is far smarter than any bear should be, or something that is far more clever and cruel than a bear or any other creature should be, sends this bear to do things he should not know how to do.

This bear does nothing by accident; the unseen human who walks with the bear knew where my primary burrow was all along, and his bear had left the body there for humans to find, knowing they would come in large numbers to avenge their dead.

He did it to get me killed by the panic-stricken humans. How else does this explain the fact that all the other bodies he took were carefully concealed, too carefully concealed, for humans to find in all of his seasons of killing them?

The humans that were in my meadow that time had hunted him, without knowing how to hunt him, or even which bear they were hunting, in their human anger, bad judgment, and lack of knowledge of how to hunt the creature this bear has become.

They hunted; but they hunted the wrong creature without realizing it, and they killed the wrong bear, and then they left satisfied far too early that they had killed the right bear and the right creature.

They were wrong on both counts; the bear has been here all along in the forest to the south, and he somehow knows where I am at all times. The human I sensed with him, the one of greed and killing and rage and far smarter and far more cunning than this bear should be, tells him and sends him to me.

The bear is driven to follow me for some reason, and I now know who drives him toward me and the ones I love, and I know from seeing him myself in the valley of the shadows of death, that the human who walks with this bear has willingly given himself to a new master of greed, and killing, and rage.

Whether the angry human did it foolishly, or for greed, or from rage at the things he could not control or kill, or for some other reasons, does not matter. He has done it, and now the human who walks with this bear is the servant of another stronger master.

I had walked into his valley, and I walked out of it. I survived the valley that he thinks he controls as the only predator there, and either he, or his master, or both, can't stand that.

He has come to kill me and the ones I love, with the bear as his servant. For some reason this angry human of the valley seems compelled to find and hunt me and my young, as if he knew that I or they would hurt him someday in some way, but I do not see how that can be.

My mother, Asaseyaa, had hinted to us of ones like this when teaching us, but she also said that we might never see one in all of our lives, and when we asked what she meant, she said not to question her.

But then she also said, "Beware the ones that are not as they should be, and who show far more cruelty and cunning than they should for their kind, who are far too fond of death, more so than even a predator should be. For these are driven ones and it is not by them they are driven, another far crueler and more vicious than they will ever be drives them to do things they should not.

"He enters them when they are damaged or weak, and becomes their master, and drives them to destruction. But there are places they can't go near, no matter how much they may want to. Those are forbidden places to them because they have rejected the thought behind those places. Find one of those places and live there if you are threatened by one such as these."

I now know that this thing and that unseen human who walks with him are one of those, and this hillock is the other. Humans can't touch this bear, for he is not truly a bear at all. Just as the angry human of the valley of the shadows of death is no longer truly human, or his own master, and let's another master drive him; this monster bear has also changed somehow for some reason.

He is no longer truly a bear in what he does or how he does it. As the predator that causes death far more often than they have to for survival is driven, so this bear is driven by another master, and until that master dies, the bear will be driven by him and will never be free of him. Asaseyaa had told us of the driven ones in the first season of my life, and we did not understand then. Now I do.

I can't fight this one or the one that walks with him, but I can outthink him and the other, for no master drives me. I am a free creature and will not be driven by anyone, much less by the one that drives this bear, or the one that drives him!

My mother, Asaseyaa, would want what I do now. I go without fear to warn those in the direction that this bear is driven by his master.

He fights for a master of evil, but I fight for myself and my own, and he goes in the direction of my own now, he goes toward Ankusha's and Ammavaru's territory. If he thought that he would go there to kill what I love without a fight, then both he and his master are wrong!

I go there, and much faster than he does. He thinks he can ramble silently to their territory and kill. I run with far more silence, and far more quickly through the brush.

Masked by shadows as I go, I pass him without his even knowing that I pass him. He is too large and has to go around things, while I run under and through the things he has to go around.

I pass and leave him behind, running for the territories of my young who are now my fellow huntresses; this one will be too late in his roaming as I reach their burrows well ahead of him.

There is no time; there is no time, as I try to get them to leave the burrows they planned on having young inside this beautiful season of new growth. There will be no growth if I do not get them out!

While they do not fully understand what I do, they both follow after I remind them of his den, what was inside it, and who is coming to see them!

We run, we run, and they run with new life inside them, I with none. But I am their life now as we run, and far behind us I hear him roar with rage as he completes the job of digging up what he thought would hold my young and their still unborn young inside them, roaring his rage at the emptiness of what he has found when he expected to find these.

Roaring rage far behind us, as we three huntresses run for the territory where there once were no badgers, but where there will be are now as these two who have the young of my young inside them go to find a new place far from where this one hunts for the innocent.

The other young of my young are there already. And there is plenty for all to share because it is a wide territory, and none of my young will starve. There, they will also help restore the forest balance that was destroyed with the destruction of predators by foolish humans in that territory.

His roars of rage grow weaker behind us as we run further from him and his rage. We run, and we find the young of my young who have gone there before us as they welcome us. There is room for all here in this territory of few predators, and food is abundant, too abundant.

The over-population of this area by prey creatures without predators to balance them out was already beginning to up-set the balance that is the forest, stripping the forest of plant growth with too many prey creatures unchecked by the presence of predators such as us.

We stay in this bright season of new growth, and I listen to Ankusha and Ammavaru giving birth inside the burrow they now share together, as I return with food for them.

My huntresses have done well with three new young between the two of them. Two for Ammavaru and one for Ankusha, and so now I know that my huntresses do not always have two each time they have young.

Ammavaru is so proud of her two males and how she did better than her sister at something for once by having two young males to Ankusha's one female, but then modesty was never Ankusha's strong point, and I am sure that Ankusha's young female will never stop hearing her mother repeat the story of the fight with the dogs and how she chased away the dogs all by herself to save Akna and her young.

I stay to teach and tell of the forest and how to survive in it, just as I stayed at Akna's with her young in the previous set of seasons to teach and train her young. I stay until the close-ness of Akna and the place where the monster roams begins to worry me, and then without letting my Ankusha or Ammavaru know, I return to my territory again.

It would be pointless to worry them, and they have young to care for and train. I will see them again if I live. Ankusha and Ammavaru have had enough lessons to train with, and experience to teach from, for the survival of their young by the time they are grown and ready to go out at dusk.

I pass into the territory of Akna, and she has her own small one to protect and care for this season when I join them as they roam in the darkness while she teaches hunting. I am careful, of course, to join slowly, and let Akna know who it is before joining.

We hunt, and we teach and tell the lessons of survival to her young one, and I do not forget to tell Akna what roams again near my meadow.

Akna tells me in return that he seems content to roam just that territory and he is strangely different from other creatures. He only ventured near Akna's territory once when she was deep inside a strong burrow below rock where he could not dig. She tells me he is insane.

"He roams as neither bear nor anything else," Akna tells me. "He roams as if driven by something that he can't control as it controls him, and sometimes he will just turn and jump in circles exposed in the open for anyone to see, as if trying to shake something off him but nothing is there to be shaken off, and when he does this I feel as if someone had just arrived alongside him. Someone human, but I can see no human there, and then the bear will paw at that thin white-furred scar on top of his head and sob, after which he suddenly rages again, as if he had lost control of himself and goes to kill again.

"The strange thing is that when he kills after this, he sometimes just leaves the prey there without eating it after he kills, and this bear never hides the dead prey for later, as other bears do when they kill but do not eat their prey. It is as if he goes out when this strange thing happens just to kill for killings sake, and not kill for prey. And always when this killing-just-to-be-killing thing happens, there is always the strange feeling that the unseen human I can sense alongside him now walks with him."

I shiver, for she has just described what I sensed myself with this bear after he returned to my meadow from the south, how an unseen human walks with this one and makes this bear far smarter and more vicious than any bear should ever be.

I have never seen this fight for control that she describes, but then she is close to where he roams since he returned to this territory.

I have been gone too long and will stay here with Akna to help her protect and care for her new young, and it will take two sets of eyes to watch for this bear as he roams.

He roams, and we watch, but we do not have to watch that often, for we usually roam at night when he sleeps.

Remembering that this one tried to kill my little Alarana and Asiaq in the darkness, we are cautious as we roam at night, and but he sleeps, which is curious since he had already showed ability to hunt in the darkness. It is as if he now tries to keep to the daylight only and has trouble roaming at night.

When the unseen human is not with him, the bear stays more toward the den he had before, which is also curious, since that would be the first place humans would come to look if they started missing their own in the forest again.

But for all his unusual smartness, the bear doesn't seem to realize that, and or perhaps he does realize it, as if he wants humans to come and find him, which is another curious thing.

Sometimes we are out in the daytime, after placing Akna's young safely deep inside the protected burrow, so we can track him and know where he is, and we see him do his strange thing of turning and jumping in circles, while shaking and pawing at the thin white scar in his head fur and sobbing as a simple bear.

Then we sense the presence of the unseen human suddenly beside him as the bear rages again, and then is no longer just a simple bear.

When this happens, the bear will go as far away from that den as he can get and stay near this territory, as if he suddenly understood how foolish it was to stay near that den.

Then the human we can't see walks with the bear as it kills, and often, when the bear kills like this, he will simply leave dead prey untouched, as if he just wanted to kill and not bother to eat.

When the human we can't see walking with him goes away, the bear is again simple bear again and wanders back to the area near the den again, as if he suddenly knows that if humans find him there they will kill him, and he wants to be found there by humans.

It is foolish, and he is insane, and we keep clear of him as he roams, and making sure we know where he roams at all times, and keeping to the darkness in our hunting and the training of Akna's young one.

We do not care how insane he is, or for what reason. If he tries to dig into our burrow he will fight two of us at once!

The season drifts into the hot one as we roam in the coolness of the night, avoiding him and his insanity.

He seems to be content with that as he roams, killing, with the unseen human beside him. He avoids me also, as if either he or the unseen human with him had some certain knowledge that I would hurt him in some way, but I do not see how I could ever hurt one such as this or his unseen human.

I could certainly not hurt him by trying to fight him, he would kill me quickly in a fight. All I can do is avoid him with Akna and her young one as we train that young one together, and the season passes into the hot one, until her young one is no longer small.

We train in all the things that my young and the young of my young have been trained in: the owl, the fox, the hawk, and dogs gone wild. We train in the plants that can be eaten and those that should not be eaten, and how to catch prey. We train in what things to eat for survival, with strong training on the word survival, for this young one of hers will not starve as Kekuit had starved.

But then I also tell the young of my young the fun that you can have when it snows, and the joys of just sitting to enjoy the last of the sun's warmth before you go to hunt in the darkness.

Until we have trained Akna's young in all the ways of the forest, and in all the ways of survival while in that forest, when her young male leaves he will leave in a safe direction. The bear, and the one who walks with him, will not have this one or his mother Akna.

We train and teach her young as the season passes onwards, until he is large enough for his own life in the forest.

He is old enough, and well trained enough, if we can ever feel any of our young to be well trained enough when they are grown, and then it is time to leave. We know he feels the call, as I had felt it so many seasons ago, and as Akna had felt it when she left me.

We go out at dusk.

Akna grooms him fiercely for the last time and gives him the same instruction I have given my own young, "Survive!"

He looks back before he enters the forest, then leaves in the safest direction he can go. We have instructed him well in this, and how to avoid the monster.

Akna cries beside me without shame, as I cried for my own young, and as Asaseyaa had cried for me, so few of our young survive in the forest to reach even her age, much less mine.

Then we return to the burrow without him, and I stay long enough to be sure that Akna will not be foolish in her new loneliness. Sometimes when we are thinking of things like young leaving we can lower our attention to the danger in the forest, and mistakes in attention can lead to death, especially living so close where the monster bear roams.

Akna will not be food for him while he still roams near here. Before leaving in the direction of my burrow, I make sure that she understands to roam for a new mate in the safest direction

If he follows me as he seems to want to, then he will follow me back there until I am safely away from Akna's territory, and I have more than enough experience in avoiding this monster by now, no matter who walks beside him.

Neither of them seems to be smart enough to have killed me, no matter how much one or the other of them may hate me.

I roam, and he follows. He follows, and the unseen human walks with him as he follows, and I watch from where I have simply doubled back inside thick forest cover, from the correct downwind side to see if he still follows.

The bear is good at tracking, but the human I can't see is too confident, and not really that good a predator. A good killer, but not a good predator; If the human were a good predator he would sense I am watching him, no matter how well I conceal myself.

Here I stay, easily concealed from his sight, watching the bear pass with his unseen human, and as they pass near where I hide, I now sense a strange fear in the unseen human's rage, as if he doesn't want me out of his sight for some reason.

I watch them go on without me, as I simply change my direction home, and once again, I am moving faster than either he or his human and am there before either arrives.

Remembering to smile at him as he walks into the meadow and sees me already here on top of this little hillock that he can't come near; the entrance of the burrow he can't dig out.

He snarls futile rage, but this time I am the one smiling at him before going inside to sleep, and I sense the human is gone before I am even inside, as I turn to look at the bear again.

The bear is once more a bear and looks like a confused, simple bear at that, as if he did not know how he came from the place he was before, to be here in this meadow again. Then he leaves in the direction of the den that will get him killed if humans ever find him near there, and I wonder just how insane he is as I go in to sleep.

Strangely, the bear now remains a simple bear in spite of his larger, more dangerous appearance, as if the unseen human who walks with him had other things to do, or other worries to attend to somewhere else.

I leave it alone. As long as he is like this, he is not a threat, other than a normal bear threat, and I have the winter to prepare for.

There is much weight to be put on, and this burrow needs to be fully lined with fresh grass to keep me warm and comfortable. There is also the last warming of the sun to enjoy, as I sit at the coming of darkness before going to hunt the night.

There is the bear to check on from time to time in the darkness when I have the advantage, but he does not change again, and whatever he has become seems to stay constant now, and I slowly put him out of my mind while I prepare for winter.

The sun becomes less in the gathering things that move across the sky, until the sun is no more, and the last of the leaves have fallen until only the always-green trees provide color to the forest, and then when the sky is a solid mass of darkness as the first snow begins to fall, I go inside to sleep while white falls from the sky.

It is a good winter, milder than most, and there are many times to come out and enjoy the sun's warmth.

There is also night hunting to do in the full moon, and both the foxes and I live well this winter when the snow glows in the moon's bright light.

There is playing to do in this whiteness, and running through snow, more for fun than to chase the few mice incautious enough to be out when I am.

There is sliding on the hard surface of the stream as I run back and forth. And of course, there is sleeping to do.

Then the sun melts the snow, the stream floods, the forest and meadow begin to turn green again, the creatures come out to mate and play, and I am lonely again.

Still I am older now, and after all, it is my eleventh spring, and I am lucky to have survived this long.

There is no sense of not having young to make me lonely this time, it is just lonely. I do not even mind the bear, and when he awakens again to roam, he seems to be a simple bear again, no matter how huge or different, and caught the same spring the rest of us have.

He does not have the human walking with him again, and so I respect his power and ability to kill me, and tolerate him in my meadow. He comes to it less and less often as spring moves onward, until one day he is simply not here.

I find his den in the darkness to check and he is there now; he is in territory on the far side of mine at the hillside, and he seems to only want that territory now, so I leave him there in his chosen territory and return.

There are things to do, many places to mark as mine, and older burrows to be cleaned out. I spend days cleaning out the older grass lining of sleeping chambers and relining them with fresh grass until I know that all of this is once more fit to be called a decent female badger's territory.

The season moves into the hotter one as we receive more rain from the sky during this season than in any other hot one I have ever known.

The stream runs heavily, and I am cautious around it, but it is nice to feel the coolness in what is normally a hot season while I sit in the sheltered entrance of the burrow, watching the rain fall outside.

The season continues to move, until it is the end of the hot one and moving into the cooler one . . . as he comes into the meadow from the south.

Our eyes may not be the best of our senses, and mine may be a little older now, but I can't miss seeing this one as he enters the meadow, and he is beautiful!

Fine, and plump, and obviously well fed and therefore, a good hunter, with lovely brown fur, and such nice whiteness to the markings on his cheeks, and to the white stripe on top of his head, with proud, black markings on either side of that head stripe of white and below the white on his cheeks.

Perfect black markings just like mine mixed into the brown of his fur on the sides like my own markings, and what fur! He waddles my way with such proud beauty on those short legs and even from here I can see this one is gorgeous. I want him, and as the handsome adult male badger enters my territory, I go see my new mate.

He wants to go through the entire meeting and mating ceremony, I simply want him, and after allowing him to indulge some fur fluffing and growling, finally convince him that I really do not need all of that to convince me, and we mate.

I have been too long without a mate to be happy, and while I know for certain by now I am barren and will never ever have young again that does not spoil the fun of having this handsome one near me at all times, and I drag him back to the burrow and try happiness again.

He is happy, also, as we enjoy each other, and he sits with me in the entrance to enjoy the sun when we rest together before going out to hunt. We hunt together, we play together, we mate and roam together, and when he finally makes his excuses to move onward, I miss him.

Still, he was fun, he was good, and he was good for me, and for the first time in far too long, I feel content. I am not training others young, and of course, there will be no young for me this next spring, but I am content.

He may or may not return, but this is now the eleventh late summer of my life, and it was good to love, and be loved again one more time. I am older now and there may not be another chance for love, and this was a good one, if it is to be my final one.

The leaves begin turning colors before falling again from the trees as I fatten myself up again for the coming winter, and fattening up for the coming winter seems easier to do than normally. Prey is abundant here, and I eat a great deal of it to prepare for the coming season of cold as I grow plumper . . . and something moves inside my plump body.

Snowfall

It is not possible, but I know my body, and after so many other seasons, I know what is inside that body. I am going to have young! Something has gone wrong inside me, and I am going to have young at this end of seasons, when they should be grown and ready to leave me.

Badgers have our mating in the late hot season or when leaves begin to fall, and then everything is delayed inside our bodies, so we will not actually begin to grow young inside us and deliver them, until the cold season is over, and it is warm again in the season of new growth.

These young have started growing inside my body far too early, and winter will soon be here. I will have to take them into a burrow, and care for them through my eleventh winter, and I have never even considered having young and actually caring for them through a winter, none of us has.

There will have to be extra food to feed them, and I will have to roam throughout the winter hunting and will have to keep them warm at a time when they should be far larger, better furred, and ready to leave as adults already!

Then, after my initial panic, I know what will have to be done. They are my young and I will care for them, and if this winter requires me to roam more than normal and hunt all the way through it, then I will.

They may be the last young I will ever have at my age, if my body is this far from being normal now. I will care for them and make it through the winter with them somehow.

I will cherish and groom them, protect them from the cold, and from any predators that might harm them, and love them, and teach them all they need to know as they prepare to leave me in the coming spring, and then when we go out at dusk, I will cry for them as my mother cried for me when I left her. From all the other young of my life, I have long since learned why she cried as I left.

I must prepare. This has to be my very best burrow ever, and these may be the last young at my age, which is already longer than most of us reach.

They will be so loved and cared for, and they will get all they need to survive this winter as they stay beside me, warm and loved and protected in our burrow. They will grow into adults on this little hillock that was my first real home, until the fire ruined it and I had to roam to the other burrow overlooking the large water place.

The newer and more open younger forest here will make it easier to hunt at night. More open areas mean fewer places for prey to hide from me, and it is my eleventh season of leaves changing color and falling, and more time is spent hunting more slowly now, with less chance of actually chasing prey down.

But those delicious ground squirrels are back in the meadow and my claws are still good. I can dig them out even in winter, and there is plenty of other food in this area.

I am not that old and can still hunt with pride. I will find the food for these young and they will have all the food they need, if I have to hunt all day and night long to get it for them.

This is the most important consideration because there will be new mouths to feed when I should be feeding only myself through the winter.

I begin making this burrow just perfect for the coming little ones. There must be lots of extra grass dragged into here to make it especially warm and comfortable for them, and my excitement builds as I work to make this so perfect for them. They are going to be the most loved badger cubs ever!

The leaves of the trees that lose them every winter have all already turned to colors and are starting to fall. I must prepare.

I take the precaution of making sure that another of my burrows near here is also well prepared. I will be roaming, exposed with young while training them, and may need to get them to shelter if danger threatens and it's impossible to make it back to this burrow.

Normally we only use one of our many burrows in the winter, but I must be sure everything is ready to keep them safe.

The leaves turn darker and fall, until the forest ground is a soft covering of reds and yellows and browns, as I wait for the arrivals and hunt as much as possible.

There will have to be lots of extra body fat to survive this winter, and probably no sleep, but I am prepared for that, and prepared for the fact that if my body has turned this wrong, I may die soon.

I am a predator, however, and will not cry for myself, and just please let my young be safe until they are trained well enough to survive on their own, and have grown large enough to survive any threats.

I eat until my body is plump enough, and in spite of all the worries, when the day arrives, I drag myself into the sleeping chamber as the sun sets outside over the forest around my hill-ock overlooking my clearing.

I have birthed so often that their birth is routine by now, and the only thing to do as my two beautiful new young ones emerge is to make so sure that their perfect little bodies are cleaned and moved gently where they can feed from me.

They feed eagerly while I admire the patterns of markings on their fur, and markings that are going to be so very much like mine. Both are males and so very beautiful as I groom them.

I never thought there would ever be little ones in my life again, but now I have these gorgeous, perfect twins, all nice and pudgy, and so much in need of me. I can see that telling these two apart as I raise and train them in what they will need to know for survival will be hard, even for a mother. They will have individual scents, of course, as they grow older, but for now, they are so identical.

One will be named Kuanja, and the other will be named Kyanna, two names that are almost the same as these two are the same in looks, and two names that both also mean the same thing to badgers, "hunting and wild animals." Such proud names for my two proud, little predators!

The need for food for myself finally drives me to the entrance only to come rushing right back at their poor pathetic cries of need. I just cannot leave until they are both sleeping again, until I am finally able to go outside: hunting as swiftly as I can at my age, before rushing back inside the burrow again with the prey still in my mouth. Not because they will be able to eat it yet, but because I am worried about them being alone while I am out selfishly hunting for myself!

Kuanja and Kyanna are both all right, and I am a foolish prey creature to worry about them so much, as I eat before removing the remains from the burrow to make sure that no other animal can scent it and come in to harm my young ones.

I am being so foolish now. Hardly a decent predator at all, but I never thought I would ever have any young again, and they are such beautiful little hunters.

For now, my two beautiful, little identical males need their own food. I roll over and let them feed from me as I fed young for the first time before, so many sets of seasons ago. I care for them, guarding them jealously until their eyes are open, and they recognize me as the large, warm thing that loves them, just as I once recognized my own mother Asaseyaa so very long ago.

When their eyes finally open, they look up at me in the darkness of our sleeping chamber, staring in wonder at the things they can now see, as I stared in wonder so long ago myself. . However, as simple as this sleeping chamber is, they are still filled with wonder at all the "new" around them, and at the sight of me, so very much like them but so very much larger. They stroke my face with their little tongues, showing me how much they love me while I groom them.

Kuanja and Kyanna grow larger, as the season becomes colder. I bring them back something to eat, and I am proud of them as they tear at it in the fierce, simple games that will later become survival when they have to hunt on their own.

They are very good at it already, even if most of this first prey is wasted in their games with it, and I bring back more.

They play with the new, dead prey I bring them anyway. Then they watch me curiously while I eat it in front of them, to show my beautiful young what to actually do with the new things I bring back to them.

I bring back more, and Kuanja and Kyanna both taste it for real, not just for play, and eat greedily, scuffling with each other for the best parts while I watch proudly.

If I can get them through the winter they will be all right. They are already such wonderful little predators! I bring back more and they eagerly wait for it, slowly growing to prefer the prey I am bringing back than the warm liquid they are used to drinking from me. Then finally I give them more prey and they have no more interest in what I provide from my body, compared to these tasty new things, and I am happy and proud of them and sad at the same time.

Outside leaves of the trees that drop them every winter are mostly gone, and this is the only thing I regret now about this late season birthing. My beautiful young will not be able to see the forest in all its glory when I take them outside for the first time.

Still they will get to see that anyway in the spring when they leave me, and suddenly I feel sad again. But their fierce play rolls across me in our snug burrow, and sorrow is forgotten as I supervise this playtime and make sure that they do not get too serious in their games with each other. I teach them as much as I can inside here, until they are old enough and it is time to go outside.

There is more than this burrow for them to explore and learn from, and it is also too close to winter now, and I do not have much time to train them on plants and other creatures, what to watch for, and what to watch out for.

It would make this instruction so much easier if there were a full, green forest outside, but all that is left of green outside are the always-green trees, and even the forest grass is now brown with winter death.

It is day outside, and I need that for full instruction in all that they must be shown and trained in. I nudge them gently up to an entrance that has been forbidden to them until now. It is time to roam, but they are to roam nowhere without me very close.

They are made to understand that clearly before they are allowed to move toward the entrance. The forest around us will be too bare now, with very little cover to hide inside, and there are also far too many predators trying to winter feed now for comfort.

What is worse for me is that, although the bear has not changed from a simple bear again, and no unseen human walks with him, the bear is still out, feeding as a bear. He will be trying to get all he can for the winter, and with all the bare shrubs and brushy plants, there is not enough cover for me to protect Kuanja and Kyanna by simply hiding in them.

We reach the entrance finally; and as I once stared in wonder so long ago, so they now stare in wonder now at the huge blue above them, at the white things moving across, and at the bright thing that makes them look away. The fall over each other and fall over me as they try to follow me, trying to look at all the new, as I once did. Then I manage to get both of them in some kind of order for traveling and instruction. The teaching is not too difficult, after all, I have done it before several times and the instruction flows smoothly now.

They are interested in everything, full of wonder at what everything means so it is not hard to get them to ask questions. My only private worry is that the blue above is far too cold for teaching this early, and the white things moving across it are far darker than they should be.

There is not much time left for instruction, or many days of sunshine to teach in before we all have to go back into our burrow for the winter. I have to teach more quickly than I would like; without the plants having all of their covering leaves to show, which ones are good to eat, and which ones should be avoided.

Above all, I teach them how to hunt and how to find and dig out the prey. I am still worried about having them so late in the seasons. Something is not right in my body, and they must learn how to survive on their own, maybe earlier than I would like them to. I am old for one of our kind now, and if I die they must be ready to live by themselves earlier than any of the rest of my young ever did; especially in a winter.

They learn to dig swiftly downward into the burrows of the prey and watch for any second entrances. Sometimes it is easier to make an obvious show of being at one entrance, then running swiftly over to the second entrance, and wait for the prey to run out when it thinks you are still at the first entrance.

They learn how to safely catch and kill the long snakes with the rattling tails, although I can only show them one because the others have already taken winter shelter.

The frogs are also not there for me to show how easy it is to catch them. I can see already that before I can let these young go out on their own, there will have to be a lot of training this coming spring.

They grow larger as the blue above us grows colder each new day, but they are still too small! I will have to shelter them all winter, and they will never leave the burrow without me.

The hawks soar above us but fear my claws and do not come down for my young as I whip my body upright and challenge them to come down and die if they dare to. The owl at night sees me, knows me, and avoids me, but it is far too open now in this bare winter forest, and that worries me.

We roam, and they learn to feed on their own, but I never allow them to roam too far or away from me, training them in all that might kill us. The bear and hawk by day and the owl by night, the wolf by day or night; as well as the humans who can kill from a distance, and who might want them not for food but just for their fur. I remember Alarana and Asiaq, as I train these two young very well in these matters. I teach them that humans do not usually hunt by night when we do, but to be very wary of humans in the daytime, and to never go near that valley!

The days grow colder as the white things move faster overhead in the blue above; the white of them grows darker now and there are many more of them.

It is coming, and they will have to learn of the whiteness and how to survive it. They are still too small for this, but I train them by the still colder nights, always making sure Kuanja and Kyanna are warm in the burrow, with me to shelter them if they even look the slightest bit cold.

Wishing that they were older and had thicker fur, wishing that they were larger because their teeth and claws are still far too small for self-defense!

We go out at dusk, and I train them how to kill others in the dark.

We go out at dusk, and it is too cold, and I take them back to the burrow.

We go out at dusk, and the huge, brown monster bear is waiting.

But not for us; he is waiting for the deer that lets its attention wander when it should not, staying with its head down at the stream for far too long as the bear charges.

I wait patiently in the best place for hiding, and as we watch the bear feed, I tell them what they need to know about eating the kill of another but not staying too long at it. Since he is their greatest enemy, they will need the most training on how to avoid him.

We wait until he is finished and moves away, then we track him from behind as the sun sets in all its reds over the bare trees around us, careful not to get too close with him until I have found where he sleeps.

I consider coming back later while he is in that deep sleep and tearing his throat out, but it is far too risky, the angry human may still walk with him and I have to think of my young first. We only track him far enough to teach my young how to track him, and then we return to the kill to eat

We feast well as I make sure both of my young understand that this may be the last good kill of the season, and they should eat even if they are full to round out their bodies as much as possible for winter.

Kuanja and Kyanna do not understand fully why I am so worried about them, but my word is law as I protect them, and they do understand that.

We awaken in our burrow in the daylight, and I tremble, for something is terribly wrong! The bear's scream is still echoing off the hillsides as I listen and try to think what could make this monster scream that horribly. It was a death scream that awakened me, but there was far too much human in that bear's scream, and it suddenly was not a bear's death scream; yet it came from where the bear stays alone, for none will live with this monster, and the scream was neither a bear nor a human scream, but both.

The bear screamed death and then in the middle of the scream, the scream became a roar of total rage and that new rage sounded more human scream of rage than bears, as if the one I had sensed walking with the bear had now been forced to become the bear against his will, and raged at the loss of what he used to be.

I gather my young close and wait, but no other scream comes and we sleep at last, until I dream strangely.

Far to the north I fly as a bird, until I see him below me, just outside his valley of the shadows of death. He is lying dead beside the stone wall that is now fallen, with his legs trapped beneath it where it had fallen on him, and where that creature was waiting for him.

He lies there with two other humans I do not know and with many dead dogs below me as I fly above him. He is ripped and torn by those dogs, as are the other two humans, and he is no more, and a thought comes to me. *Someone innocent is coming to me, and I will care for her in the cold around us.*

I wake up trembling and do not know why. I should be glad if he is dead, but somehow, I know there is more that will happen before he is truly dead. I tremble in fear and can't understand why as my young sleep peacefully beside me until it is dark.

Only after darkness is here to hide us, and my young are awake do I tell them to stay in the burrow while I roam alone to the place of the bear's den to find what has happened to the bear.

He is there inside his den, sleeping and sobbing in his sleep. He sobs first in human anger and then as a simple bear, until the bear awakens to scream rage again, and is lost as he screams.

That strange, screaming roar again sounds both mixed bear and human. It sounds like two creatures are trapped inside the bear; the trapped one is the bear, and it wants to die.

I keep my two young roam close to me as we go to hunt and teach, and never far from the burrow on the hillock. It is far too strong for the bear to dig out, and I remember now that he can't come near to it for some reason that is impossible for me to understand. He may rage forever, but he will not dig into the burrow.

When I see the bear roaming over the next two days, I think Akna was right. The bear is insane; he sobs as he roams, and then suddenly roars that scream of rage, before he begins to sob again.

We sleep and wake to the growing cold, and there is no sun or blue above, only the now dark things gathered into a solid mass as they move quickly above us.

We go out at dusk and approach the bear's kill cautiously, but he is not there, so we feast. Strangely, he did not eat, only killed and left the prey untouched, just as in the valley where I had seen the angry human kill and leave prey untouched.

Still there is more than enough food for us, and we feast well, before I lead carefully to where he dens; watch cautiously for him to emerge, and when he does not, I close with the entrance to his den.

He is sleeping in that deep winter sleep already, and I am satisfied. He is asleep for the winter and it is one less worry for me in guarding my young.

There are few other creatures that will risk my claws and teeth in close combat, and I feel secure for the first time about predators that might harm my little ones.

I must keep them close to me as we roam, but now we can roam in the day also, and we can enjoy the sun as a welcome relief from the cold of the snow that will soon fall.

Kuanja and Kyanna have begged me to see this thing that I have told them about, this thing of snow falling, and so I will give them one last day outside, just so they can watch snowfall.

They stroke my face in gratitude with their little tongues to show me how much they appreciate this extra time outside and this new thing to see.

Shortly after the day begins, we roam from the burrow and explore, roaming in the open areas where the sun breaks through the dark things moving above us from time to time.

Enjoying sun warmth on our bodies in the cold, when the sun does appear through the darkness above; until it appears less and less, then is gone into a solid mass of moving darkness above.

The day will not be done for some time yet, but I know we will not see the sun again as the first flakes of falling white begin to appear.

We roam and my young play in wonder at each falling piece of snow, standing upright to slap with their paws at every white flake that falls near their heads, falling over in their excitement at this new game. But then I feel a sudden sense of "wrong."; nothing I can see or smell, just a sense that something is not right somehow.

I do not understand the reason for my growing concern. There are no other creatures around, but my nervousness grows because we are too far into the open, barren winter areas of this forest, with only the always-green trees spreading sheltering limbs above us.

I have experienced the snow falling many times before, that is not the problem, but we are too far from our burrow in the hillock. I do not want Kuanja and Kyanna to worry . . . but something is not right? There are no creatures around?

I feel the growing "Wrong" more strongly as I consider that.

Winter is here, white and falling now, growing thicker before I realize with a shiver not from the cold why it is so wrong; there are no other creatures around!

Even with the ones that seek snug dens for this time of seasons there should be other creatures around, and even the birds that remain are silent. But they should be warning of our approach because we are predators to them. Yet the birds are silent because another predator other than us is already here among them.

I suddenly have the same feeling from so long ago when the brown bear had tried to dig me out of my burrow, but he is sleeping now, I know it. The white is falling from the sky in flurries as I turn my young back toward our burrow. Something is wrong, and I want them inside.

They want to stay and watch the snow falling, but I snarl at them and move them back toward safety by force. Something is here! No sounds, no scent, but something is here! I do not run with Kuanja and Kyanna, for they would only worry and it would not be a good example to show them fear. I still do not actually know what the danger might be, but the instinct of danger is too strong to ignore, and I will not take a chance with their lives.

I hurry my young faster, heading for our burrow on the hillock; I have another one closer, but I want the warmest and safest one for my young and that closer burrow is covered only with ground.

The one we are hurrying to is on my hillock, and if the bear cannot come near it, then the danger may not be able to come near it, either, and the old, fallen tree is still on top of it to prevent them from digging it out. It will be impossible to dig out! I know that the bear is sleeping, I know it! I smell nothing, but whatever it is could be upwind.

The snow falls faster as I try to keep my young under the limbs of the always-green trees to keep them dry and safe while we move homeward. I am afraid; something is here that can kill us, but it is not the bear. I have the scent . . . Dogs!

Human dogs gone wild; I have their scent. They are in front of us, between the burrow and us!

The falling white is covering the open areas as I turn my young and run them for the next nearest burrow, thankful I had made so many. They can kill any of us, even the bear in packs and this is a pack! I have the scents better now, but still can't make out how many there are.

They are close, but I do not think they know we are here yet as I run my young for the safety of the burrow; and the dogs suddenly begin to howl behind me in the falling white as they find the scent.

They have our scent they are coming! They are many, I can tell by the howls, running my young before me as they run for us!

I run my young, I run my young; I snarl my rage, and prepare to kill!

The dog's legs are too long. They are coming too quickly behind me, coming too fast to outrun. I find the place I need for what is coming, turn my young to have their backs against a fallen tree, and turn myself in a tight circle of fury to kill.

Staying in front, keeping my body between them and the threat, prepared to use every skill I have ever learned in my long life as the dogs come running to kill what I love. I will die here before these predators dumped in my forest by their human masters take my young from me!

They break through the falling white in front of me, and I count five as I wait, and they realize far too late in their charge for us that what they have found is predator; and one of the fiercest predators in the forest, not some running prey they can kill with ease!

But they are also coming far too fast to stop their charge. Judging their five to my one as they come running to kill my young, they still think they have the advantage with superior size and numbers.

Until I pick the leading one and show him what a badger can do at high speed with claws; standing suddenly upright on my hind legs to give me more reach with my fore claws, and ripping the nose of the one in front of the pack as he rushes to get by me for my young! Bleeding, howling pain, he suddenly realizes just how badly his nose is ripped; jumping backward from me as the others who thought I was easy prey for them break their charge on either side, dodging away from this new thing that can hurt them in the white that falls on us equally, as I scream rage, and they understand that this is not the easy kill they first thought it was!

He howls pain from his ripped nose and forgets caution in his anger at what I have done to him; running for me again, as his companions wait behind to judge his charge and my defense against it before coming after him.

In his anger he is too foolish to fight correctly, and he is too slow as I rip him again, and he bleeds more; scrambling backward away again to avoid this thing that has hurt him twice before he could react to its moves. They all back from me, suddenly afraid of this snarling creature that waits to kill them, instead of fleeing like they are accustomed to.

I take advantage of their cowardice, turning my young and running them in front of me, away from these cowards that refuse to close with me.

I run my young, I run my young! Running through the falling white as those behind try to catch us, and I turn again suddenly to rip through the air at another with my claws!

He backs from me barely in time to be able to still use his nose.

I run with my young again and the dogs close again, too confidant, because I am still running from them, and in their minds, that is fear.

I scream rage while turning and ripping air with my claws to prevent them from closing with my young; stopping their charge and turning again to run my young before me for the burrow!

The dogs try to take advantage of their numbers and circle me as they run behind us and I run back and forth between them and my fleeing young to block them!

Turning, rising, ripping, and screaming our rage sound into their faces as I rip at them with claws and teeth; bleeding another too slow to avoid my claws, turning and running from these incompetent predators when I would love to stay and kill all of them instead.

Stopping suddenly as Kuanja and Kyanna run onwards; turning, rising again on my hind legs, and clawing at air as they refuse to fight, dodging my claws and teeth.

If I am lucky these cowards will not remember that I am only one, and they can simply go around me on each side with a single rush; they are stupid human dogs gone wild, I am a true predator and I will kill them all!

I run my young through the white of the open areas where the snow falls heavily now, leaving too many tracks behind us for these to follow, turn and fight again on winter dead forest grass beneath the trees as we claw and rip at each other; and another is foolish enough to think that I am weak, gets too close as he tries to go around me, and loses part of an ear.

He screams and they back off again as I turn to run my young who have stopped to watch me with pride while I fight.

They are proud of me, and I feel the incredible pride of fighting five at once, and keeping my little ones safe from this death coming for all three of us as I run them.

Run them past the trees and through the brush of this winter dead forest of leafless brown; trying to make distance from these dogs behind us, trying to use the advantage of our smaller size to slow them as they are forced to run around the same brush instead of through it, and the bleeding ones behind me prove themselves to be true cowards, running safely behind their still unhurt companions as all five dogs' charge again.

I turn to fight as they try to rush around me, and bleed another down his side, and, slip on the white and fall; grabbing one of them with my teeth by a back leg as he flies by me for my young, ripping my teeth into his leg, feeling the taste of blood and flesh in my mouth as he screams pain and forgets my young to turn for me instead.

Grabbing me also, lifting me off the ground with his mouth around my head as I lock all four sets of my claws around his front body before he can have the time to bite down or realize what I have just done to him! He has just given himself to me, he is a fool to place my mouth inside his, and he is too slow to make the decision to bite as inside his mouth I use my teeth!

He suddenly realizes his error far too late to save his tongue and screams raw pain, throwing his head back and my head out of his mouth!

It is his last mistake as blood from his ripped tongue floods his throat and with all four sets of my claws locked around his body holding him to me I whip my head over his. Screaming rage as I hold on to him, ripping and tearing as he tries desperately to get away from this thing locked onto his body ripping at his head!

Screaming desperately to escape me, he throws that head further backward, and that mistake kills him, as I whip my mouth under his head, find his throat with my teeth, and rip!

A warm stream of red pumps across me and over the white around us as he falls; and I do not have time for him as I jump from this twitching soon to be dead one and rush to where my young have backed against a tall rock, ripping at the air with their far too little claws against the four dogs that remain, and the cowards are afraid to take the chance even on someone as small as my young.

Running yelping fear as I charge them screaming rage, charge through them and stop in front of my young again, turning and rising to kill these cowards!

They are four now and I have a chance!

They and I both bleed red on white snowfall as they circle and try to find the advantage.

I shake the blood from my eyes, flowing from where the one that had my head in his mouth damaged me, and prepare to kill these four also.

I did not even know that I was injured until now, but think it is only a small rip and will heal. No it is more than a small rip; there is too much blood, but I can still fight and that is the only important thing as I shake more blood flowing down my scalp away from my eyes. I must see!

The dogs refuse to close and I turn my young and run them while the dogs howl frustration behind me, and foolishly decide to continue the chase.

I am so close to the burrow now!

They run behind me with much more respect for this thing that they now know can kill them, but they still run for the prey they want so badly, and they are willing to die for it; as the ones I have bled the least close me from both sides at once, ripping at my sides, and bleeding me again!

I endure it, running onwards; ripping my own body back and forth at them as we run, snarling rage at them when they rip in to bite, and dodge away outwards again to avoid my teeth and claws; trying to drop me so they can have my young unopposed.

I run behind my young; running back and forth, blocking these incompetent predators from my Kuanja and Kyanna, trying to keep the dogs interested in me only, keeping them behind me, letting them think that they should fight me instead of going around me for my young as they could do at any time if they were thinking.

Until I can't endure it any longer, as I turn and show them again how fast I can still move from one side to the other; while standing on my hind legs and bleeding them back with my claws! Then run behind my young again as these incompetents these would be killers bleeding behind me, back away again in cowardice, recover their nerve, and chase us. I turn and stop before them all to scream rage as my young run onwards and the dogs see only me and back off to stand raging at this thing that hurts them in spite of its much smaller size as I take advantage of their confusion to run again for my young.

The dogs close with me again in an area not covered with the white already, under the sheltering branches of one of the always-green trees; and we rip at each other while scrambling for position to kill, until they back off again!

My young learn fast; they try to stay behind me as I rage and scream at these killers and claw at them every time they try to close with us.

Ripping ground and dead grass around me with my claws in this too open area, as they rip it also with their paws while trying to dodge me and attack me at the same time.

But there is nothing to put my young's backs against other than the tree, and it is not thick enough, and far too easy for these to get around. I have to run back and forth to cover my young and I am tiring; I am too old and I am tiring!

We all bleed now as brown winter dead grass around us turns red while we scramble for advantage and rip at each other!

My advantage is that they are fools and fail to rush me all at once; I can take one or two at a time. Their advantage is numbers, even hurt now they are still too many for me to cover all at once!

They back off fearing my power, and I run my young as they wait until they realize they are more hungry and angry than they are afraid or damaged; howling rage behind me they give chase again through the falling whiteness, and I trick him!

He is ahead of the rest of his pack, the least hurt by me, and too angry to think; as I run Kuanja and Kyanna around a wide tree, tell them to keep running, and then wait for him.

He is a fool; he only sees them still running, follows, and I slam into his side as he passes, the impact knocking him over with me on top of him, and he will never get up again as he screams and tries to reach back with his teeth to bite me on top of him.

My claws shred his face faster than he can react to avoid them, and then return to his body underneath me as his companions break to run in fear from this thing killing one of their own.

"Dog; your humans did not train you well enough, before they dumped you in my forest!"

He dies screaming as I run from the ones now afraid to follow me, and now there are only three.

I run for my young as these cowards behind me try to get their nerve up enough to chase me again while I find my still running young and run with them!

I am so tired now, and the blood from my head and sides is leaving an obvious trial in the falling whiteness.

I think with satisfaction that my young have not been touched, and two of the three dogs that remain do not really have good noses to smell with anymore as we run through the white for the burrow and safety, and the dogs howl rage at what a smaller creature has done to them and resume the chase.

They are fools, I have already killed two of them, and the others all bleed, and I will kill these three also!

I bleed as they do, the trial reddening the whiteness behind me as we flee together; the surviving dogs leaving their own trials of blood as they chase me, and white reddens behind all of us as we run.

I try to avoid the deeper areas to avoid slowing; the snow is falling quickly now, and my breath gasps from me in agony. I am so tired, and my body and head hurt where I have been bitten, but I will die before I give my young to these!

Kyanna does not know how to run in snow; slipping and falling in white before me, as we run through deep falling whiteness and I scramble frantically to get him upright again while my Kuanja waits for us.

My brave little badger does not run for himself, Kuanja waits for us; I love him, I am proud of him! We run, and the surviving dogs run behind us following the blood trail I am leaving.

My young can't run this fast, and their legs are still too short; I can hear their breaths gasping from them, see their tiredness, they can't run this fast! Too fast; the dog's legs are too long, they are too fast, I will have to stand and fight again.

"Good!" I think in fury; whirling around in this far too open area; throwing blood from me in a circle spray of red drops across the white as I turn in rage to fight the last of their survivors, and the dogs break through falling whiteness coming for my loves!

I scream my rage and invite them in to die, and they remember their injuries and fear, backing from me as the white falls upon us equally in this open area.

This is the worst thing that could happen, now they are thinking not just charging me blindly; I will have to outthink them and there are still three to my one, they are all larger and I am tired as they begin trying to circle me.

Snarling fury I move in my own circle; keeping my young in the center of it, remembering to be ready for a charge from three sides at once, and so proud of my young.

They have no fear, and their little claws are ready also as they snarl behind me ready to help kill. But they are still far too small for this and I keep them behind me as I turn snarling; noting with great satisfaction as I turn to keep facing them, that all three of my enemies in front of me bleed very nicely, and they fear me.

Each refuses to be the first one to rush my young, no matter how much each may want us.

The white falls, and we turn it red with our blood as we wait for someone to make a choice and rush; they are still not sure of me, even with their still superior numbers.

I wait ready for the rush, snarling death; I will have to kill as quickly as possible; white falls on us and around us equally as we wait to kill each other and bleed on it, and they hang together, afraid now to leave the protection of each other to try for me individually.

But they want me so badly now; I have done more than just bleed them, I have humiliated them! Five to one, and smaller than any of them, and they still could not take me; and now there are only three of them left from what used to be the full pack of five; the three who still live snarl rage at me; the smaller one who has hurt them so badly, while I simply wait to kill the survivors.

They suddenly go together to plan, and I watch as they split into two groups; the least hurt one moves toward me as the other two remain together. I invite the one foolish enough to move toward me in to die.

He declines, and stays away snarling rage as the other two begin backing off; and I concentrate on the fool that wants to die now, as the other two suddenly decide to leave, and disappear into the falling whiteness.

Probably running from this creature they assumed was smaller and weaker, but this creature has bled all of them and killed two of them. They are cowards!

He refuses to close with me, possibly something about the way my bloody face is smiling at him now.

I drip blood into the white; but so does he as I shake my head again to keep it out of my eyes, spraying it around me in another circle of red droplets on whiteness. Shaking my head again just to clear my thinking; I am so tired, but I know I can kill this one he is alone now.

He comes charging quickly for me through the falling snow; trying to get around me as he comes, and I am there when he does. Blocking him faster than he can react to my speed as he jumps backward and I just miss his nose!

He comes charging again; breaking at the last second to the other side, certain that I am tired by now and he can get around me this time by tricking me!

I am tired; but am still in front of him as he tries and almost loses his life as I slip on the white beneath my bloodied paws, and just miss raking my claws across his face as my jaw snaps shut below his neck!

I still have speed left, and he realizes it backing off again.

Picking myself up quickly; it is so hard to move quickly now, but I can still do it and he sees that. Moving slowly back just out of reach while I follow him through the falling whiteness to kill him; I want this one now for the harm he intended and for the damage he has done.

The dog senses that I am not ready to be his meat yet and backs from me as I move toward him; he does not want to be my meat and stays just beyond my reach.

Behind me Kuanja and Kyanna cheer me on; they are proud of me, and I bask in the warmth of that pride in the falling white coldness around us as I move to kill this one.

He refuses to close and backs away, as I follow through the white on the ground, while blood drips from my face and body making the whiteness red where it drips.

He backs snarling, I follow. He backs snarling, I follow. He backs snarling, I follow. He backs snarling, I wait.

He is confused, he thought I would still follow and he moves closer snarling, daring me to charge, and I wait.

He is indeed a fool, and he moves closer as I try not to smile at him with my bloody face; he is doing so well now; so well at letting me move him as he comes closer, snarling through the falling snow, probably thinking I am now too weak to resist his charge if he dares.

I tense slowly not to alarm him; and gather my legs under me, as the snow falls on us both.

He closes snarling, satisfied now that I am too weak to fight. I wonder where his companions went; I might go hunt them down after killing him and getting my young to safety.

He closes, I jump!

Far too late he realizes what I have done by letting him get this close and screams as he tries to back away, all four paws scrambling for a grip in the white stuff around us as he falls away from me.

I jump but I am too tired now as my rear paws also slip on the white and I do not get what I want, but I do get him; he screams again as part of his neck fur comes away in my teeth as my front claws rake his face; trying to get a grip so I can do to him what I did to the first dog I killed.

He screams and manages to get back on his feet as I rush and he runs, but I am lower to the ground than he is, have my paws back under me before he does and far too close to him now as I rip his rear leg!

He screams again in fear and pain, turning to fight me on his three remaining good legs; giving me what I want his neck, as I rise from the ground in one quick tearing motion, rip savagely with my teeth, and he screams again and breaks free from me with part of that neck still in my teeth as I fall away from him!

He runs into the forest on three good legs and one bad one to die with blood pumping from his ruined neck as I hear Kuanja and Kyanna scream behind me; and whirl around to them, too old, too slow, too tired, and see the other two dogs killing them!

They tricked me! They let him lead me off as they circled and came back behind me! They have my young; I shriek my terrible rage and charge, they are dead fools, they refuse to leave the kill, I am a fool I let my young die, I am a fool, I am a fool!

I hit the first one on the side just as he starts to look up from his kill! Hit him hard enough to knock him over, as he realizes his mistake far too late and dies screaming while I rip his throat.

Leave him and jump for the one next to him who still stands above my dead young! Screaming total killing rage as I jump for the foolish other one who wants to keep his kill, waits too long to try to defend it, and also far too late realizes that death is coming!

Hitting him hard in the face with all my weight and all my rage, and ripping, clawing, and driving him backward off his paws, into the white he falls on and colors bright red as I land on top of him.

Screaming and screaming rage as I kill him; until I remember my young, and scream grief, and turn to see what is left in this open area which was white before we entered it, and is now scattered red upon that whiteness in far too many places.

What was once white around us is now colored red; I am colored red all over my fur, both from my blood and the blood of dead dogs as I go to my young, bleeding head lowered in shame and wailing my grief!

I failed in my duty as their mother; I failed to protect Kuanja and Kyanna. I failed to realize the two dogs were tricking me so obviously when they appeared to leave. I failed my young, my beautiful young identical males, the last young I may ever have; my beautiful too late in the season young, my beautiful young, my beautiful dead young.

Too old, too slow, too weak, too foolish to protect those that needed me; I scream my grief into the falling white; trying desperately to groom their far too small bodies, dead and bloody now in the white that melts and turns red where it falls on them.

Cleaning the blood from them as best I can in my shame at failing them, while still wailing my grief; and sense movement at the edge of the forest near me.

Screaming rage as I whirl from my young to face the new threat; prepared to kill any predator that might find them good to eat. *"You will eat death first!"*

Then for the first time see the small brown rabbit watching me from the edge of the barren forest.

She is not of consequence, she is prey. I turn to my young again and wail my grief over their small bodies; trying frantically to keep the falling white off Kuanja's and Kyanna's little bodies, so they will be warm as I once tried to warm my little Kekuit.

I wail, and, and near the edge of the forest she turns to leave as I sense the movement, and look at her again in my grief to watch her go; and note four things at once with a predator's instincts and eyes.

First, her brown fur will stand out against the white and every predator around will see her. Second, even if a predator does not get her it is too late for her to dig a burrow in this cold hard ground and she will freeze tonight. Third, she is small and young and helpless. Lastly, she will die.

She is as small and young and helpless as my own young were small and young and helpless, and she will die as they died. She is prey and I should not care for her, but she is so small and weak, and some other one will kill her as these dogs killed my beautiful small helpless young ones. She leaves, as I begin to follow.

Against my will to stay and die beside Kuanja and Kyanna I begin to follow her. I do not know why.

Follow her through the white falling on us; falling on my dead behind, and falling on their killers.

Follow her as I leave a trail of blood leading back to my dead; and the white falls equally on my dead, and the ones that killed them as I follow her.

Covering the red back there, covering all of them, covering the trail of red I leave to mark the location of my dead.

I want to stay and die with my young in the snowfall covering them, but she is so small and weak, she is innocent, she is prey, someone will kill her, and I have to follow her.

I wail my grief to her and she runs from me, and I wail and she stops to watch me, and then tries to leave me again; and I wail, and she looks at me curiously, and leaves again.

I follow behind, trying to make her understand I only want to see her not eat her, and she is so small and helpless in this freezing winter white.

I follow, and she leads, and then I begin to lead by moving to her side while following behind her. If I can get her to my burrow she will be safe, and no one will kill her, and this little young one will not die as mine died.

She moves as I want; until she realizes what I am doing then runs again, and I wail my grief behind her until she stops.

I move again and she moves the way I want. I am so old, so tired, so bloody, and hurt so badly not just in my body; I want to die, but she will not.

I move more to her side and she is careful to stay well ahead of me while still moving the way I want her to go.

I try desperately hard to keep my head in the lowered submissive position as I follow; so she will understand and not just flee to her death tonight.

I have to shake the blood from my head less now to see; soon it stops dripping into my eyes and down across my nose from my head, and then I just feel numb where I have been bitten.

It is so cold, she will die; I try to hurry her without frightening her. She moves in the right direction, and I breathe relief as I lead from behind, and she follows from in front, and we move until we are there.

Then she knows suddenly where I want her to go, and I see the hesitation and the urge to flee me in her eyes as I cry softly to her; wanting her to understand what I need now so badly, and she understands and comes to me.

She comes to me in fear still, and I regret ever eating any of her kind before, and I need this small weak innocent one to be safe tonight so badly, and I cry softly with my head down in the submissive position.

Until she understands finally; and comes to me without fear, and begins to clean the terrible wounds on my head and body.

I did not ask her to do that, and we can't speak the same language anyway; but somehow she understands what I need now, and I try not to whimper with pain as my wounds are cleaned.

I still have pride, even if I am now reduced to asking a prey creature to help me. We lick our wounds to clean them and prevent infection; sickness kills predator and prey so quickly in the wild as I know far too well from my own life, and now she cleans my wounds to help me. I am her enemy, and she is helping me.

I cry softly for my young; and for this prey creature that wants to help me, even if I am her mortal enemy.

She cares for me, the killer of her kind; her kind can't stand blood, but now she cleans mine from me without complaint.

Cleaning me until the wounds are soothed, and I indicate to her with my head in the submissive position that she can be warm in my burrow tonight.

She hesitates; and how can I blame her, I am the one that kills her kind. She then enters as I sigh with a strange relief; strange because for the first time ever I want to care for prey instead of eating it, and I will kill anyone that tries to eat this small prey one now.

She is so small and helpless, and I make sure she has the warmest inside spot in the sleeping chamber before we sleep; keeping my body close to keep her warm, although I hurt in the colder outside spot.

My burrow is well made, and well lined with grass, and neither of us will be cold tonight, but she will still have the best inside spot to sleep in.

I awaken from my bad dreams of young dying in burrows, and young dying after they leave my protection because I have not taught them well enough to survive, and, young stripped of their fur by humans, and young dying in the snowfall.

Whimpering in anguish, I awaken and discover that she is grooming me in the darkness; comforting and soothing me, while I pretend to be still asleep so she will continue doing it.

She continues while I marvel at how this prey creature could ever care for one such as me. She is alone, and would not be traveling in the winter if she had others to share her life with and a snug warm burrow.

I sense that we are somehow sisters in grief, and cry softly; while she grooms me in the darkness of my lonely burrow, where my young were going to be so safe and so happy beside me this winter.

"Caring for prey"

She awakens, and that awakens me. She jumps upright inside the burrow and I sense her sudden fear of me and of being trapped in here with me.

Moving aside quickly to let her out, I can tell from the light coming down the entrance tunnel that it is daylight and I should be sleeping. I ache all over, and my head and sides hurt. I should rest now, but she wants to go out and she will not do that without me alongside for protection.

Only when we are outside in sunlight do I realize just how different she is. This is not a totally wild rabbit, with fur of mostly one color. Her brown fur has fine lines of black stretching along her sides and joining over the top of her rear, while on top of her head; other fine black lines merge to look like the face of a bear looking outwards. Her body fur is black around both the sides of her ears and on her rear, but her nose tip is white, not the brown it should be, and her ears are slightly shorter than the ears of a wild rabbit. Her dark fur will stand out against winter whiteness, and the first predator that sees her will be able to chase her down.

I never really stopped to look at prey before eating them until now, but this one puzzles me. Why would she be traveling alone in the winter instead of staying in one place with other rabbits in their burrows for the winter? Either she does not know how lucky she is to survive, or she is better at protecting herself from predators than I think she is.

The first predator that tries to chase her down while she is under my protection will die, and anyone chasing her will think the dogs died easily. Then I remember . . . The dogs, my young. I have to know! This young prey I am the mother of now has finished eating, but I have to find my own, and I have to know if they are alive.

Beginning to break a path through the white around us; wanting to see them one more time. Maybe they are not really dead. Maybe I was wrong. Maybe they have survived and need me!

The snow flows past my body as I try to find landmarks in winter's new look. I find them and move through the snow in the direction my young. She follows.

I know she is curious in what I am doing, but I can't explain it to her. How can I? We do not even speak the same language. I am predator and she is prey, and how can we talk with each other? What am I doing helping prey to survive? My young might have survived, and I must find them!

I break through barren, white-covered brush and find the open place where we fought and they died, and give up hope. Snowfall covers everything, but the lumps under it are plain to my predator eyes. They died. My young died.

I feel grief at first, looking at the open area, feeling shame at having been tricked so easily, and not being good enough save them, and then I feel a strange sense of relief.

Kuanja and Kyanna are dead and are not cold. I did not abandon them in the cold. They are dead and it is over. They died, the dogs that killed them died, and there is nothing left for me here. I turn and leave as she follows again.

My habits are as strange to her as hers are to me. She is prey, I am predator, and we are natural enemies. What am I doing? It does not matter. She is small and maybe not so weak after all to have survived this far, exposed in strange territory, but she is mine to protect now, and I will kill anyone that tries to touch her!

I stay close to protect her from other winter predators, watching curiously as she finds food. I have never bothered to study the habits of prey before, other than the habits that allowed me to find and eat them, but just as I know exactly where prey is hiding down in its burrow, so she seems to be able to tell where grass is under the snow.

She can't possibly see it or have been here before to know where any grass might be, yet she knows exactly where it is every time and covers me with snow trying to find it.

I watch fascinated from behind her the first time she digs; and as she forgets that the snow she is digging has to go somewhere, when she shoves it behind her with those powerful rear paws of hers.

The snow does go somewhere; all over me as she realizes her mistake and turns to look at me cautiously, unsure if now is the time to run.

I can tell from the look on her face and the poise of her body that she is ready to run, but all I feel is that my little one has been naughty, and has taught me something at the same time. I smile at her, remembering too late that my toothy predator smile might scare her more than if I snarled at her.

She seems to understand my intentions, however, and relaxes, returning to digging through the white, as I remember to stay to one side behind her this time while she is digging. I protect her as we wander out each new day as she feeds. She has no reserves of winter body fat to sustain her as I do; and needs to feed, and needs my protection when she does.

True, I am a creature of darkness, and should be sleeping in the daytime for most of this winter. But my life has always been so different from the ordinary, and since I am now living with prey in my burrow, why try being normal now?

I am now reduced to sneaking out of my own burrow in the dark when I know she is sleeping to hunt; returning with any prey blood cleaned off my mouth before she can awaken, hoping that she will not detect any other remnants of prey on me.

She needs me because that dark-brown fur of hers, with its black markings, stands out so much against the white around us in this barren winter forest that she would be prey for the first predator that came along. I do not care how well she survived up until now; my new little one is not some predator's meal, and the fool of a fox almost dies thinking that she is.

We are out for our normal walk to find food and drink for her, and some discrete predator food for me.

A fox has been shadowing us for some time as we wander this day, and I know that he is near somewhere, but he is not as clever as he thinks he is, while tracking us.

I do not know exactly where he is; becoming even more nervous while trying to watch all sides at once as we draw closer to the natural ambush point I have used so many times before in the past myself . . . the stream.

I did catch a glimpse of him in the forest while he was tracking us; but then he was gone, slipping quietly away into the bare winter brush when he noticed my attention to him. He is not enough of a fool to try to take on an alert adult female badger with young directly. But I know that he wants her, and we are almost at the stream so she can drink when he makes his rush for the new helpless young one I care for.

He is not as quiet as he thinks he is in the whiteness he is rushing through; I already hear him coming through the snow before she sees him, and realizes that she is far too exposed in the open as my new young one shrieks alarm!

I already know he is coming for her, and already beginning to turn in a whirling circle of fury as she screams. Screaming my rage, turning, plowing back through the whiteness to kill him as I knock her aside into a deep pile of snow while running for him! I may be older now; but speed is still with me, he will die today!

His winter luck is still with him; unlike the dogs, this fox is not a fool. He manages to use those longer legs to get out of my way and outrun me as I come for him.

I snarl toward the forest where he disappeared; inviting him to come back so I can have him for food, but he declines and stays hidden, which is probably the wisest thing he can do near me right now.

Then I remember the lesson of the dogs tricking me and turn frantically again to see if she is all right or if he has tricked me also!

Rushing frantically back in time to see her trying to dig herself out of all the deep whiteness I accidentally knocked her into in my rush past her to kill him. She splutters the white out of her mouth as I smile to let my little young prey know that I just saved her life, and paid her back for throwing the white all over me that time before.

She sneezes and splutters white as I smile, and we depart together for the food she needs to dig out of the whiteness, my heavier body easily pushing through the white for her to break a trial.

I think that she could just as easily hop over the top of this snow, but she is letting me do this for her so I will feel useful to her. My life revolves around caring for a prey creature now; my life is so messed up, and the cold seems to affect me more this winter as we wander.

However, I am now seeing eleven sets of seasons in my life end with this winter. This coming spring will be my twelfth spring, and few of us ever reach that length in life in the forest. My fur is grayer now, with less brown, and the dark black streaks running down my sides over that brown are now black and gray, but there's still some nice black fur in there with the gray.

I just hope when mating season is here again, someone else will also like this graying fur. It would be nice to have some more young, even at my advanced age.

My legs are also sore sometimes when I wake up in the cold, but I can still chase prey around the forest, and hunting in the darkness helps if I can catch that prey while it sleeps.

I may have to resign myself to becoming an elderly root digger and planteater. I shudder at the thought of no longer being able to catch prey, having to eat only dead prey others have killed for meat, and having to grub for roots instead of being able to chase prey down.

But for now my new young finds a treat for me with that uncanny sense she has of where food is under the snow, as she finds some late season berries still under the snow.

It is a treat for both of us, and to my amazement, she shares it with me, not trying to keep it just for herself. We both eat greedily until the last ones have been uncovered, and then it is back to the burrow for some sleep. I really must rethink this whole predator-prey thing, living together.

The winter moves onward, and we go to hunt, each of us for our own food, sometimes going out just to roam. We watch the sunsets together over the hills around this meadow and spend more of our time sleeping, until the day when spring warms our meadow, and I feel the call.

We will part soon, maybe not at dusk, but we will part soon. I know she has someplace to go, and I drop the brief thought that perhaps she will stay and we will have an unlikely companionship from now on. But we each have our own lives to live, and she is getting restless. I suspect she is ready to go for her own life and is spending her time with me now just so I will feel better after losing my young.

And the call comes strongly to me on one our trips outside. A male badger is near, and the need to go to him is so strong.

The call, and the prospect of new young to replace my dead ones, is impossible to resist. I begin to walk in the direction of this new male, walking more quickly as I get the first real scent of him while the young female rabbit follows curiously.

This is not my last lover; this is a new one, and he is young and strong, I can tell that by his scent markings. As I hurry through the freshly growing spring forest to meet this new one, I hope that I am not too old for him.

He might not find me suitable because I am older, with this gray spreading through the browns of my fur where the markings used to be black, and he might not even have any interest in meeting me at all. He might already have a younger mate, although I do not detect the scent of any rival as I try not to look too desperate.

We push through the brush, and he is there in a clear area and. He is so handsome, perfectly strong, and so young, and so powerful! I ruffle my fur, hoping that it does not look too gray; but then he looks at my companion, and he is a predator!

At his look, I move to stand between him and her, ready to defend her no matter how much it hurts me to give this male up, and he looks puzzled.

Obviously, it is hard for him to understand how I could be with prey as a companion and not eat her. But my teeth are showing now, as he considers her, and then forgets it. Young with a badger mother are young with a badger mother, and he knows better than to think too hard about the how or why of what he sees.

I bless him for understanding, and she does something that makes me bless her also, she comes to me, grooms me for one last time, and turns to the forest.

I feel sadness as she leaves, and I hope she makes it to wherever she is called, but for now, I have my own call. And he likes me. I suddenly feel shy with this one because he is younger than I am by half as many sets of seasons.

But he is also strong and plump, just as a badger should be. He has lovely long claws and teeth and is so well furred with proud black stripes mixed with the smooth brown of his sides and has such beautiful, black face markings!

There is a bond. We can both feel it, and he is interested. His name is Akycha, and we return to my burrow together in this season of new growth, as the forest comes alive into springtime again . . . and I rejoice in having a new mate.

"Aataentsic"

Akycha stays with me, and this is not the stay of male and female badger together as our kind normally knows it. This is not some quick thing of finding a mate in spring or summer, giving new life, and then leaving, as males of our kind normally do.

This is a longer stay of friendship and love in this beautiful place where food is so abundant. Akycha is happy to be settled with a mate for life.

A forever home is unusual for our kind, but we love each other, and this new thing works for us both, so we settle in together to share the new growth of the springtime meadow around our burrow on our little together hillock.

It is my twelfth spring of the seasons in my life, and when I awaken in the dark, my legs remind me I am old for one of my kind. It is harder to chase prey, and more time is now spent trying to hide and pounce quickly instead of getting into a chase for prey.

Prey can outrun me more often lately if I do get into a chase for food, and now I know that someday I will be reduced to catching and killing plants and roots for food instead. While that may not be much of a chase, that will at least allow me to survive another season or two.

It also seems so much easier to just go out in the sunshine and bask than it is to hunt at night. Now, I let the sun warm my body until I feel like hunting. It is harder to see in the darkness anyway because my eyes are older. Therefore, I look for the easier prey now instead of digging as much for those ground squirrels.

Akycha is wonderful at helping me, as I once helped Thamuatz when he was crippled. When it is too hard for me to hunt, Akycha is more than willing to roam and bring prey for both of us.

We share the season of new growth together as plants cover the forest under the trees and grow thick in the rain falling from the sky. The thickness hides me well as I wait for incautious mice or others to come by where I hide, and sometimes I find the eggs of ground-nesting birds as a treat. Eggs are a real treat for me now because they do not run or fly away, and I still have pride as I hunt for myself.

We snuggle together at the end of the day, watching the sunset over the hills across our large water below the burrow we share, and then sleep together in the comfort of our sleeping chamber as the season warm into the hot one.

Sitting in the entrance as the day ends; waiting for the cooler night to hunt in; finding prey on our travels and sharing it with each other, as Akycha lets me have pride by allowing me to find most of it even if he sometimes has to do the actual chasing of it.

We mate in the sleeping chamber, waiting for coolness of night, and mate in the coolness of night, but I am sure now. So much time has passed since I had Ankusha and Ammavaru and Kuanja and Kyanna.

Something happened to my body after Ankusha and Ammavaru, and then Kuanja and Kyanna came at the wrong season when they should have waited until spring. Something is wrong inside me, and now there will probably be no young for me ever again. I put the thought aside and enjoy the time with Akycha as we roam and hunt with each other in darkness now that it is warmer, exploring the territory that is ours, and marking boundaries as we go to let any rivals know this is ours. I am grateful to Akycha.

This body is far too old to be able to defend territory by myself. Any younger rival could easily take it, and I would not know where to go if that happened. If I lost this burrow I love so much on the little hillock overlooking this meadow, I would die. But Akycha is strong and proud with wonderful claws and teeth that few rivals would think of trying to take this away from him.

We roam and hunt, and slowly hope builds inside me that I will have more young in spite of my age, and in spite of anything that might be wrong inside me. As with Thamuatz, I know that Akycha will not be a threat to young, and I want to have more young with him so badly.

As the hot season passes, I roam with him, and we mate again in the coolness of night as hope continues to build; until the night when she comes through the meadow again.

I forgot the moon was also full like the last time I saw this thing happen seasons ago. Akycha and I are sitting in the burrow entrance looking at all that is ours in the full moon's light. The moon suddenly shifts in the sky to a new place, startling both of us as the first one comes through the edge of forest at the north end of our meadow, walking into this meadow as he walked into it once before in the moonlight as memory suddenly returns.

I gasp then shiver beside Akycha as he wonders what is wrong. To him, this is just a human coming into our meadow from the forest edge, but to me, it is something that should not be there again.

The smaller, darker human wearing things of the skin of the deer and carrying the strange, long upright curving thing with the sharp, stone-tipped stick held in it, and somehow, I know now that this is a human weapon. I do not have to know what will follow as the second, wearing the same and holding the same, appears into the meadow from the north, and the next, and the next, and the next.

Walking slowly with caution, as if afraid of discovery, the smaller, darker people come through my meadow again, walking south together as they did before. Akycha snarls beside me at them as he senses my mood and sees me shiver.

He does not know what I saw when I went to the valley of the angry human in the north and saw the creatures that were there but not there as they fled the fire, which was there but not there. He does not know what I know from before, seeing these smaller, dark humans roaming through my meadow in the moonlight. Akycha does not know that he can't harm these with teeth and claws, even if they threaten me, for they are not there. These humans had passed through this meadow long ago, and whatever happened to them happened long ago.

Silently, they move south, without scent and without disturbing the grass their lower paws pass through without touching. Fear and desperation is in their dark eyes again as it was before. Male and female, with all of their young, they move south, trying to escape what follows them.

Death is coming behind them and coming for all of them. I can feel it now as before, and know who will follow as before and know these humans have no chance to escape those that follow them.

Akycha can feel it also. He has finally noticed that the grass does not move under their lower human paws as they pass through it; they simple pass through it. He has also noticed there is neither noise nor scent from these while they move south across this meadow in the moonlight. He shivers too alongside me when he finally realizes the wrong of what he sees.

She is there with them again, on the side to me as before. She will again pass alongside our hillock burrow, and, as before, even without knowing what human standards of beauty are, I know that in human terms she would be considered beautiful.

She carries her young female in her arms as before, while walking in deerskin-clad lower paws, and while none of these others traveling south through our meadow show any sign they can see Akycha or me, somehow, she sees me again as she had before.

She sees me, smiles gently at me, and shows me the small, young human female in her arms as she passes next to our burrow with the others, and I cry softly as she shows her young to me, for I already know that it died as my own young had died.

Then she smiles and speaks to me as she says, "Aataentsic," and her voice is of the wind as it drifts like the spring wind through the meadow's grass toward me.

I don't understand. Aataentsic is my young, one of the three males and two females born in the fifth spring of my life. Aataentsic had gone south to find the large water and make his territory there, in the same direction she is now going.

I shiver, for this is almost the same as what happened to me in the valley to the north where the angry human ruled, and if these humans walking through this meadow now are long dead, then my Aataentsic must be dead also.

I grieve for my dead Aataentsic who should not have gone seeking the large water. As I do, she stops to smile at me as the others walk on through her body as if she were not there, and I understand her again as she sooths in a voice that is soft warm wind through trees.

She says, "Your Aataentsic is not dead. I only give you my name. I am Aataentsic, also, and your Aataentsic has found your place of large water where I also dwell. I have been left behind for a reason, but he is alive, and you will see him in this next season of new growth after the coming winter when you will finally end the pain of one who does not deserve it and give final justice to one who does deserve it. No matter what happens to you, always remember that the others who have loved you wait for you at the end of your journey."

I am puzzled, knowing of no one who waits to the south for me, other than, maybe, my own Aataentsic.

She smiles as if she suddenly pities me, and then turns to walk with the others.

I watch as she moves with her people, moving south to her death, and I do not understand what she meant by "left behind" or "the others who have loved you wait for you at the end of your journey."

They pass into the forest on the south side of our meadow and are gone.

Akycha moves beside me to find tracks or scent from these, but I stop him.

He is curious, but I know what follows and do not want him to be in the meadow when the others come following these, and he sits again to watch me curiously.

They come into our meadow from the north as before, the ones that carry death with them; and I know from the last time this happened that these are no more here than the ones who passed before them, and what happened to these, as what happened to those, happened long ago.

As before, these are also wearing the body coverings humans wear, but not the same as the others who had passed through here before them These human body coverings are again the looser, brighter-colored ones, and these humans again have things on their chests and backs that shine in the moonlight like the things on their heads rising to a ridge from front to back across the top of their heads, which also shine in the moonlight.

Some of them again ride on the tall, long-legged creatures with thick tails and long noses, and again, the others follow on foot around them with things that kill.

The killing sticks again are different from the ones I have seen in the forest; these killing sticks are wider and simpler somehow, but I can't say how, and there is a thing smoking and glowing red above the back top of these killing sticks.

Others carry the long, sharpened stick things that shine in the moonlight like the things they wear on chests, backs, and heads shine in the moonlight. Again, the others who do not carry the strange-looking killing sticks with the glowing thing on top of them, or the long upright stick things have other things I know that are used to kill, even without my having seen one of them kill. The killing things look like shorter curving things on their sides, with shorter sticks set into them.

The other two are with them again, and again do not carry killing sticks or the other things that kill the others among these carry, and again, they do not even wear the same human body coverings as the others with them do. These two again have a deadly sense of what they want about them. They want all the others to want what they want, to believe what they believe, and their anger is toward the smaller people that had passed before, who somehow did not want what they want or want to believe what these two believe.

Without knowing how I know this, I sense all of this while the two wearing the flowing, all-black body coverings urge in angry tones at the ones that ride and the ones that walk onward, with no sound of their angry tones in my ears as they do.

The others talk also, but again, there is no sound as they do so. These humans are not here for me to hear; only she was here for me to hear, and I do not know why.

The smaller, darker humans had carried fear with them as they passed. These humans also carry emotions with them, the same emotions that I sensed from the angry human in the valley to the north: anger, greed, and killing for the sake of killing. These are as the angry human of the valley was; but he was only one, and these are many.

Silently, without disturbing the grass their lower human paws pass through, they move through our meadow.

We both shiver as we watch, for Akycha and I both know they follow the smaller, darker people, and we know without being able to see it happen, that these humans found the smaller, darker humans somewhere to the south, and all of them passed into death long ago. Now, as the last of these all pass south into the forest as the moon suddenly shifts back to where it should be in the sky.

We do not feel like hunting this night and choose to go back into the burrow and cuddle together until it is light again outside. It is the good light of day, not the light of last night's moon, and I know now I will never have young again.

The memory of that night fades as the season moves onward, and the thing that happened for the second time in my life does not repeat itself. There are no smaller, darker people moving through the meadow in the moonlight ever again, or others following them.

Akycha cares for me and helps me to forget about people wandering through this meadow, who are not there. He did ask me curiously about the "Aataentsic" of mine she had mentioned or ask what the "large water" place she had mentioned.

I tell him, of course, and he has no jealousy. In fact, he is curious about how large this place of large water is, and we may eventually go there to live. But for now, we fatten ourselves for the coming winter. The signs are already there that this will be worse than the last one because it is getting colder earlier in the season and the leaves are almost gone from the trees that lose them.

As the first flakes of white start to fall, it becomes obvious that we did the right thing in making sure we had extra body fat stored up as the day ends early in a solid mass of darkness moving above. We return to the sleeping chamber after the first flakes begin.

The air outside is cold, even for the start of winter, and neither of us is surprised when we awaken after two days to find that we have to dig our way out of here to hunt, but there is nothing to hunt.

The meadow is a deep mass of cold whiteness covering everything in sight, including the branches of all the trees, as we push our way through it to the stream, only to find that it also is a solid mass of white on what was once running stream water.

We have to go through all of the snow to find a soft place to break through just to be able to drink, and then our hunting turns out to be useless.

The mice burrow in tunnels under the snow, and while we normally can hear them and dig down to them quickly enough, this is just too deep, and they are gone into other tunnels by the time we get there.

The birds are not on the ground as prey, either, and most of them are gone for the winter, and the ones that remain are too smart to come down to us, or they stay on the top of the snow just long enough for us to stalk them.

Finally, after much useless searching for food, we return to the burrow through the thick whiteness to get some sleep. We snuggle together and comfortable in our well-lined sleeping chamber and dream of prey, until it is time to come out again.

We awaken to find the snow is not as bad as it had been in the past. Some of it has either blown away by the wind or melted in the sunlight as we slept, and even with our thick layers of hair and skin and fat, we can feel the cold.

This will be a bad winter for all the forest creatures, but we roam anyway, looking for food, and there is none as we roam further, searching for until finally giving up.

The next time we awaken, it is still cold, but enough snow has cleared from the solid top of the stream to let me have fun with Akycha, who has no idea what I am going to do. I slide out on it and turn to urge him to do the same. The old trick I learned in my first winter is still fun, even if I do have to clear some snow off the top of the solid, cold thing that was the stream.

Akycha is still not too sure of this as he watches me run back and forth, until I lose my balance and slide over the top of this solid cold.

Realizing this strange, new thing of mine might actually be fun, he finally comes clumsily to join me, and after a few tries to keep his feet under him as we run and play and slide, he learns how to do it.

Then we run, shrieking delight as we slide and bump into both each other and the stream banks. We lose control of our paws and chase each other like young badgers back and forth, until we are tired, and it is time to go back to the burrow to sleep.

It would be nice to have food also, but we have enough built up in our fat layers to survive the winter, should we not be able to find any prey this winter.

We have fun, instead, as I teach Akycha the trick of gathering the snow on top of your nose and throwing it in a huge curving arc of whiteness into the air, then trying to run underneath the arc of snow before it reaches the ground.

I teach him the trick of waiting until your mate is near a thick layer of snow on top of the ground, then pushing them into it. This draws a startled, upset gasp from him the first time I do it. But then he discovers that it is fun to do it to me also. I have trouble walking outside for a day without being pushed into the snow, and he smiles at me each time he does it.

But I am older now, and our playtime outside is shorter when Akycha pushes me into the snow, suddenly drawing a painful gasp from me instead of a happy cry, and only then does realization occur to me that what I used to love to do is now harder, and what used to be fun before now hurts.

Akycha stops to look worriedly at me as I walk out of the snow, shake it off, and realize I am also out of breath. I used to be able to do this all day long, but now it tires me early. And I thought it was just snow on this fur, making it look gray, until I tried to shake it off. But it is not, and I realize sadly that the black fur of the stripes, which once contrasted so well in the brown fur down my sides, is no longer black. What is left is gray, and I am old.

Akycha grooms me with worry, certain he has hurt me, but I push him away impatiently. I will not be some weak prey creature, and I resume the play just to let him know that it is still fun, even if my body does ache a little in the cold.

That night, we sleep cuddled together. I stay awake beside him as he sleeps peacefully against me. I am afraid to lose speed and agility and become prey instead of predator. I am afraid to become the meat of some other faster or larger predator, or even worse, not to become prey at all, but slowly starve to death because you can no longer hunt for food. This is the greatest fear of all predators.

I knew that it would come someday, but not this early. I wanted a few more sets of seasons to be with Akycha. I wanted to share more fun with him, to hunt together, and to show him the place of large water where my burrow used to be and make territory with him there.

Not in the same place, of course, as I remember with a guilty twinge that my two little huntresses, Cetnenn and Caoineag, are still inside that burrow where I had told them to wait for me to return.

I should have stayed that night and should not have gone off hunting, but what has happened has happened. There could be another burrow near there.

It would be nice to be able to see the sun setting again over the green hills on the other far side of the large water again and watch that sun turn the large water all golden as it sets behind the green hills on the other side, turning the things that move across the sky overhead all red behind it, until it disappears.

Maybe I could even see my Aataentsic again. It has only been seven or eight sets of seasons since he left to find the large water. Then I realize with a shudder that I don't remember the exact number of sets of seasons since he left me. It has been seven or eight, but I can't remember. I don't remember that many sets of seasons passing this quickly. Where did they all go?

I wish the human female, Aataentsic, with the voice of the wind would not have come through this meadow and talked to me. I wish I could not have understood her, and still do not know how it was possible to have understood human when she did talk to me. I do not talk human, and they do not talk our language, and now I am too old to even remember when my young left to go make his own burrow.

I give up, sigh sadly, and go to sleep against my lover, sharing his warmth to comfort me.

I dream, and something is wrong. I am outside the burrow and know it is a dream I am in, but it is so real. The day is beautiful and warm, as if it was spring again, and in the meadow, all the trees and plants are once more full and green.

Oddly enough, I can't tell where the sun is. It is daylight, but there are no shadows underneath the meadow's plants and trees, and it is evenly the same light everywhere. Still, it is so nice, and I want to walk in the meadow to enjoy the day; but I can't walk for some reason, and I am hungry.

I sit and watch, instead, as creatures come toward me from the north, entering this meadow in countless numbers and types; all the creatures that would be in a forest or meadow, including many creatures of types I do not know, as my mother, Asaseyaa, walks in front of them and they follow, all moving south behind her.

Asaseyaa turns her head to smile at me as she passes, and then walks onward leading the rest, and I wonder how my mother can be here. It has been so long, she must be dead by now. She does not talk, only smiles at me and walks onward south, as predator and prey walk together, all the creatures in their countless numbers, following her south; birds of all types flying overhead, keeping slow pace in the air with the creatures of the ground below.

None of them sees me as they pass; none of them see anything, they only look straight ahead, following her. Kekuit, Red Fur, Cetnenn, Caoineag, Alarana, Asiaq, Atsentma, Thamuatz, Sesondowah, Kuanja, Kyanna all walk with the rest of the many creatures, and though I call to them as they walk past where I sit watching, they do not see me, do not answer, or even notice me as they walk by.

There are other badgers among them, walking with the ones I know. But even though they all walk past beside the ones I know are dead; I can't see the faces of these other badgers, as if those faces were hidden from me for some reason.

The slow procession moves onwards through the meadow; endlessly following my mother Asaseyaa south, as I sit and watch unable to move.

Then the thought comes in what I know is a dream as I dream it, "I have to join and follow them."

But I can't stand up to follow; for some reason my rear legs don't work and there is something wrong with my back and I am hungry, terribly hungry.

I wake up shivering next to Akycha as he grooms me in the darkness of our winter burrow. He wants to know why I was disturbed in my sleep, awakening him, and I can't tell him.

There was no fear in the dream, but for some reason it makes me shiver, and even with Akycha helping by grooming me it still takes a while to fall asleep again, and then there are no dreams that I remember until we awaken to go hunt again.

The dream seemed so real that I almost expect to see the meadow covered with warmth and new growing things as we break through the snow covering our entrance again.

It is still the same winter meadow; just a little deeper this time, and a struggle for us to work our way through as we try to find food in this vast whiteness the forest has become.

Food is not easy. The prey is either gone or better at running swiftly across the top of the snow than we are at catching it, until we finally give up hunting to have fun, but even that is hard in the thickness of snow.

We also give up that idea and return to the burrow for some more sleep. Next time we will come out in the darkness to find prey because it is always easier to hunt at night than to hunt in the daylight.

We sleep again until the call for food comes from our bellies as we awaken in darkness . . . or we thought it would be darkness, but there is far too much light coming through the snow piled over the entrance. It should be night based on our body's way of finding the time, but there is too much light as we go up the entrance tunnel together.

We find out why when we finally manage to break through the snow over our entrance. We have lost track of our days and nights, sleeping in the burrow. The moon is up, and the meadow glows in full moonlight as the moon hangs in the sky above us.

We hunt and are rewarded by prey, smaller creatures that are not cautious enough in this night of light. We catch a few mice that run too incautiously on top of the snow. Then we find a large, white rabbit of the snows roaming in the light of the full moon, roaming to find food as we are, and I stop.

Akycha prepares to stalk and kill, but I can't. I can't kill rabbit, even if this is a large, white one of the snows, and not the small, young brown female one with the strange markings I had protected. I can't kill this one, and suddenly for no reason I am afraid!

Akycha is puzzled beside me at my hesitation, thinking that I am only tired again, and prepares to run it down himself and bring some back to me. But I stop him. I can't kill this one or have it killed for me, and we return to the burrow with only the mice in our bellies.

I shiver beside my sleeping, puzzled lover. He still cannot understand why I could not kill a rabbit or why I would not let him do it instead, especially since it was a nice, plump one at that.

I shiver because something is wrong, and something is coming. Someone told me that, but I forget who, and I know it is coming, and do not know what it is, and I am afraid. There was something someone said to me many seasons ago that I should remember, about a young, brown female rabbit with strange, black markings, and snow or cold; except it was not exactly about her or the snow or cold. I do not remember what it was; that was so many seasons ago and memory fades, but it was important, and I can't remember it now.

I shiver and try to fall asleep beside Akycha, grateful for his warmth. Sometimes when I wake up and my legs are stiff, it feels better to keep them tucked against Akycha's warmth while we sleep, as I had once kept Thamuatz tucked against me while we slept together in the cold.

That was almost seven full sets of seasons ago I remember suddenly; where did all the seasons go behind me? I finally manage to fall asleep; but the fear is there again before I do, I am old.

Akycha and I awaken to roam the night for food, and the moon is almost as full as the last time we came out to hunt, turning the snow around us into glowing white light as it gives us more than enough light by which to hunt.

We find the fox was hungry also, as we roam for prey. The large white rabbit of the snows, that I could not kill and did not want Akycha to kill, is freshly dead, torn apart and eaten with the scent of the fox on it.

There is little left, but we share it together, and then roam for other prey. There are a few mice but not enough, and the snow now makes it difficult to catch them as they run across the top of it. But there are two of us, and we make a good set of predators as we chase them to each other until one of us can catch them. Then we share what little there is with each other.

The rest of our night is spent trying to break a hole in the cold, solid top of the stream until finally we give up and accept that we have to take the cold snow into our mouths and wait for it to melt to get a drink this night. Akycha and I both hate this but we need to drink so we do it. We both realize that it will be a hungry winter as we trek back to our burrow to sleep again.

Then I see her again as we go inside.

Akycha goes inside first as I stop for one last look at the beauty of the forest, looking at the trees and the snow on the ground reflecting bright moonlight, admiring the beauty of moonlight on snow as I look back the way we came from.

Suddenly receiving the predator's instinct that tells me I am being watched; and see her for the first time, as she smiles up at me from where she stands just below the hillock in our meadow.

My mother, Asaseyaa, is standing below the hillock, watching me and smiling upward from where we have just walked, with a large white rabbit of the snows waiting beside her without fear of her. She must know it is there beside her, but she doesn't turn to kill it. She only smiles up at me; turns, and walks slowly south through the snow-covered meadow in the moonlight with the large white rabbit of the snows following her.

I stare astonished at them; as my mother Asaseyaa walks south, with this prey creature hopping behind when it should be fleeing her.

I know this is not a dream. I am seeing this happen as I watch them, until she disappears into the edge of the forest to the south, with the white rabbit of the snows following.

Only then do I realize there are no tracks in the snow behind them, and my mother looked only a season or two older than the last time I saw her; she should be older than I am by at least several sets of seasons, an impossible age for one of us.

I shiver in the cold moonlight and go inside to try to sleep. It is hard to sleep. Akycha stirs restlessly beside me as we sleep, as if sensing I am disturbed by something. I try to let him sleep. He is our main provider of prey now and may be the only provider soon.

I let him sleep and will not tell him of the thing that happened outside as he waited patiently for me to come inside the sleeping chamber. I am old, and I am afraid.

My legs don't ache when I awaken, and for which I am grateful, while trying to understand why I awakened.

Nothing is wrong inside the sleeping chamber, and there is no predator warning instinct of danger outside, I am just awake for some reason while Akycha slumbers peacefully alongside me.

Then I remember there was a dream, but I can't remember what it was, although it was important. What I do remember is that there was something in the dream about the small young brown female rabbit I had cared for in the coldness around us.

Strange I should say it that way, but then it is strange why I had sheltered her in the first place. She was prey and I am predator but somehow that did not matter. My own two young were dead in the falling snow, and she was so weak and helpless I had to help her. I wonder what happened to her, if she found a new burrow somewhere safe where she could be cared for and loved, or if she died after she left me.

I give up and go back to sleep.

We awaken in the night, and Akycha is curious about why I am so slow to leave the burrow, and why I insist on first looking carefully around the meadow before leaving the entrance, as if expecting to see someone else waiting outside. But no one else is there, and I leave the safety of the burrow entrance to go hunt with him.

We are a little luckier this night, but it is still only mice and they are still too small for a good meal: we feast as much as one can on too little prey and then just decide to roam.

Badgers normally seldom leave the area of their primary winter burrow, spring brings the time of roaming and extending territory. Spring is also the time of making sure that all your old burrows, as well as the new ones, are clean and well prepared in case you need them for safety or sleep. Winter is when you only use a small amount of the territory you have claimed to roam and hunt in, and spend most of your time sleeping in the burrow you have chosen as your primary winter burrow.

But tonight, we are both curious to see if there is more prey to be found in other areas close by. We roam until the sky begins to lighten, and by then, we both know the answer. The forest will give us what it gives us this winter, and no more, but fortunately, the fat layers we built up for this winter are still good, depleted, but still good. Those fat layers will see us through the winter with what we can catch for prey, but we will have to feed heavily this coming spring to build our bodies back up to the plumpness they should be.

As the sky turns to light around us, we return to the burrow to go inside to sleep.

I cast a nervous glance behind me as I enter, but Asaseyaa is not there, and the forest is light enough now to be dangerous to us with our darker fur standing out against the whiteness of winter snows, and so I go inside to tuck comfortably against Akycha after we both groom each other and sleep.

There are no dreams this time and we awaken to hunt again, return to the burrow, sleep, awaken to hunt again, return to the burrow, and sleep. Our winter passes slowly as I wonder if I will see my mother again, and I try to puzzle what I did see of Asaseyaa that night. For my mother, who was the greatest predator I have ever known, to let a simple prey creature roam behind her as she left this meadow is something I still can't understand.

Winter is a struggle for food for every creature in the forest, but my mother, Asaseyaa, simply walked away to the south in the moonlight, with that prey creature hopping as peacefully behind her as if she were its own mother instead of mine. Maybe she found some rabbit prey to shelter as I had done, but hers was a full-grown winter white rabbit, not a young one like I found. The full-grown rabbit would hardly need sheltering by a predator.

I give up this puzzle, and simply resume the winter hunt for food with my lover with little luck.

The snow falls again, and it is too much trouble to go outside, so we simply sleep, cuddled together instead. The snow stops, and we go outside to hunt, but it is too deep for hunting, or even to bother chasing mice across the top of, since they have their tunnels well under it now. The sky clears, and the nights are dark with no moon, then the moon returns slowly to full again, and passes into darkness again as we hunt. The days turn to darkness and back to day as we roam at night, and the season of cold passes into warmer days, then returns to more snow and colder days and nights.

We roam and sleep, and the days become hunting times for us, even if our darker fur does stand out against the snow. We are simply more cautious as we roam for food. The winter passes and the days begin to warm as the sun returns more and more often from the dark mass that is the sky overhead in the daytime. Waking early to go outside and get some sunlight warmth before we hunt the night that follows each day, we now spend more time at the end of the day in front of our burrow entrance. Our winter passes more swiftly into warmer days and nights as we wait anxiously for the spring to return with its creatures, where we can feed again the way that we are used to doing, and as we sleep, the days warm into the ones we have been waiting for.

Pain

Spring roams warm and perfect into our meadow as we emerge from our burrow together to watch. The days pass, the meadow grows greener, and we hunt to seek food again to fill our bodies.

This day is warm already, and Akycha and I travel as one while enjoying the warm sunshine and the joy of closeness. I know now that we will always be different from the rest of our kind. I will no longer be solitary. Akycha and I will share our lives together, and I will take him to the burrow overlooking my large water where we can watch the sunsets together. I will return there for the first time since the deaths of my two little huntresses, and will spend my last days there with my lover.

At the most, I have maybe one or two full sets of seasons left in my life, and want him to enjoy them there with me, to watch the sunset turn the large water golden and the sky red, and sit on the flat area in front of our burrow and warm ourselves in the late afternoon sunlight. Or we may watch rain falling from the sky upon the large water, and see those things arc up in colors across the sky from the water when the rain falls when it is sunny, and I hope Akycha will realize it is the most beautiful place of all for us to live together.

We find a fresh deer kill in an open area near the stream where a predator must have surprised it while drinking. There is bear scent around it, so we know what killed the deer and are cautious.

I know that bear scent, but I am older now, and my memory fades and my nose is not what it used to be. It is not important; the bear has eaten his fill and gone, leaving both of us a nice feast after a long winter of not eating very much. We do not have to worry about winter now because judging by the heat of today, it will be a very warm spring indeed. We feast, filling our tummies and grunting in satisfaction, stopping at last to sit in the grass and enjoy the warmth of the sunlight.

I enjoy just sitting in the sun so much now, for I tire more easily, making it harder to chase prey, and sometimes I forget things from time to time. It is now the thirteenth spring of my life, but Akycha does not care. We are bonded for life and will share it until I die some season from now at the place of large water I loved so much.

Akycha also does not mind the scars that will always be on my face and body from the human dogs gone wild that killed my young the winter before he found me, the winter I sheltered the young rabbit. There is something about the death of my young from the dogs gone wild and the sheltering of her that is important from somewhere in my past, but it is too much trouble to try and remember that during this present happiness.

We sit in satisfaction, glad to be with each other during another fresh spring. Akycha says I am his mate, and even if I am never able to have his young, he will still stay with me and care for me until I die.

We sniff the fresh breeze, and there is another faint scent somewhere close, from the downwind side of us so we can't quite catch its source or type. But we do not care as we groom each other. He grooms me so very well, not minding my age difference at all. The noise of cracking branches nearby makes us alert, but then it is still again, and we go back to happiness together. Still . . . a scent is there.

I know that scent, which is closer now but still too faint to really smell from its downwind side. I know that scent . . . I know that scent . . . I know that scent. . . .

The bear . . . the bear!

I scream the alert to my new mate. I know that scent now, but Akycha has been too busy grooming me to be aware of it!

We turn together, whirling around, moving as one with my lover, standing together to face the threat, our teeth and claws ready as the huge brown monster that is both bear and human comes. But we are too exposed in the open!

Feet pounding the ground, roaring with fury, the huge brown bear is already charging us! Roaring his rage at me, I see the old, ripped scars on one side of his face, and the thin white scar on top of his head from front to rear as he charges us.

It is my old enemy, the one that tried so hard to kill me when I was younger, the one that tried to kill Alarana and Asiaq, and the one that may have killed my brother Tigranuhi!

I wasn't alert enough, I wasn't alert enough! I curse myself for stupidity as we wait the charge together. It is far too late to run. He has us in the open. We have been eating his kill, enraging him, and this thing that is not truly bear at all hates me for what I had done!

I had entered his valley and walked away; he did not walk from that valley but he did leave it. He covers the distance to us quickly now, as I wait with pride beside my lover to meet him.

If my lover dies, I die with him, and if I die, my lover falls beside me, and neither of us will abandon the other now as we scream our rage at the thing coming to kill us. We rise to meet it with our claws and teeth!

The bear hits us as we jump; springing to each side of the bear, trying to go around both sides of it at the same time to confuse the bear with our move, the move Tigranuhi and I did together when we fought it. But that was at night, and night's concealment helped us, and now it is daylight, and I am too old and too slow!

It knows, remembers me, and turns toward me first; almost casually reaching out and hitting me with one massive paw as I try to dodge around it, but do not succeed!

The terrible blow knocks breath out of me and rips four long bloody furrows in my side, as I try to get my feet back into the right position while flying through the air, and I hear Akycha's scream of terrible rage behind me, with a sudden roar of deep pain from the bear as I go end over end through air with my side hurting terribly where its claws ripped my side!

Hit the wrong way, backward and hard against the tree, and something cracks inside me! Pain! Pain!

My back is pure, raw pain, and I scream the pain to the forest and fall, hitting the ground and scream again from the pain in my back as both my rear legs thrash out of control, giving me more pain, and then I see my lover and scream in grief!

Akycha has tried to distract the bear from me and stayed too long with his teeth buried in its too thick hide; ripping and tearing at it with claws and teeth! It reaches down and grabs him with both front paws; lifts him easily and puts his head in its mouth and I scream in grief as my beautiful lovers body pumps blood and falls from the bear's paws; as the bear spits my lover's head out, looks at me, and smiles!

I scream in rage, trying to move and go kill it or die with Akycha; then scream the vicious terrible pain, as my back sends its message of now useless rear legs horribly up my spine!

I want to kill this creature; but can only sob with pain, and try to crawl away to hide as the bear begins to eat my wonderful lover!

And through my pain as I crawl helplessly away; I cry at the sounds of Akycha being devoured behind me, as the bear ignores me and eats my love.

I crawl like some pathetic prey creature, every movement raw agony as I cry from the pain, and cry from the new fear of being so totally helpless when the bear comes for me also, and I know it will come for me as soon as it finishes my lover; and I crawl trying not to scream from the terrible pain of each movement, as I crawl desperately for our burrow, and cry as I remember my lover beside me in that burrow, and cry from the pain, and my rear legs will not work, and my side hurts so badly bleeding from where claws ripped it!

I know that it is coming for me now; I hear it coming as I crawl into the burrow entrance, crawl inside as deep as I can go, and faint from the pain. It will dig me out and kill me now, but at least I will not feel it.

I awaken in agony and whimper with the pain! My hips will not work my rear legs are useless my side has stopped bleeding but hurts, and I know that I will starve to death; I can no longer hunt or dig for food.

The pain becomes too much as my mind wanders into unconsciousness again.

The dogs are coming! I run my young, I run my young! I stayed out far too late with my young as I tried to show them the snow falling, and gather a last bit of body fat with them before going done into our den for the winter.

The dogs are coming through the falling snow for my two little hunters, and I will die to defend them from these human-bred predators! I scream my rage as I whirl around in the falling whiteness, turning to fight, and waking up screaming in agony in my burrow alone!

I hurt so badly; oh my back hurts so badly! I have never even dreamed of pain like this before, even when the dogs that killed my young tore me up as I fought them to protect my young, and then fought them to avenge my dead young murdered by these killers turned loose on my forest by the humans! Pain! I faint again.

I turn to fight; trying to keep my young behind me as I fight and the dogs try to circle me as snow falls on us all equally. They are five to one; but they are still afraid of my claws and teeth, and the total rage with which I greet them as they try to close with me, get around my teeth and claws, and take my young from me!

I wake up and cry from the pain, and try to move, and scream as I try to turn! I can't move without pain, I wonder where the bear went, he must have followed me here; I wish he would find me now, anything but this pain! The pain drives me back into the past again as I faint.

The dogs close with me; appearing through the falling snow to rush what they thought was helpless prey with helpless young! I rip savagely at the first dog that rushes through the falling whiteness, and, too confident because he thought five to one was good odds for him. He is wrong; my claws rip his face as he yelps and jumps backward to escape his pain!

He is foolish enough to lose his temper and close again as I rip his face again!

The others try to circle and I tear at every one that tries to get around me for my young; trying to keep Kuanja and Kyanna safe behind me, while still matching the circles of the dogs around where I stand ready to kill! They try to trick me, and I bleed another one who is too confident; and I wake up sobbing, knowing that I lost and my young died anyway, and I can't move anymore through the pain, and I faint again.

They are in the burrow waiting for me to come back with prey and I have; this fat rabbit was just sitting out in the open sleeping this night, and it is almost dawn now.

I will be back to the burrow overlooking our beautiful large water to share it with Cetnenn and Caoineag by the time the sun is up. I told them to wait for my return before they could leave the burrow, and when it is dark we will go out later to give them more instruction.

Remembering not to tell them that I caught this one sleeping, thinking how proud they will be of their mother for catching this fine plump prey as I enter the burrow, reach the sleeping chamber, and they wait in the sleeping chamber together to greet me as I enter, and they are proud of me; two perfect little skeletons with all their bones showing, walking toward me as their skulls smile proudly at their mother, and I drop the prey from my mouth and scream!

I am wandering through the meadow below this little hillock that is my home with my mother Asaseyaa; and she is trying to tell me something, something very important about letting go. She wants me to come to her, tells me to let go and we will walk south through the meadow together; and I wake up screaming through the pain!

Sobbing at my helplessness, and sobbing at the death of my lover Akycha who died trying to save me; and I was too old, and too slow, and caused him to die for nothing!

If only Akycha would have run away and left me to die instead; and I faint from the pain again.

The young brown rabbit that watched me as I grieved over my young in the falling snow grooms me as she tends to my wounds.

I have to protect her she is so helpless like my young; who I could not protect, who died because I was old and weak and slow!

I have no pride left and cry with grief as the young rabbit cares for me; tending to my terrible face wounds in the falling snow around us, as she cleans the blood from there and from my body. I am her enemy and she is still caring for my wounds and trying to comfort me; we can't even speak the same language and she is caring for me.

I wake up again and the pain is not so bad now; I feel numb along my back and it only hurts when I try to move, then everything drifts away into pain again.

I hear the call again in my mind not in my ears, looking up from the prey I have stopped to eat in this frozen white winter forest near my burrow above the large water.

Someone was beside me but there is no one beside me? Suddenly realizing I know the one who called, know the unseen one who was beside me, and begin to run frantically for the top of the hill behind my burrow overlooking the large water.

I ran here before, I know I did, but this time it will be different, this time he will still be alive if I run fast enough! And I scream my grief as I see Kekuit lying in the snow of this barren snow-covered frozen field he tried so hard to crawl through with the last of his strength to reach his mother again; the only one he truly knew could hunt, the one who might have kept him from starving to death if she had only trained him better or kept him with her longer.

My mother Asaseyaa is trying so hard to tell me something and I try to listen, but something is wrong and I can't follow her. Asaseyaa wants me to come to her now.

Tells me "Relax and walk south with me, it is time to go." as she turns to leave, walking south through the meadow without me.

And I scream for her to wait for me, and try to walk as she leaves but can only drag myself, and there are no shadows even below the nearby small trees, and I can't tell where the sun is above me, and my rear legs don't work as I beg her to not leave me alone! I am still too young to be on my own; but she is walking away, and I try to crawl to her, and I wake up.

The pain is there again; and it throbs through my body, but my rear body is becoming numb now and I don't feel my rear legs until I move and pain rips through me again as I faint again.

The young rabbit sooths me, and tries to tell me something about where she has to go; but we do not speak the same language, and she has to go without me as she gives me a final parting kiss.

Alarana and Asiaq are walking in front of me and their fur is gone, and they are all bloody bodies, with no fur to cover them! I scream for them to come back to the burrow with me and put their fur back on; and they smile bloody red stripped of all fur smiles at me, as they turn to come back with their red bodies stripped of fur and I scream!

My new lover Akycha is here, handsome and strong.

Akycha likes me in spite of my greater age, sooths and comforts me, wants me, and I love him as I cuddle beside him safe and warm in our burrow as he grooms me. It was only a dream, everything was only a dream!

I look up as he softly grooms me. He has no head!

I wake up again screaming, and cry from grief for my lover and grief for myself. To be helpless is the worst of all fates for a predator; we of all the forest creatures know what it means to be helpless.

It means the first predator that finds you will kill you, or you will starve to death slowly. The grass eaters can find grass and hide near burrows if they are lucky enough to be injured near food and water, but I have to hunt my food; I am a meat eater. I can't eat grass like the young female rabbit could.

The deer kill, it is probably still there; I can crawl to the deer kill, or find grubs.

My mind is working again and I am thinking of survival not death; if I crawl to the deer kill I can eat again, and I am so thirsty. I need water so badly now, and the stream is near the deer kill, I can eat and drink.

I try to get out of my den and the pain is numbness now if I do not move in certain ways. I scream in agony as I learn what ways not to try to move my body, as my screams bounce off the walls of our burrow and mock me by screaming back to me. The burrow I shared with my handsome younger lover Akycha.

I try to stop even thinking of him; he is dead, I must survive!

Crawling

The bear is arrogant. He is not even there when I manage to work my painful way back up to the light at the burrow entrance, crying not from the pain, but from the knowledge that my lover Akycha will never see the wonderful burrow overlooking my large water, and I want so much to go back to it now.

I will. If I am to die, then I will die there and not here. My rear is a useless weight dragging behind as I begin to crawl. It hurts less if the side the bear ripped is upward, but I fear the flies. If they come and land on the ripped part where his claws tore me, I can't reach back there to clean my body, and the young of the flies will hatch on my body and grow into things that look like small worms that will eat at the wounds, and then the smell of my wounds will bring more flies and still more crawling young to feast on me, and I will die in misery. I must clean the side but can't reach back to do it.

The answer is the stream. I will let it clean me, as it cleaned and soothed my wounds so long ago when I had my first fight for territory. If I can reach the stream, the bear's kill is the only food available right now, and it is near the stream also, but where is the bear?

He can kill me easily, but hunger and thirst are my desperation right now, and my injured side must be cleaned, or the young flies will devour me. I crawl for the deer kill. If I die there, at least I will die quickly.

But the kill is gone; the bear as taken it away to hide it from any other predators that may try to rob him of it, or to deliberately hide it from me.

I weep and crawl for the stream. The flies are coming. Crawling, I find that at least the stream is still there, and I crawl into the water slowly to let it clean me.

Pain! The water finds my back in its coldness, and the shock of pain in that back lets me know I have made a mistake. I howl with the pain, and ride it, crawling deeper into the stream. I must clean my side, and I whimper in agony as the stream's water finally becomes deep enough to flow across me, hoping no prey creatures have seen me whimpering.

I am a predator, I will not give up now, so I wait in pain as water flows across me and washes my back along with my injured side.

When my side is clean and my back simply becomes a dull, numb, throbbing reminder of my new helplessness, it is time to crawl out, but I remember to drink as deeply as possible before leaving the stream.

I am going south. There is nothing left for me here, where my favorite burrow in the little hillock is. I am returning to my two little huntresses, Cetnenn and Caoineag, so we can watch the sunset in front of my burrow overlooking the large water.

I crawl, moving south in the remaining daylight.

Night is far too dangerous for me now, because others hunt in darkness also, and I can't fight them. Even day is too dangerous for me unless I can bluff any daytime predators into thinking that I am not actually helpless. I am prey, not predator now, and have no pride left as I drag myself south for the place I must go.

The ground drags slowly past as my body drags over it. My front paws were never intended to hold all of my weight to pull me along the ground; they are already tired, and I have come so slowly for such a short distance. It took days to get up here from that burrow, and it will take far longer to go back. Being forced to stay near the stream, dragging myself south is the worst part because predators lurk near the water to take their prey.

I do not want to be prey, but I need the stream for water to drink and water to keep my wounds clean. Having to go back into the stream from time to time as I drag myself south, I make sure flies can't settle on the wounds where the bear's claws ripped me.

Having to go back into the stream and fainting once in it from the pain of my back when cold water hits it. I wake up in time to keep from drowning, and force myself to still stay inside the water while gasping, coughing, and trying not to faint again.

Food will be the problem; hunting is out of the question, food will have to be whatever creatures are really incautious, or whatever is available. Some plants and some roots are good, but I never really concentrated on plants before. Prey was always available. Eating the wrong plants can poison me and leave me even more than helpless now.

Nighttime solves part of the problem as I manage to find some smaller grubs out near the stream. But it is not enough; my winter fat layers are depleted, and there will have to be more food than this to survive. I sleep finally in the most protected, thick brush I can drag myself into, because digging a safe burrow is impossible for me now.

Hunger is the first awareness I have upon waking. Dawn is not here yet; but the hunger is there, tightening my stomach. I have to find food today.

I begin crawling again; the stream is the first thing I have to do, and the water is colder in the early morning air.

Gasping, riding the pain, I let my front paws ease my useless body into it. I must remember to wait until the sun is higher and the water is warmer from now on as I whimper from the pulses of pain and manage to get my side covered with flowing water again.

The claw wounds are healing, but there will be scars there forever, or at least as long as forever is for me now, though I suspect not long. In a few days I will not have to make sure that they are clean, but right now I endure the pain to concentrate on other things.

I can tell that already by the heat that the sun will be hotter today, and I will need food soon, and food that can't escape me or outrun me. Since I can't run at all that limits the types of prey to be found and caught but there has to be something in this forest roaming that I can catch . . . ground squirrels!

No, I can't dig, at least not fast enough to catch them.

I find a patch of fresh brush next to the stream, but it's far too thin this soon after winter to hide me well, yet if I stay still, I can blend in with the shadows anyway. I blend into the shadows and wait as the sun moves higher in the sky above, and wait until the tree squirrel comes to drink too far away from me.

I force myself to wait and not try to rush him anyway as he begins to look for any food he might have hidden near the brush where I am waiting inside. I force myself to remain still in spite of the hunger as he comes near me, then I lunge for him and miss!

He runs back to his tree, chattering alarm, and I curse myself. I could almost taste him in my mouth. Now my hunger is worse. I could almost taste him in my mouth.

Missing him has also made my back spasm again; as I try not to scream and grit my teeth in agony until my rear legs stop thrashing helplessly out of control, and my back returns to the familiar, dull, throbbing pain. Then I begin to drag myself south beside the stream again.

The day passes, but the hunger does not. The sun heats me as I crawl through the grass and plants, trying to stay under the cool cover of sheltering ferns near the stream as much as possible. If they are too thick, I have to drag myself around them, and my front paws are so tired already, but I will not stop until I am back where my two little huntresses wait for my return. I told them to wait there for my return; I have to get back to them

I crawl back into the stream again for water, and my back hurts when I do, but the hunger is worse, I will settle for any food now even plants.

Red Fur walks in front of me; guiding me to the nearest edible ones as I crawl behind him, following as best I can.

Red fur is dead!

I blink, clearing my head by shaking it. He is gone, but the plants are here, and I eat greedily of what I can; but plants are not real food to my kind, and can only fill my stomach until I can find prey again.

It was Red Fur. I know it was Red Fur, he was right in front of me; but he lies dead long ago, torn apart in the red leaves falling around his body. He was my first mate in this life, and he gave the first young to me; but he is dead and can't walk with me, it was a waking dream. I sigh through the dull throbbing pain of my back and begin dragging myself south again.

The loose ground near the stream is the easiest if I stay on it or on the grass. My lower side is sore from being dragged, and I look for the easiest ways to travel without having to leave the stream as my guide. Brush is no longer something to conceal inside; now it is an obstacle. The traveling is horribly slow, and the sunlight is brighter and hotter than I thought it would be; it may be necessary to risk night predators and travel by night instead of during the day.

I find myself needing the stream more and more for drink; dragging this useless body into it for healing and drinking, then dragging myself back out of it again, slowly but surely moving south.

The day passes, but the hunger does not, and I see so many prey creatures now. The squirrels that mock me from the trees, and the rabbit that almost runs into me, simply runs away, but stops when it realizes I am helpless.

I am so hungry, and it is far too early for any ground-nesting birds to leave eggs, otherwise I would look for them. As I continue to drag myself south, I try to ignore the food appearing around me. The food that is available now is also now sure of me and keeping its distance, there is nothing to eat.

I sleep hungry this night, then move slowly south again at next light. It is harder to concentrate now, and I simply drag myself. The going is hard and slow, one rear side is rubbing against the ground as I drag my useless rear body with my front paws, and the sun is hot upon me again.

Alarana and Asiaq walk in front as I drag myself behind them. They are walking too fast; I can't keep up with them. I beg them to slow down for me; as they turn, all their fur falls off leaving them smiling bloody bodies as they walk back toward me!

I wake up screaming; lying in the grass, exposed to any predator out in the open under the sun's heat. Cursing myself for stupidity; dragging this useless body to the stream again to wash the wounds on my side, and to drink as hunger gnaws at my stomach while I drink. Then I just lay in the stream to let the water relax my pain.

Night is coming; I do not know how long I lay exposed in the open, but night is coming. I start to drag this useless body from the stream to begin crawling south again and look up; and he smiles at me.

His face scarred forever by my claws, the bear sits beside the stream smiling at me, sure of this, ready to kill me. And I know that the unseen human who walked beside the bear is now no longer beside him; he is now inside him, and he is the bear.

I will die fighting as best I can; teeth ready for him, body unable to rise and fight him, as the huge brown bear simply smiles and then walks away. He has been watching me, he knows that I am helpless, he has time.

The scars on his face are still there where my claws ripped him as a bear when he tried to take my Alarana and my Asiaq; and he remembers who gave the scars to him before I entered his valley when he was there as a human, and walked away untouched by him. He will be back.

I begin to crawl; dragging myself, clawing my way south with my front paws dragging my side along the ground. My front paws hurt from the work of dragging myself; they were never meant to pull my entire body weight along and I am old anyway. I will have to rest soon and need safety; let the bear work for this meal.

One of my burrows is not too far from here, and, if I can reach it he will have trouble digging me out; the sleeping chamber is under the roots of one of the tall wide trees that lose their leaves each winter, with an entrance on either side of it, and if he can dig that up he can have me!

Whatever he is now, the human inside this bear is arrogant and has forgotten that I am a true predator and not whatever he is now. He thinks that he can just return and take me at his pleasure when he is ready, but he will have a great deal of difficult digging to do, and an entire tree to move!

It is still there, and there is a prey creature inside it in residence. Food! I drag myself through the entrance as quickly as I can, but I make too much noise and am far too slow. It flees out the other entrance.

I curse myself for that because it would have been so good, and I am so hungry. I begin to eat the old grass in here where I had lined this sleeping chamber long ago. It is long dead and tasteless, but it gives me something to eat at least.

He is outside when I awaken; not bothering to dig, he does not have to; I must come out of here for water and food and he knows it, he only has to wait for me.

He waits patiently for me to come out as day becomes night, becomes day, becomes night again.

I have never been this thirsty before, he waits.

I have never been this hungry before, he waits.

He waits patiently for me to come outside to be eaten, and I will not give him the satisfaction; I will die down here first of thirst and hunger. He is death; let him come to me, I will not go out to him!

Day becomes night, becomes day, becomes night, becomes day, becomes night.

I whimper in my sleep as I starve and die of thirst; and my dead come back to me in my sleep.

I whimper as my mother Asaseyaa tries to tell me something about, "Letting go," and I do not want to! I want to go back to my burrow overlooking the large water and see the sun set again, and see my two little huntresses who are talking to me; but then I remember that Cetnenn and Caoineag are dead, and are not really talking to me as I awaken.

My back hurts again, and I am so very hungry and thirsty, and Tigranuhi can be not talking to me either in the darkness of this burrow. Tigranuhi is gone and has been gone since we fought this huge brown monster together to save Asiaq and Alarana.

It is dark outside; I can tell from the darkness coming down the entrance tunnel into this darker burrow.

Darkness within darkness within darkness my black-furred dark brother Tigranuhi sits across from me in the sleeping chamber, and I wonder if it is another dream as he speaks to me again.

"We have to leave now," he says softly.

I try to concentrate *"Leave?"*

"We have to leave." he repeats, "We have to leave if you want to go home."

I try to focus, *"What about the monster?"*

"The bear is sleeping; he could not stay awake forever, and if what you want to do more than anything else is to go back to the burrow overlooking your large water then we have to leave now."

I start to move; then suddenly remember that Tigranuhi was never at that burrow, and I never mentioned it to him. It doesn't matter; I am so hungry and thirsty, it no longer matters.

Tigranuhi leads to the entrance, and I see him clearly crawling behind him. This is not a dream.

The bear sleeps outside, snoring heavily, while I crawl quietly past him with Tigranuhi in front. I must have some water from the stream first.

We stop, but only I drink as Tigranuhi waits, and I wonder briefly why he does not thirst as I do. But then it is time to leave, and I crawl, with my brother leading and guiding me through the forest.

Tigranuhi's dark body blends so well into shadows and darkness I have trouble seeing him from time to time in the darkness around us, but I know that he is there roaming with us, and it is comforting to know that another fighter is with me on our journey. The darkness of the night covers us well as we go, and only the uneasy feeling I have about how my life seems to be so joined now with the life of this huge brown monster of a bear that worries me.

I stop crawling and shiver, and for I suddenly remember that was exactly what I had thought the last time I saw Tigranuhi when we fled together with my young from the place where my dark brother's mate Atida was killed, and where we fought this huge brown monster bear together, trying to save Alarana and Asiaq.

Tigranuhi does not look as aged as I do. He looks the same now as he looked on that night, and he has no scent. Tigranuhi has no scent!

He roams just ahead of me through some brush as I try to follow; dragging my useless body with my front paws, clearing the brush just after he does. He is gone.

It is clear beyond the brush for a small area; Tigranuhi did not have time to roam to the next brush beyond that area; he is simply gone, as he was gone after we fought the bear together.

I begin to crawl again; so hungry so very hungry, and trying to outthink the bear. He follows me, but I have all of this night to get clear of him as he follows.

If he continues to sleep, and if he still thinks I am down in the burrow when he awakens, and if I can keep moving, there may be even more time to lose him. But he still has his nose.

I ignore the hunger in my stomach and the pain in my back, and crawl back for the stream again. I am going to destroy my scent, which is the only way he can be tracking me.

The night-cold stream is raw cold pain again as I crawl into it; but the hunger is worse, and I gasp from the reminder that I am so very hungry as cold water clears my head. There must be something in the water to eat, but it is too early for frogs, and the fish are too quick for me.

I crawl into deeper flowing water and let the water carry me downstream, trying not to shriek like some pathetic prey creature every time I bump into something in the darkness as my back reminds me how foolish this idea is.

All that is important is that the stream is carrying me downstream in the direction I want to go, and destroying any scent trail as it does.

The bear is smarter than any bear should be now, but I do not think he is this smart. His only hope is to remember the direction he last saw me traveling in, follow the stream south, and try to find where I left the water, because my scent trail will only tell him where I entered.

Gasping from the pain, I float downstream in the coldness of the water, bumping into things as I go, until I have had enough. Too much pain, too little food; I must get out, or faint and drown.

I crawl from the side of the stream, trying not to whimper. My back is throbbing pain again, and the coldness of the streams nighttime water made it worse. I wait for the pain to become less, and my rear legs to stop thrashing helplessly out of control, and then begin dragging myself slowly south again.

It is daylight; he will awaken soon, and will wait for a while before he realizes I am not there anymore, and then he will be on the move also. He wants me very badly, and if he is smart enough to remember which direction I was going, he will come south.

The sun is getting hotter, but at least it will be warm, which seems to help my back, even if it does make me thirsty.

My front paws reach and pull, reach and pull, reach and pull; my lower rear side drags against the ground as I gnash my teeth and pull with front paws, dragging myself, crawling slowly as best as possible and moving slowly south.

I know there is another burrow this way to hide in, but the most important thing is food. I am starving and unable to feed myself as Thamuatz had starved when he was unable to feed himself before he found me to help him.

There will be no such luck of finding another badger to care for me, and I will not risk the life of one of my young by leading this monster into their territories, for if I did, the bear would follow and kill them. There is no one I can crawl to without putting them in danger. I must keep crawling.

I crawl, and far behind me, I hear a deep roar of rage as the bear discovers, probably after digging up the entire tree to get into the burrow beneath, that I am gone. Despite pain and hunger, I still manage a happy *"Good!"* as I drag myself along.

He may be stronger and larger, but his arrogance in believing I would simply wait forever down there in the burrow for him to dig me out has made him lose me.

The roars of rage echo off the hillsides far behind me as I crawl, dragging my useless body along with my front paws.

He will be searching, and if I have gained enough lead I may have lost him, or he may not be able to find me again. But if he is smart enough to actually think to use his bear nose to find where I entered the stream, or smart enough to remember the direction I was traveling in, then that will decide whether I survive and reach my burrow overlooking the large water, or not.

I make it through the day somehow. Hunger eats at my stomach and devours muscle since there is nothing else in my body for it to feed on, and I crawl. I crawl until dark and find a rotting tree that has fallen into the stream. I crawl toward it eagerly for I know what that means!

Grubs! They are there, deep under the rotting part of the tree on the bank. Enough to feed me a little, and the stream bank is soft enough to let me dig under the tree to pull more grubs out from under it. I eat greedily, trying to get all of them, but there are so few. At least there were some, and I drink from the stream before crawling further in the darkness to the next nearest burrow. It is not a good one, not yet fully finished, but it will be shelter, and I must rest.

Resting is easy; after dragging my body inside, I simply faint inside the sleeping chamber.

The valley burns behind me as I run screaming with the rest; none of us predators or prey now as we run together from the red wall coming to kill us all.

Trees are exploding and throwing flame before the fire even touches them; turning trees into towers of flames instantly, cutting off escape routes as I dodge frantically in the only direction I can see that is open, and it closes with fire!

I dodge again, and run for another direction as burning embers fall from the sky. The heat is terrible, and the fire is running at us far faster than the slow and weak can run from it. They scream and die behind me as I run; my lungs in agony, my heart ready to burst inside my chest as I run screaming with the rest!

Birds catch fire and burn in front of the flames, falling from the sky around us! The wind is wrong; it has turned from pushing the fire before it faster than the slow can run to now roaring savagely back into the fire, it sucks at me trying to feed me back into the flames. I scream and wake up shaking.

The burrow is darkness as I shake, and he is here. I do not know how long I slept, but I know that he is outside waiting for me; and this burrow is not under a tree, he can dig it out! It was darkness when I crawled in here and it is darkness now, he could not possibly have traveled this far that fast, or found me this quickly!

Then I realize that truth as my stomach tells it to me, I must have been unconscious for more than one dark to light time. I did get some food from the grubs before crawling into here, but that is gone now, and I hunger again badly.

This is not the darkness I went to sleep in; this is at least the next darkness after it, maybe even the one after that. He has had ample time to find where I left the stream and track my scent to here. He did follow the stream south after all to find me; he is too little bear, and too much human now.

Outside I hear the slow deep sound of his steady breathing as he waits rumbling with satisfaction. He will only wait a little while before starting to dig, and this time he will get me; I did not dig this burrow well enough, there is no second safety entrance and it is not under a tree.

Even if there were a second entrance I could not run from the second entrance fast enough to escape, only crawl from it, and this burrow was dug too shallow; the bear will see me crawling to escape as he digs, he has me.

"Why?" she asks softly.

Curious as to why her mother; the source of all food and protection and training, would worry about something so small as a huge monster killer of humans bear waiting outside her poorly made burrow.

Menhit sits across from me, as she waits patiently for me to stop laughing insanely.

Menhit is only three sets of seasons old across from me; Menhit should be ten sets of seasons old, and she has no scent.

"I don't think we can wait for him to fall asleep like last time." I giggle to her.

"Stop that." Menhit sighs patiently, as I once sighed patiently to her when she made a mistake. I, her mother, obey her.

"The bear has his own reasons for rage," she continues softly, "and they have nothing to do with you or with the bear that is now trapped inside this more ancient bear."

"More ancient?" I ask, without understanding what my daughter is talking about, and I shiver as she tells me what I do understand.

"As anger, greed, and a lack of caring for others built inside the human of the valley, he lost his right to be saved by his own choice, and he has fallen back into a more ancient and evil control. He perverted this creature, so he could have the pleasure of using it as his killing thing while he walked with it to watch, and as he perverted it into his personal killing thing, this creature has fallen back into the form of a far more ancient and lethal bear, the ancient creature humans of learning call Arctodus Simus."

"You know the human's learning terms for bears?" I ask, confused how my daughter could know human terms of learning, when we cannot understand human words.

"The Great Cave Bear," she answers, without answering my question, "it is an old enemy of humans. The human chose that form for this bear because he likes to kill as the most ferocious of all bears. This bear's free will and its form as the creature it should be was taken from it by the human, who willingly gave his own free will to others even more evil than he. This bear rages because of another's anger, greed, and evil, and it rages because of the old, thin, white scar you have seen on the bear's head."

"The human who is trapped inside this bear gave him that scar when the human took what the bear loved most in life, and almost took the bear's life. This bear's head is damaged below that thin scar, and another controls him now, as others control the human now. The bear controls neither its rage nor its killing and is not responsible for its rage or its killing. The human who killed this bear's mate, and did that to him, then left him alive to suffer is responsible, and that one will soon have ample time to regret all his actions."

"The human?" I ask, already knowing who we are talking about.

Menhit replies, "He has already received part of his justice and will soon receive the rest. After death came for the ones you never thought you would have in your life again, you sheltered an innocent in the cold around you, and she and one who waited for him at a wall, brought justice to him together when he came to that wall one time too many to kill the innocent. The remainder of this human's justice will be forever, and others will bring that to him, as they bring rest to the bear. You bring him to where they wait for you, without knowing they wait."

I shiver, as if Menhit knew my thoughts, and yet there is something else I remember from seasons ago about someone saying that before, but in my pain and hunger I can't quite remember it now.

"We leave," Menhit says softly, although it is a command.

"How; he waits outside, and he can kill us."

"Oh, I doubt he can bring death to me." Menhit smiles "See."

And I shiver in fear, and for I suddenly remember the other who said that word "see" to me three times in the valley, and what he said with it. Shivering again, I remember the one that only looked like an unnaturally black rabbit with eyes of fire.

Menhit smiles again, and I suddenly know from her smile that she does know my thoughts, and has met the black rabbit herself, and she knows why I shiver! She stands and walks from the sleeping chamber, and I fear, for the bear is outside!

I scream for her to stop, but Menhit shows no sign of caring as she walks out the entrance toward him.

The bear roars in rage as I drag myself frantically in pain up the tunnel, to at least try to distract him from her so she can escape, and crawl outside just in time to see the bear slam a huge paw down through her!

She only smiles up at him unconcerned; for his paw does not hit her, it passes through her as she mocks him by smiling up at him.

Then Menhit simply walks away; while he slams his paw futilely again and again downward through her, bites savagely at nothing, and follows her roaring rage at this smaller thing he can't kill or touch. While she mocks him by simply walking away; as I crawl the other way crying softly.

I know that she is dead; as Tigranuhi is dead, as Kekuit is dead, as Red Fur is dead, as Cetnenn and Caoineag are dead, as Alarana and Asiaq are dead, as Thamuatz is dead, as Atsentma is dead, as Sesondowah is dead, as Kuanja and Kyanna are dead. Death has always been with me, and it has been very busy with me.

I crawl; trying not to whimper with pain and hunger as my back tells me I should not be crawling, and my belly tells me I need food desperately. I have crawled for so long now; I must be close to where I have to go, but my mind is wandering and the bear will not be distracted for very long by whatever my daughter has now become.

He was smart enough to realize that I would come out of the stream somewhere; and if the scream flowed south, then I was moving south, and would continue crawling south once I left the stream.

He was also smart enough to follow the stream to wherever I would have to come out of it, and then to find my scent again, and track to the burrow I was hiding inside. He will simply dig the next one out immediately instead of waiting.

There will be no stopping now; I will have to hide as best possible, and try to break the scent trail somehow.

Another trip south in the stream will kill me, and I learned from my stay in the burrow overlooking the large water that the stream I am following falls in a waterfall down into the place of large water. If I lose track of where I am in the stream while trying to let it carry me south to the large water place, and go over the waterfall; that will certainly kill me.

I crawl as close to the stream as I can; only going into it to drink and sooth my side, before crawling south again as my mind drifts. Remembering, "Life comes from the north, and goes south to die." as I cry from the pain and crawl south.

Front paws in front and pull, front paws in front and pull, the sun heats, and my lower rear side drags along the ground, stripping fur from my body, and my top side heats and pains where the bear ripped me.

I enter the stream, trying to cool myself again, and then drag this useless body from the stream again to crawl south, and hunger as I reach and pull, reach and pull, reach and pull.

There are rocks, and it hurts crawling through them. The sun-heated rocks burn my front paws and hurt my lower rear side as it slides over them, dragging along behind my reaching, pulling front paws. The stream is rocks and bare stone now along the sides of the stream in this area.

I drag myself out of the rocks and try to stay as close as possible to the stream while still crawling south for my burrow. I need the stream for guidance, and the burrow overlooking the large water can't be that far now, even at this slow-crawling pace.

Some of the landmarks around me look familiar, but it is hard to tell when I hurt so badly and am so hungry. I must return to my burrow because Cetnenn and Caoineag are waiting in our burrow. I told them to wait there for my return, and if I can reach the burrow in time, we can watch the sunset together.

Cetnenn and Caoineag are dead . . . I remember, and cry from the pain of loss and the pain of crawling as I drag myself toward the burrow. I want to go home; please let me go home.

The bear follows behind. He is patient and waiting for something. He could kill me at any time, but he waits, and I know that there is something he wants to do that will really hurt me before he kills me. He has never forgotten who ripped his face open that night when he thought he had small, easy prey, but found Tigranuhi and I instead.

Then I understand clearly.

He wants revenge, and he wants to hurt me, not just kill me, and he knows I am going somewhere. He will let me get almost where I am going, and then he will kill me just before I can reach it. He is playing with his prey, just as some forest predators play with their prey before killing it.

My mother, Asaseyaa, walks beside me as I crawl in pain and misery, urging, "Let go, walk with me."

"I will not. I have to go to my burrow and see my daughters again!"

She tells me, "It isn't important anymore, let go! I can't stand to see one of my many daughters suffer like this. Let go and walk with me."

I want to obey and walk with her again so badly; but Cetnenn and Caoineag are waiting for me in our burrow, and we are going to watch the sunset together, and my mother, Asaseyaa, walks south away from me as I wake up.

I have been lying in the sun again, and I burn. I try to drag myself to the stream again, but everything is rock now, and the stream is lower in that rock. I can't reach water unless I let myself fall down into it, and then I may never get out.

There is no way to climb out if I go down there, and if the stream does not have lower stream banks where I can crawl out of it then somewhere ahead of me, the waterfall at the end of it will eat me, and I will never see my burrow that overlooks the large water again.

It is the hottest part of the day now as I crawl, but Thamuatz walks beside me, and he walks very nicely. His front leg is back again, and he has no scent. He is also dead, of course, and I am not surprised he is here now. I am hungry beyond belief, so very thirsty, and badly in pain, but not surprised. I wish him well as he walks alongside. He smiles at me, and I collapse.

He grooms me gently, loving me, as I lay on the hard ground, and he shields me from the sun with his body. His body is at least real enough to shield me. I no longer burn in the sunlight.

"I want to go home and see my two little huntresses again!" I sob to Thamuatz. And as I say that, my thought is, *Not like when I sheltered you; now I am so old and tired, and my back and side and front paws hurt so badly, I am not going to make it!*

He soothes, "Just as you sheltered me then, so I shelter you now, and you will make it."

I am not surprised that, like Menhit, he too can read my thoughts as I remind my lover, "The bear won't let me, and he intends to kill me before I reach it!"

Thamuatz soothes and comforts me, "You are going to where you must go, and taking him where he must be, and the one who hides inside this bear only thinks that he has found shelter from what awaits him."

"Him?" I ask, meaning the monster inside the bear that follows closely behind us, and I am not sure if Thamuatz means the same him, or means the bear-him.

Thamuatz smiles at me. "You go, and where you go he will follow as you take him to where others you have known before wait without knowing they wait for you and him to arrive together. Justice is walking with you, and his rage is almost over, as is your roaming. I will see you again where I and the others wait for you." Then Thamuatz is gone, and it is hot again.

I am too old, too tired, hurt too badly, and my back throbs with the reminder that I can't make it. I am not some weakling prey creature that surrenders so easily to death! I grit my teeth, reach and pull with my front paws, reach and pull with my front paws on the heated ground, and crawl toward where I must be.

I crawl until I can reach water again, as rock gives way to dirt, as the banks of the stream become lower until they are level with water again. I crawl desperately to the water and drink long with thirst that I have never experienced or dreamed about. I drink until I am full; and then am reminded that I have not had anything to eat in longer than I care to remember and am starving to death.

I crawl, and he follows. The sun crosses the sky and heats my body, and the bear follows patiently, waiting to see where I am going, choosing where he will kill me as the landmarks become a field with trees on the other side of it. I know these trees! They are taller now, but I know them.

I drink one last time for as long as possible and then crawl away from the stream; my burrow is close and I am going home to it.

Crawling through the grass past the four, thin, hard things stretched overhead from short not-tree to short not-tree and into the field. I crawl through the short grass of the field, and it is too high for me. Before, I could see easily over this grass as I walked through this field, but now I do not walk, I crawl. Trying to find my way past grass I can't see over. Confused by pain and hunger, I crawl across my own trail in the grass, and try again and crawl across my own trail in the grass again, and try again and crawl across my own trail in the grass again, and then stop this useless journey home to weep in frustration, pain, and hunger.

I am lost and crawling in circles, and I will not be going home to my burrow ever again!

Then the pride of the predator sets in, as I curse myself for having the weakness of prey. Reaching and pulling with my front paws, as I drag my useless, rear, lower side across the grass of this field I am lost in and try yet again. I crawl in pain and hunger, grit my teeth, and reach and pull with front paws.

Looking up in another return to my own useless circle trail in the grass, and noticing for the first time that there is something in the flattened grass of my crawling circle ahead of me; a far too thin brown lump with black stripes lies on its side, waiting in stillness for me to reach it as I crawl, and I know that far too thin lump.

I saw him lying in this field once before in the snow of a barren freezing winter. I see him clearly, and cry as I crawl to my poor starved dead little Kekuit who did not learn to how to hunt well enough to survive, and poor starved dead little Kekuit raises his head to look at me as I crawl to him.

He raises his front body as I reach him, and we crawl together through the grass as he leads me across this field; dragging ourselves toward home where the only one he truly knew could hunt wants him to be so she can care for him again and find him the food he needs.

We crawl together; Kekuit far too thin to walk anymore, me far too weak and injured to walk anymore, as Kekuit crawls with me across this field guiding me home.

The bear is behind us. He has seen me crawling in circles and now he waits for me at the edge of the forest; waiting for me to circle close to him again, so he can finish this at last.

I do not complete the circle again for him; Kekuit guides me home, as we leave the bear behind to wait in puzzlement. Wondering how a creature as weak and helpless as I am now could have avoided him.

The ground is higher here on this other side of the field, rising slightly to meet the edge of the forested hill; the edge I need to crawl over to make my way down the forested hillside to the burrow I need.

I can see the entire field we crawled through behind me, and see the humans in front of me.

They stand together; waiting at the other side of the field with killing sticks over their shoulders. They wait watching as I crawl with Kekuit toward them, and I do not care if they are real or just another waking dream, I am going home.

Kekuit and I crawl together as the two humans wearing coverings on their bodies that are the colors and shapes of the forest wait for me; I know these two from somewhere?

Behind me I hear a low rumble of hatred from the edge of the forest; he sees them also, and he sees me being lost to him.

The two humans that I know from somewhere come to me as I crawl from the field to the edge of the forest, to go the little way down the hill to where my burrow is. They do not seem to see Kekuit beside me; they only seem to see me as they come. I smell food!

One human passes right through Kekuit without noticing him, as they come to where I am. And I am not surprised at this either; for some reason these humans can't see Kekuit, he is not there for them only for me.

They look down at me where I have to stop to rest as Kekuit crawls to rest beside me with a human's lower human paw passing through his body to the solid ground below it.

They have food! The two humans have food with them; I smell meat!

They see my thinness; see I have not had food or been able to hunt in so long a time, as they also see my twisted back.

See that my rear legs are useless now.

See I have been dragging myself for too long on my front paws.

See the pads on my front paws are worn raw.

See that the lower side of me is also raw where it has been dragging as they bend down and look carefully at me.

See the fresh upper side wounds where the claws of the bear ripped me.

See the old wounds on me where the dogs gone wild fought me to the death in the snow.

I should know these two humans, but I can't remember.

However, both of these humans seem to know me well as they kneel down beside me. They make noises of knowing me with their human mouths, noises of worry, and noises of sorrow that I don't understand. I only want to go home, where my two little huntresses are waiting for me to return.

I know these two, and they know me, but I am so old and so confused now, and my mind is wandering again, and I can't remember from where I know them.

They make human-mouth noises to each other as they kneel beside me and reach into things next to them. There is meat!

They have meat and they give it to me. They give me their food! It is between two white pieces of things like the smaller round things they made for me over a fire somewhere, but I can't remember where, or what that tasted like.

This tastes strange, and there is something on it, but I don't care, it is meat, and I eat greedily for the first time in so long.

They give me all that they have, until only the white things the meat was in between are left, and as they see that I am still so hungry for more, the two humans give me the white things also, and I eat greedily again.

It tastes strange, and has the same taste as the meat, but it is so good, and I cry with joy as I eat.

They take other things that they carry, and there is water again!

The crawl across the field in this late afternoon sunlight was hot, and the water I drank from the stream was not enough. One of them holds his paws together below my mouth as he kneels beside me, while the other pours water from the human holding thing into his friend's paws, and I drink from these human paws as the water flows generously into them.

Another low rumble of total hatred comes to me from the other side of the field as I drink. He is enraged; he has lost me, they are helping me, and I am his prey, the one he hates most of all, the one he must kill.

The two humans do not hear it; their human ears are not good enough, and not good enough to hear the sound of his paws as he begins to move.

The two humans I know from somewhere stand up from where they comfort me, and they do know me from somewhere, and I knew them and respected them as they shared with me before. I wish I could remember.

Both humans are standing facing me with their backs to the field as I lie on my side and see between them; see him begin his charge.

"He Charges! He Charges!" The two humans do not see him, they face me, and they do not hear him yet, their ears are not good enough. No creature as large as he is now should be able to charge that quietly!

He comes, mouth foaming with rage, silently through the grass of this field, covering the distance to us quickly.

I scream my rage to him, lifting my front body to die. Screaming my rage and waiting to die, but the two humans look down at me, startled and confused. They do not see what is coming behind them!

I scream for them to turn, and they are still confused; we do not speak the same language, they do not know, and I scream my death scream to let him know I will bleed him when he kills me!

He attacks silently, huge and deadly, both to my kind and the humans' kind, and these two humans have good predator instincts after all. They see that I am not just insane, there is something I scream rage at behind them, and they turn.

The instinct is good between the two of them; they do not question, there is no time he comes too quickly! Human paws snatch human killing sticks up and off human shoulders as one, just as on the day I watched them kill the deer in the forest the first time I saw them. These two humans think as one. I remember them now and scream my rage at the death coming for the three of us; as he sees that we see him, and screams raging roar!

He roars a far too human scream of rage; no longer bothering to hide his charge now that he is sure of us. His roar shakes the forest and the grass of this field with its power, as his paws shake the ground of the field in his charge.

The two human's killing sticks reach their human shoulders again, with the wide ends against those shoulders, the narrow ends facing him as he comes! They can't stop him he is too large!

Human paws reach a small thing on the killing sticks under their faces near their shoulders sticking out from the side of each killing stick, lift it up and back, then push it forward and down again with a click, click, noise I have heard before, and both killing sticks roar in a solid single *"Crack!"*

It makes my ears ring, and I feel a sudden pressure cross my body, as solid crack noise and flash of hot red comes from the front of each killing stick facing him!

The bear shifts slightly in his charge and comes onward to kill us!

They have bled him, they have bled him! He bleeds, but he is not stopping!

Roaring rage, he comes pounding the ground, and now even the humans can hear his size as the ground pounds beneath charging paws, eating the distance between us rapidly in fury and killing rage. Both human paws lift and pull the small thing up and backward again from the side of the killing sticks near their heads. Click.

And this time as they lift up and back, something small and shiny flies up and out of each killing stick as the human paws go forward and down again, click, *"Crack!"*

The roar of killing sticks comes as one solid noise, making my ears ring again!

He bleeds again! He bleeds, and roars powerfully again on his way in to kill us, and this time there is no bear at all in that strange screaming roar, it is all human, and I sense the fear of both humans at the sound of the far too human roar, that they have never heard from any living creature before!

He bleeds, and he comes, roaring his rage, and now there is pain in that rage. But he does not slow, he eats the distance between us too quickly, as behind the two humans I suddenly realize a terrible truth the killing sticks they have brought with them are not large enough!

Their killing sticks are only intended to hunt the smaller, simpler deer of this forest, not a monster such as this, and I sense the fear as both humans suddenly realize the same thing in front of me.

They have not stopped him, he is too large! He is too big, there is no time! I scream my own rage, trying to rise on my paws, inviting him to me to die with my teeth in him while both human paws lift and pull back again, click, and the small shiny things fly up and out of the killing sticks again as the paws go forward and down again as one, click, *"Crack"!*

I feel their fear grow stronger as he comes without stopping, but they have courage; these humans refuse to run and abandon me as they pull the thing up and back again on each killing stick with one paw! Click, the small shiny things fly up and out near their heads, the human's paws push the small thing sticking out forward and down again, click, and I feel their fear increase, but they do not turn and run!

They will not abandon me to this thing that even they know now is not truly a bear at all, and I cheer for these two, as my Kuanja and Kyanna once cheered for me in the falling snow

Kuanja and Kyanna died!

"Crack"!

The roar is as one again, and my ears ring again from the solid roar of the killing sticks. A sudden pressure wave crosses my body again, and he shakes in his charge again as something hits him and bleeds him again. *"He is here!"*

He bleeds well, but they have not stopped him as he roars rage and stands erect, huge paws ready to rip both humans apart with claws, and there is no room left between him and them to escape those paws as I scream my rage at this thing from behind and between the humans and he suddenly remembers who he hates the most.

Shifting his attention down to me instead of them; and giving them one brief moment, as this huge thing that is not really a bear at all looks down at me, and that moment is all the humans need as human paws lift and pull.

Click, something shiny flies up and outwards again from each killing stick again, and both humans quickly use the paw that lifted and pulled the small thing to reach down to the side of their human's covering things, as each human grabs something small and shiny with a pointed tip on it as one motion together, and throws that small shiny thing with that pointed tip on it into their killing sticks with the pointed end forward!

Hands go forward and down again on the small thing on the side of each killing stick, click, he is so close they are aiming upwards at him now as he stands erect to kill, *"Crack"!*

Red fire from the front of both killing sticks smokes fur on his upper chest as they roar together again into him, and something hits and rips through him, in two places close together!

He suddenly shakes as he roars death to us; mouth foaming with fury, paws extended to kill, he shakes again, and then suddenly looks confused.

Paws still raised; he looks down at his chest where both killing sticks have just bled him and burned his fur with the fire flash from the front of them.

His upraised paws fall to his sides as he looks confused at his chest where it pumps blood across burned fur while the white foam in his mouth turns red and one of his legs begins to give way to the side.

He falls!

He shakes the ground as he falls; and his body trembles as the monster looks at us, the weak ones that he was used to killing so easily.

His mouth opens to rage, but blood comes out instead as he shakes again and dies; and as he dies, something leaves him, screaming in desperate human fear of what awaits it, as his body shifts and changes back to something he once was before as a brown bear.

Then he is only a simple dead brown bear.

The two humans shake also; as both suddenly sit down in front of me, clutching their killing sticks tightly enough to show the tenseness in their paws where human paws clutch those sticks.

They shake, tremble, and gasp for breath, but they did not run, and I am proud of them. They are true predators, as am I again.

I tremble myself; but it would not do to let humans see me do this, and I am thankful that both of them still face the monster bear as my back reminds me that I should not have tried to stand up and fight. The pain rips through me as I faint.

Humans sit with me when I awaken; one of them holding me, the other checking me with worry.

I should know these two humans; but my side, back, and front paws, hurt so badly, and I am confused. The knowledge of who they are is just out of reach inside my mind. I am old and tired and it is time to go somewhere and rest.

There is a huge monster of a bear, dead in front of me, but I am confused, and don't remember killing it. No, I could not possibly have killed something this huge.

My mind comes slowly out of confusion, and I weep as the humans hold and comfort me, one of them holding me, the other stroking me, and both thanking me over and over.

This is the monster that killed my dark brother Tigranuhi; the killer of my last chance for love Akycha, the killer of humans, the one that tried to kill humans once too often, and the one that always threatened those I loved.

Something else is confusing me, but it is just too hard to think, and then I realize I can't remember my name.

Closure, Psalm 23

I can't remember my name. No, I do remember. My name is Melanie, and I remember my mother gave me that name a long time ago. Remember also that my mother is gone because I left her long ago to become a forest dweller, with my own burrow and territory. She used to cradle me beside her and comfort me when I cried before my eyes were even open, and now this human cradles me beside him and comforts me, and it is so hard to keep my eyes open.

He holds my graying older fur gently as the other human sitting alongside us strokes me with his own human paws. Their eyes are wet, and I do not know why their eyes would be wet, but do I know these humans from somewhere. They should stroke me because I have just saved their lives with my warning scream of rage.

Once again I am allowed to be proud predator instead of a weak prey thing. I can have pride again, and not go without the pride any female badger should have. Not crawling through the forest in pain like some lower prey creature and not trying to find anything to eat while starving slowly, instead of hunting prey on four good paws.

Kekuit waits beside me. For some reason the humans can't see him waiting patiently beside me, even though I see him clearly. He crawled across this field today to guide me home, he crawled here once before.

The monster is dead, and I am proudest of that. I have pride and try not to whimper with gratitude as the human holding me strokes me. It is just so hard to think now. I lick his human paws as he strokes me and tries to ease the journey we both know I am going on. The humans know, as I know, what is coming for me because I am a predator. I know death when it calls. Kekuit waits beside me, and I know he is beside me to help me answer death's call.

They gave me something to eat! These humans gave me their food instead of keeping it for themselves when they saw my need for it, saw how thin my sides were, saw how impossible it would be for me to ever hunt properly again.

Both humans gave me something to eat, and it was so delicious and so wonderful to actually have meat again. I have not had enough food for so long, and am so old and useless a prey not a predator anymore reduced to licking the paws of humans in gratitude. Kekuit waits beside me.

I know both humans, but it is just so hard to remember. Their human scents are familiar as their stroking human paws follow the traces of the scars that have never left my face and body from the murderers of my young more than a full set of seasons ago. Their stroking human paws follow the four furrows in my side that the monster gave me in this season of warmth and new growth; four deep furrows, unable to heal properly because I could not turn enough to clean them.

Their stroking human paws follow the twisted thing that is now my back. The two humans stroke me gently, and their eyes are wet. Why are their eyes making water? Why would these humans sorrow for me? Kekuit waits beside me.

My lover Akycha strokes me, grooming me gently at sunset in the heat of this season as we sit together outside our burrow watching darkness grow around us. Waiting for it to be cool enough to hunt, as he tells me I am not too old, and he will love me no matter how strange and different our lives are now from the common habits of our badger kind.

He came to me so late in life and is younger than I, but he is the one that chose me, and I am happy with him. I remember that he came to me after the young female rabbit left.

She and I are so different, I the predator and she the prey. No, the young female rabbit left me when Akycha arrived. No, Akycha is dead, killed by this huge monster that took him from me when he was my last chance in life for love and new young, and the monster that followed tried to kill me in hate and anger for what I did.

It lays dead where they stopped its charge as it prepared to kill all three of us; and this time there will be no extra chance for him to survive, to kill again in any form. The humans are stroking me, my mind is drifting so much, I am so very old, and I have been hurt so very badly. Kekuit waits beside me.

The young rabbit strokes me with her tongue in the falling white coldness around us, grooming my injuries where my face and body are ripped and torn by the human-bred creatures that slaughtered my young, the last young I might have so late in life. She cares for me even though I am her enemy.

How can I let prey care for me? I do not know her name, and how can I know her name when I do not speak the same language as prey?

But she is so small and young, and my own small young lay dead behind us, being covered by the falling snow along with their killers.

I want her to be my new young so badly, as I whimper with pain and loss, and she cares for me, her enemy. No, she is gone, and she left early last spring when I found my lover Akycha. He strokes me instead of her, grooming me gently. No, he is dead. It is so hard to think. Kekuit waits beside me.

My young stroke me in our snug burrow with their little tongues as the leaves change colors and fall outside. My young show me how much they love me even though it should be impossible for me to have had them so late in the seasons, so close to the winter. They should have waited inside me to arrive in the spring, not arrived this early, not now. How can I see them through the coming winter when they should be grown and gone by this season?

No, they are all dead, and snow is covering them, along with their murderers. I fought so many so hard with all the fierceness that is ours and I failed to save my young. I am so useless; a poor prey creature that has to be held by humans and stroked by them and it is so hard to concentrate anymore. Kekuit waits beside me.

I try not to whimper with gratitude for the gentleness with which the two humans stroke me. I remind myself sternly that I am predator and not prey. Predators do not whimper, and I will not cry for myself!

The humans stroke me, and they seem to know this also, because their eyes are wet as they both try to help me, the predator that saved them. Kekuit waits beside me.

I remember now. I do know both humans trying to comfort me because they shared food with me in the forest after they took the deer seasons ago when we first met, and they shared with me in seasons whenever we met again. We have an understanding, these two humans and I. We are both predators in the forest, and we are the same under the fur, or at least we would be if humans had decent fur.

I could not save my young and I could not save my lover, but I saved them. They remember me. They know me. They cry for me. I tremble in human paws as he holds me, strokes me, comforts me, and cries for me. Kekuit waits beside me.

Their human paws touch me as they try to sooth me, and I would have let few humans touch me before. But now I am some pathetic prey instead of a decent predator, and they helped me to kill the monster. No. They killed it. I had no choice; I could only wait to die and scream my rage at it from behind and below the humans as it came charging, roaring rage across the fresh spring grass of the field to kill the three of us.

I lick this human hand as he strokes me. My mind is drifting so badly. I am so old, and my back hurts so badly.

I hear my mother calling me from so many seasons ago.

She is so beautiful and fierce. No predator will dare touch us with her around.

No, she must be dead; that was so long ago.

She strokes me, grooming and cleaning me. She is calling me, and I have to go to her.

Kekuit is still beside me, waiting patiently for me to join him in our final hunt together. He grooms me gently, comforting me on this last journey while reminding me that his mother must be stronger than this. I must go with him soon.

The young rabbit strokes me in the cold, winter whiteness around us as she cleans my wounds. The humans stroke me in this new spring grass I crawled through to come here as they comfort me. My lover strokes me in the heat of summer as we love and then sit together to wait for the darkness to come. My young stroke me as the leaves change colors and fall around us.

They all stroke me as one; and Kekuit, who once could not stand, now stands up beside me.

I must go with him now. I begin to crawl and the human tries to hold me still. I snap at him. There will be pride in this final trip home to the burrow!

He yanks his hand back from my teeth in time to save his fingers and jumps up.

Both of them watch me with curiosity, standing beside me as I begin the painful crawl past the edge of the field to the edge of the hillside that leads to where I must go.

The humans talk to each other and try to reach for me again, which draws another angry snap.

I thank them for their food, but I must do this thing now and will not be stopped from it by any human, even one who has saved my life.

The ground moves slowly past me as I wince from the pain of trying to crawl on what has already been rubbed raw, but it is there, I can see it now through the forest around us.

My large water, my beautiful large water at the bottom of this hillside with the beautiful green of the hills on the other side of it, as I drag myself downhill toward it, past trees, through brush, while the two humans follow, still curious.

But then they can't know how important this is to me. My two little huntresses, Cetnenn and Caoineag, are waiting for me inside our burrow.

I drag myself while the humans follow me down the hillside, and Kekuit walks alongside me.

Plumper now, no longer starved, no longer dragging himself beside me, Kekuit walks plump and sleek again, and I am happy as I drag my poor, useless prey body downhill through the fresh spring growth of green until I see the place I need.

The flat area in front of its entrance is now covered with old leaves, twigs, and loose dirt. I must clean that off when I have the time, but for now, I just want to see the sunset again.

The humans are not foolish. They see the old hole of the burrow entrance, see the flat area I had made in front of it for watching the sunsets I loved so much, and seem to realize now where I have to be.

They let me go to it, simply watching as I drag myself to the flat area in front of my burrow, and turn to clear a small area for myself, feeling my body relax as I finally rest after a long crawl to come here.

I am here where I wanted to be, and I must remember to clean the burrow out after watching the sunset because I want it to look nice for my two little huntresses when they return home.

No, they are home already I remember, and suddenly I hear the voice of my daughter Menhit in my head, as if she were here again. "No, they have gone on now, after you returned for them as you promised."

Menhit is not here, she is dead, and the voice is wrong, of course. My two little huntresses are waiting patiently inside for me to join them and have waited patiently inside for all of these many seasons for me to return.

But the sunset is here now, and I turn my body to watch it. Lifting my head to see better with these old eyes; and it is still the most beautiful thing I have ever seen, as the humans sit beside me staring at it in awe also as they stroke me to comfort me.

I let them; they do not spoil my view, and I am content with them doing so while Kekuit sits watching the sunset with me. As he sat here watching it long ago with his sisters, as my two little huntresses who are still inside the burrow waiting for me watched it with me before.

We are content together as the red sun dips into the tops of the green hills across from us; turning the sky red, and the large water golden; dipping deeper behind the green hills; while the white things that move across the sky above turn red behind it.

The two humans watch it with Kekuit and me; four predators bonded together at this beauty of nature, as I hear the humans gasp at the sight of it.

Their human reaction to this sight I have known of myself for so long does not surprise me. We are not so different in our own ways, as their human paws stroke me gently while we watch it together, and for the first time I think these two humans finally understand why it was so important for me to come here and watch this one last time.

It is almost behind the hills when Kekuit stands again beside me; as I sigh at the beauty, resting my head on my front paws, and the sigh becomes breath leaving me.

There is a soft letting go inside my body; distanced as if it were not my body anymore, and the pains of paws, side, and back, drift gently away.

I stand up from the thing that was me, to wait patiently beside Kekuit as the two humans call me in the gathering darkness, and I watch with Kekuit as human eyes run with water and human mouths make sad noises. Then I feel someone else watching us, and I look up the hillside.

My Aataentsic is there at the edge of the hill looking down at me, and he sees me! Somehow, he can see me as I am now.

He looks so strong and proud. My young one has done well here. He looks down and sees the old broken used up thing that was once me, lying behind me; and sees me also as I stand new again before it, trying to understand what he sees.

I smile, and he smiles back, still trying to understand. I am glad he found this place, but it is time, and I have to go elsewhere.

It is darkness now, and there is only one thing left for the two humans to do for me, and both humans understand what that one thing is.

I know that both of them are truly grateful for my warning them of the bear's attack, the warning that saved them, and now they understand what I need from them, to complete this last needed thing for me. I am truly grateful to them in return. We are not different at all; these human predators and I, we both have things to complete in our lives.

They use one of the long killing sticks that they killed my enemy the bear with to push the thing that was me into the burrow I loved so much, until the thing that was me is deep inside the sleeping chamber, and close to the bones of my two little huntresses who waited so long for my return.

Then Kekuit and I watch together, as the humans fill the burrow entrance in with bare human paws in darkness.

They can't see me waiting patiently outside the burrow with Kekuit as they do this, they can't see Kekuit beside me, and they can't feel my last gift to them as they complete the filling of the entrance tunnel.

Both humans are still kneeling in front of my burrow entrance, saying something to that entrance as I stand up on my rear paws, giving each human a last kiss, grooming both humans softly in front of the burrow that now holds what was my two little huntresses and I safely together. Just as I used to groom both young and lovers for the love we shared in our lives, so I now groom both kneeling humans, grateful to them for understanding and for doing this last thing for me.

It is time. My mother, Asaseyaa, is calling me to join her, and Kekuit is here to guide me as the entrance opens into light. It is light, but there are no shadows; the same light is everywhere, and she is waiting for me.

My mother, Asaseyaa, waits for me, and the vast beautiful meadow she waits in holds more creatures than I can ever count in its infinite length and width; and I suddenly know that other deep forests and other meadows, and other places that are not forest or meadow, each in their own infinite lengths and widths, hold still more.

There are humans here also, more than I can ever count, with no aged or infirm among them. They are all young and strong; as if they had been made so when they came into this infinite garden that is the new home for all of us.

Predator, prey, and humans, all mingle together with one another, and there is no anger, hunger, jealousy, or territories, and there is no reason to kill for any reason.

I know this, just as I know that our stomachs will always be as full as we wish without having to kill, just as I can now feel the infinite, understanding love for all creatures from the one who gives all of us this.

I feel strength in my new, younger body, and know my scars are gone without having to look. I run through the entrance with Kekuit, and the entrance closes behind us. The two humans have seen nothing as they depart into the darkness behind us.

Those that have waited for me now run to greet me as I run to them. My two little huntresses, Cetnenn and Caoineag, and Tigranuhi, my dark brother with his dark mate, Atida, and

Shareesa, my sister, and Asiaq and Alarana, their fur now so beautiful and perfect again.

Thamuatz runs, young handsome and strong on four, good, strong legs with Red Fur and Sesondowah running alongside him, none jealous of the other.

Atsentma, Menhit, Kuanja, Kyanna, and all the ones who have come here before me come running, as Kekuit brings me home to the ones I love!

A large, adult rabbit smiles at me from alongside his beautiful brown mate as I run past him. Instead of terrible fiery eyes, his eyes are now happy and bright, and his beautiful fur is a soft dark brown instead of that unnatural black.

"See?" he says softly, and I do see fully, understanding for the first time.

There will be a young brown rabbit with strange, black markings on her body here someday, and then it will be both my duty and my pleasure go to greet her just as he greets me now, as she in turn will greet those who follow her here.

I will show her my two little hunters, Kuanja and Kyanna, who had died in the snow. The last time she saw me with them, I was wailing over their torn bodies in the falling snow. Then when it is her time to come here, she will see how beautiful Kuanja and Kyanna both look as they run with the others to greet me!

She will see me, just as I see that the huge brown bear I had once called monster is also here.

His body as it should be now, the scars on his face are gone, and also gone is the thin white scar that ran from front to rear through the fur on top of his head, as is the damage below that thin white scar. And his rage is gone.

Younger and gentler now, he runs, crying with joy to meet his own long-lost love who had died beside him when he received that scar from the angry human's killing stick.

That angry human is not here, and I do not think he will ever see this place because he has gone elsewhere.

The dogs I once fought to the death in falling snow now play tamely in the meadow before me. I no longer hate the bear, or them, or anyone; for there is no hatred here.

I run through the meadow with Kekuit beside me, running to meet those I have loved before and now can love again.

And for any who may doubt that they can all live together in peace and love, may this remind them that it is indeed possible to live in peace and love together. Isaiah 11: 6–9.